PENGUIN

Bobby on

Pamela Rhodes is one of the two runners-up in the hugely
popular and *Saga* magazine life-story competition,
beating over 5,000 other entrants to a place in the top three.
She continues to live in North Yorkshire where she was one of
the first WPCs in the country, and this is her first book.

Bobby on the Beat

PAMELA RHODES
with JO WHEELER

PENGUIN BOOKS

PENGUIN BOOKS

Published by the Penguin Group
Penguin Books Ltd, 80 Strand, London WC2R ORL, England
Penguin Group (USA) Inc., 375 Hudson Street, New York, New York 10014, USA
Penguin Group (Canada), 90 Eglinton Avenue East, Suite 700, Toronto, Ontario, Canada M4P 2Y3
(a division of Pearson Penguin Canada Inc.)
Penguin Ireland, 25 St Stephen's Green, Dublin 2, Ireland (a division of Penguin Books Ltd)
Penguin Group (Australia), 707 Collins Street, Melbourne, Victoria 3008, Australia
(a division of Pearson Australia Group Pty Ltd)
Penguin Books India Pvt Ltd, 11 Community Centre, Panchsheel Park, New Delhi – 110 017, India
Penguin Group (NZ), 67 Apollo Drive, Rosedale, Auckland 0632, New Zealand
(a division of Pearson New Zealand Ltd)
Penguin Books (South Africa) (Pty) Ltd, Block D, Rosebank Office Park,
181 Jan Smuts Avenue, Parktown North, Gauteng 2193, South Africa

Penguin Books Ltd, Registered Offices: 80 Strand, London WC2R ORL, England

Printed in Great Britain by Clays Ltd, St Ives plc

ISBN: 978-1-405-90946-4

www.greenpenguin.co.uk

MIX
Paper from
responsible sources
FSC™ C018179

Penguin Books is committed to a sustainable
future for our business, our readers and our planet.
This book is made from Forest Stewardship
Council™ certified paper.

ALWAYS LEARNING   **PEARSON**

In loving memory of my parents, Mathew and
Eveline, and my brother Peter.

This book is dedicated to my daughter, Pauline, who
gave me the inspiration to jot down the memories, and
to my colleagues, the members of the North Riding
Constabulary in the 1950s.

Introduction

1st October 1951. We've founded a Welfare State and fought a war. Britain stands on the brink of a new age, full of optimism and the wonders of labour-saving devices, convenience foods and television. But in Yorkshire, just as it's been for billions of years, the heavens don't give two hoots for optimism. They open up, just as they always have, and pour their watery offering across every hillock, cobbled street and country lane. What's more, I'm nearly late for my first day at work and running full pelt in the biggest rainstorm I've ever witnessed in my short life.

Water finds its way onto and into everything, including up my nose and down the back of my shirt. It seems to slither up drainpipes and over things that could have no conceivable use for it: dustbins, tin roofs, a pair of old boots. The rain pours relentlessly across everything in its path as I leg it towards Newbiggin on my way to Richmond police station.

I hold firmly on to my regulation handbag, leather with a broad strap, which contains my whistle and a notebook, all now thoroughly soaked through. But it's my precious shoes, which I have stayed up half the night shining, that are the wettest of all. And they certainly aren't shiny any more as I slosh through the tidal wave now making its way down the road.

What will Sarge say? He's such a stickler for punctuality

and smartness. I've been warned that every morning there's an inspection and all the officers on duty line up in a row while he walks up and down to check the length of the lads' hair, the crispness of their shirts and the shine on their shoes. Dripping with mud, I shake off my feet one by one and carry on up the hill towards the station as fast as I can.

Towards me, running the other way, a figure in a huge brown coat, floppy hat and corduroy trousers tied at the ankles with brown string is running down the hill with his arms waving.

'Miss! Miss! Look out! He's on his way. My Bertie. I couldn't restrain him, by Lord, I couldn't. He's got a will of steel, that lad.'

This was the last thing I needed, some batty old farmer to deal with, making me even wetter and even later for inspection. But the man grabs me by the shoulders.

'Miss, run for it! He's on his way and there'll be no stopping him now. He's got a firecracker up his . . .'

'Sir, heavens, please. Stop shaking me!' He is now spraying a fountain of spittle across my face.

'Oh, sorry, Miss. I . . . only you must hurry. It's the new bairn. He's escaped and he's wild.'

'The new baby?'

'The bullock. My Bessie's bullock! He's got the devil in him, I swear it.'

As I look up I can see the massive animal rounding the corner, nostrils snorting, water streaming down his coat in sheets. He runs this way and that, slithering and slipping on the cobbles but managing to build up a fearsome speed. He's heading right for us, past the post office and on towards Market Place.

'Quick. Run!' I grab hold of the old man's coat, which is ominously sticky, and pull him along behind me. As we run, his breath, a heady mix of whisky and swede, washes over me in dizzying waves.

'I don't know why he's being like this. His sister's an angel, by Lord. I only turned my back for a minute, and then he turned on me!'

'Come on. Hurry.'

I can practically feel the bullock's snorting nostrils at my back. But before he reaches us, I catch sight of a red telephone box in Market Place. It's one of the boxes which will become as familiar to me as my own home over the next few months. But for now it's nothing less than heaven-sent.

I pull the farmer in behind me, heaving the door firmly shut. I lean back, trying to stop the old man from falling onto me in the cramped booth, when the animal slides to a stop in the muddy water and crashes up against the door in front of us, his huge flaring nostrils puffing steam onto the glass, brown eyes looking up, terrified. He lets out a long whine as though someone has slowly and deliberately stepped on his tail, then slumps down head first in the mud and gives up the chase.

And that's why I was late for my first day at work, and why I failed my first inspection.

A loud bang at the front door woke me from the deepest of sleeps. Rubbing my eyes, I stretched, noticing that the rain had finally stopped after weeks of constant downpour. The first frost of the year was sparkling round the edge of the window and it was a clear starry night. Between the trees a yellow half-moon lit up the clock – ten past three in the morning. I looked out of the window and down at the front garden, where a figure in a black helmet and greatcoat was shifting from foot to foot.

Shivering, I got dressed quickly and ran downstairs, trying not to wake my landlady, then peeped round the door. A twitchy young policeman stood on the front step, breathless from running.

'Grab your things. We need you down at the station. We've got a situation.'

'Hello, Bill! What is it?' I whispered. My words puffed out in white clouds.

'We've picked someone up on the Great North Road. She's in a bit of trouble. Sarge says you're to come right away. And bring your coat.'

I grabbed my hat and bag, and we walked at a brisk pace into town. There wasn't another person in sight, not even the milkman, or a hint of morning sun. The only sounds were the shop shutters swinging and the clatter of our boots.

As we walked, PC Bill Bryant explained to me that the woman they had brought in was, as he put it, a 'lady of the night'. He said they were often picked up on the Great North Road near the army barracks, 'selling their wares' along the roadside. I had never seen one of these women in real life and was a bit apprehensive. But as the only female police officer at the station, it was my job to be there when a woman was brought in, so I had to put on a brave face. I soon got used to getting dragged out like this at all hours.

Bill chattered on excitedly.

'She was found by Traffic Patrol wandering onto the road, drunk as a lark. She could have been killed.'

He revelled for a moment in the drama.

As he spoke, I tried to remember all the offences it might be possible she had committed. I'd just spent the last thirteen weeks at the training centre, learning the ins and outs of every angle of policing, and I scanned my mind, thinking back to the big textbooks we'd had to memorize. Drunk and incapable? It would be at least that, surely, but at that time in the morning, groggy with sleep, everything seemed a blurry haze.

Richmond police station consisted of two small stone cottages knocked through into one. The main room was more like a cosy sitting room, with, amongst other things, two chairs at a table and a blazing open fire.

As we walked in Sergeant Cleese, the duty sergeant in charge of the night shift, was holding up a woman at the front desk. In the flickering firelight, she looked a bit worse for wear, though she was very tall and elegant, a bit like a young Bette Davis, with lavender silk gloves right up to the elbows, a silver fox fur with a real fox's head draped over one shoulder and with her hair piled up in high curls. I noticed that the make-up round her eyes had smudged and there was a large, bloody cut on her lip.

As we came in she made a dash for the door, shouted something incoherent, burst out laughing, then into tears, and collapsed onto the floor at my feet.

'What a lovely hat!' she slurred, then slumped over.

'Oh good, Rhodes, you're here.' Sergeant Cleese never lost his cool; he always responded with military precision. 'If you lift her arm there, you can help me get her down to the cells, like so.'

We half carried the woman, who was surprisingly heavy, down a narrow stone passageway and into the cells.

An overpowering smell of damp and vinegar hit me as we entered the cell. To this day, I still don't know why it smelled of vinegar. I walked over to the little iron bed, where we sat her down and I used the handkerchief in my pocket to clean off some of the blood from the woman's face as she slurred and nodded. It was rather tricky, as she kept grabbing out at imaginary adversaries and trying to say something.

'Don't hit me, I didn't mean to!' she said, followed by a plaintive, 'Why me?'

When she fell asleep, I realized that she couldn't be much older than twenty, about the same age as me. What different lives we must have led, I thought. After all, I'd never even kissed a man. I wondered what it meant, in real life, to be a lady of the night. But I couldn't imagine it.

'Righto, we'll check her in an hour or so, see if she's sobered up,' said Cleese, and he shooed me out. Then he shut the door and turned the key.

The next day, Pearl, as she called herself (though her real name, we later found out, was Mary Brown), sat in the office cradling a strong mug of tea. The cut on her lip was still bleeding a little, but she was more concerned with getting hold of some hair curlers.

'Be a dear, will you, and get me something for this mess?' she said. 'I can't let him see me like this.'

She was genuinely quite distressed at the thought of being witnessed in such a state of disarray. In the heat of the moment, I remembered an old trick I'd learnt from one of the girls at training school, a cunning method using pipe-cleaners in place of curlers, so I went into the office and found some, and she fixed them in place before Sarge came back in with his notebook and pen.

When she was settled, Cleese asked her a series of questions – why was she out that late? Had she been drinking? and so on – and I took down the statement later as carefully as I could in my neatest handwriting on the statement sheet.

It turned out that Pearl was a dancer from Leeds who had auditioned for a big training school in London and got a place too, but she needed more money to pay the fees.

'I met this lad, Reg, who said he owned a few night-clubs. He could have charmed the rattle from a snake. Anyway, he said he'd get me a job dancing at an exclusive revue bar.'

So he swept her off her feet, and then up the aisle. But it wasn't long before he wanted her to earn money in other ways. And if she refused, he hit her.

'That night, I said I was having none of it any more,' she said, pausing to consider how much she should tell us. 'Anyway, he got a bit angry, if you know what I mean. And one thing led to another and here I am with a bloody lip and Reg is nowhere to be seen. So I drank the rest of the gin and then the next thing I know I'm in here with you lot gawping at me.'

Sergeant Cleese and I listened patiently.

'He's all right really,' she laughed. 'He can't help it. He'll change. I'm sure.'

She looked down and twirled the ring round her finger sadly.

'I probably deserve it, in any case.'

Eventually the Sergeant went out and conferred with the Inspector for a while in his office. Cleese gave her a good talking to, about the dangers of being a young woman on the streets, and told her to be sure to take care.

Suddenly a man burst in through the front door, demanding to see his wife. I have to admit he was quite handsome, with slicked-back black hair, piercing eyes and a neat pencil moustache. But he had a strange way about him that I didn't trust a jot.

'A lady policeman, eh?' he said, eyeing me up and down. 'That's a bit weird, in't it? Nice hat, by the way.'

Before I could reply, Pearl ran over and flung her arms round him.

'Reggie! Darrrrling! Where have you been all my life?'

'Right here, Pusskins. Right here, always.'

As the pair embraced, Reg looked back over his shoulder and gave me a deliberate wink.

When they had left, Sergeant Cleese shuffled some papers together and took a slug of his tea.

'Nice girl that,' he said. 'I doubt that's the last time we'll see her in here. But then what can you do, eh? What can you do?'

As they walked off up the street, Pearl with her fox fur swinging, Reg in his pinstriped suit and upturned collar, they could have been film stars, the happiest couple on earth as the credits rolled. But as the newest bobby in Richmond, I was about to learn that things are very rarely what they seem.

I

I never really dreamt of joining the police; it certainly wasn't the kind of ambition they encouraged in a young girl from North Riding in the 1940s. In fact, I would hardly have known what the police force was if it wasn't for an incident one summer, back in 1939, my one and only brush with the law.

I was nine years old and it was the school holidays. My best friend Mary and I had thoroughly exhausted every game our little village had on offer.

We'd flung a big rope over an old gas lamp on the main street and spent hours swinging up and down and laughing until our sides ached. When we got tired of that, we hitched a ride with Farmer Brian up the road on his hay truck and sat in his field while he and the lads loaded up the hay in great heavy bales. When that was done, we watched the cows and gave them human names and characters, deciding which people in the village they were.

'That one looks like Mr Gordon,' Mary said.

'He's got the same silly cross face,' I agreed.

'And the same hairy nose.' We both collapsed into a pile of laughter.

When the cows wandered off, we lay back on the grass, picking daisies and popping their heads off. I tried to catch a cricket to discover how it made that noise with its legs, but when it evaded my clutches I gave up and we lay back in the sun, staring at passing clouds. After a while, Mary jumped up. 'Come on,' she said. 'I've got an idea,' and she pushed up her sleeves.

Mary was always pulling pranks. Once she had posted a piece of dried cow dung through Mr Gordon's letterbox, and I'm sure he thought it was me. Another time she left a live frog on our schoolteacher's chair. Mrs Allen was so alarmed she jumped right up onto the chair with the frog, which just looked at her, croaked and bounced off up the corridor. The whole class got the ruler for that. But life was never boring with Mary, so I followed to see what she would do next.

When we got to the main row of houses in our village she paused, looked this way and that and skipped along the road, banging all the door knockers along the whole row one by one with a loud slam. Then, with a whoop, she disappeared off round the corner.

I was so startled I froze right there on the spot. My knees felt like jellyfish but the rest of me was stuck to the ground with imaginary iron weights.

One by one, the doors started opening. A row of heads peered out, looking up and down. Mr Gordon, who had been a merchant seaman but who now spent most of the time walking his two dogs and generally being cross, shouted over to Mrs Phillips, the baker's wife, a few doors down.

'What was that all about?' said Gordon, shaving foam smeared across his face.

'I've no idea, I must say. I heard a knock at the door, and then not a soul.'

Then she caught sight of me, standing across the street. I tried my best to look innocent, but failed miserably.

'Is that that Rhodes lass over there, causing trouble again?' Her three young children peered out round her skirts to see where all the fun was.

Mr Gordon looked like he was about to burst into angry flames. He bellowed over to me: 'If I get hold of you, you'll see the end of next week. I've warned you about this. You little . . .'

Then, before I knew it, two creatures ran out of the house with their tongues hanging out, teeth bared, and I legged it as fast as I could, the gnashing animals, followed by a panting Mr Gordon, in hot pursuit.

Where was Mary? She'd left me right in it this time.

A few other neighbours had now come out of their houses and, just when I thought things couldn't get any worse, I bumped into a giant of a man and fell flat on my back on the road.

It took me a few seconds to come round and when I looked up, it wasn't a giant at all but the village bobby, PC Bennett, pushing his bicycle. He towered upwards and upwards, from his great big shiny shoes, long coat, big nose and pointy chin, right up to his hat with its badge glinting in the sun. He was the scariest vision I had ever seen, apart from Mr Gordon, that is, who came running over shortly after, his face by now beyond boiling point.

'That girl there, that Rhodes girl, has been disturbing the peace,' he said. 'She has also been posting unmentionable items through my door, *and* tormenting the village. What's next, eh? Stealing? Or worse. Murder! She ought to be locked up and the key thrown in the Humber.'

'Thank you, Mr Gordon. I can deal with it now. I'm sure the lass meant no harm.'

A forum of neighbours now stood with their arms folded, discussing my fate and simultaneously deciding how best to solve the crisis of morally corrupt and out of control children sweeping the country at that very moment. PC Bennett put his arm round my shoulder and steered me away, up the street towards my own house. The crowd looked disappointed.

'Well, just see she's punished right and proper!' shouted Mr Gordon after us, the dogs circling wildly at his feet.

It would have been a great sin, breaking all known codes of loyalty, to tell PC Bennett it was Mary and not I who had committed the misdemeanour, so when he asked I had no choice but to confess to the whole affair. All the while I was imagining with horror what might happen to me next. Thrown in jail and forced to eat bread and water, stretched out on the rack, or worse, hanged, drawn and quartered.

But none of these was to be my fate. Instead PC Bennett gave me a stern telling off, but also agreed not tell my parents, just this once, but I was to promise to steer clear of Mr Gordon, and if he ever caught me door-knocking again, there would be trouble. Perhaps PC Bennett wasn't so bad after all.

Of course, nothing stayed secret in that village for long, and when Mam and Dad found out, which of course they did, Mary agreed to tell them that it was really her who had planned and executed the whole affair. And we soon forgot about my little brush with the law: in 1939 there was something much bigger on everyone's minds.

*

Mary and I were on our way home from school, smarting from the ruler for getting our sums wrong again. I had a penny in my pocket, earned by helping Mam, so we decided to buy some sweets to soothe the pain. Mary had her eye on some jelly babies while I was drooling at the thought of Liquorice Allsorts or acid drops. As we were stood at the counter, surveying the delights, a little wireless on the shelf crackled and a serious voice interrupted the broadcast.

The whole shop went quiet for a moment, and then hushed conversations started up. A man called Hitler wanted someone's land, the voices chattered, and they had known it was only a matter of time. Mary and I hadn't a clue what it all meant and why everyone looked so serious all of a sudden, so we skipped off and sucked on the sweets and didn't worry much about anything, until I got home and saw Mam and Dad standing in the living room, looking very grave indeed. The man's voice droned over the wireless.

'What does it mean "at war with Germany"? Who is Hitler and why does he want someone's land?' I demanded, arms folded, waiting for an explanation for this sudden turn of events.

'Don't worry, little mouse. Come here, you,' said my Dad and he ruffled my hair. He had just got home from work; he ran his own business in a nearby town. 'It'll all be all right. It won't last, they say.'

My little brother Peter came in from the garden, running round us in circles, whooping, wearing Red Indian feathers and brandishing his new homemade bow and arrow.

'Get down, all of you, or I'll shoot!' he said.

We were silent. I hoped this war thing would turn out to be just that, a big game of Cowboys and Indians.

Everything changed. Food and even clothes were rationed and everyone had to muck in: 'Dig for Victory' said the posters. Then there were soldiers. They came to the village to take down the road signs, and Mam made them tea and sardine sandwiches. I went along with her, intrigued to see them, all smart in their uniforms.

'Mrs Rhodes, your sarnies are a lifesaver,' they'd say as they gulped down the hot tea. 'And who's this pretty little thing?' they'd ask, looking at me, and I would blush and look down at my shoes.

One day, as we were walking back from a delivery of sandwiches, we came across a huge parachute stuck in a tree, puffing in and out in the wind like a huge sleeping bird.

'I wonder who that belongs to?' said Mam, looking thoughtful. She ran her fingers through the silk. 'You could make a few dozen dresses out of that. Anyway, I hope the pilot's not hurt, whoever he is'.

We both stood and watched the parachute as it fluttered in and out for what seemed like hours. I suppose we'll never know whose it was, or what happened to him.

Luckily for us, Dad didn't have to go away to war because when they checked him out he had a heart murmur. I think he felt a bit guilty though when a lot of his friends went off to fight for king and country.

The first time I heard an air-raid siren it was exciting and scary. We'd all been warned about what to do, but nothing prepares you for the noise. Everyone in the neighbouring cottages and houses had agreed to go to a house nearby which had a cellar and stay in there until it passed. We did have an Anderson shelter in the garden, but Mam didn't trust it.

'That wouldn't stop an incoming pigeon,' she said, and she made sure we all got a place up at the big house.

When the siren sounded one night, we met Mary with her mam, Mrs Green, on the way up the lane. Mary and I pulled ghostly faces with the torches and tried to scare each other as we walked up the path. Then we scrambled over a wall and through the back garden, down into the stuffy old cellar where Mrs Tench, who owned the house, brought us all cups of tea. There was an eerie silence when the door slammed shut, and I could only just make out people's faces in the torchlight. Then, after a while, we relaxed a little as our eyes got used to the dark, and people started chatting.

'I mean, what does Hitler want with Gomersal anyway?' asked Mr Gordon, trying to control his two dogs, who kept jumping up and down on people's laps.

'If a Jerry pilot lands here, we might all get captured!' said Mrs Phillips, in her dressing gown and with her hair still in curlers, positively revelling in the idea.

My mam was quiet, staring into her tea cup. Dad was still outside, helping to make sure everyone's lights were out.

Mrs Green started to panic. 'What if a bomb lands on the house? The piano. My china! I saved for years.'

Mary and I looked at each other and didn't say a word.

'They said on the wireless that in London whole streets are being taken out. In one hit,' she went on, 'leaving massive craters in the road, bigger than a bus!'

But we never did see any bombs over our village that night or any other, so we were the lucky ones.

*

The war may have been on everyone's mind, but I had another enemy in my sights: Eric Willis. He lived opposite us and would shout names at us from across the street. We ignored him most of the time and went off to play in the field up the lane. But he sometimes followed us.

'Oh no, it's you,' said Eric on one occasion as he approached us, pretending he hadn't known we would be there. 'Why are you in *my* field?'

'It's not *your* field, we were here first,' I said, standing in his way with my hands on my hips.

'Well, you're just girls anyway, what do you want being out here?' He pushed me aside. 'You should be playing with dolls or knitting or something.'

I turned away and ignored him.

'Did you catch that cricket yet, Mary?'

'No, he got away,' she said sadly.

I had a jar all ready and we were going to take one home to show my dad how they make that noise with their legs.

'Well, me and Peter's gonna play in the stream and you better not bother us with your boring girl's stuff,' said Eric.

'Yeah,' agreed Peter, and I realized that my brother was there too. So he has joined the enemy, I thought. Well, we'll see about that.

When they had walked away, we picked blades of grass and blew them to make high-pitched squeaks. It was deadly serious stuff. We nearly forgot about Eric and my brother's defection. Anyway, I knew that they'd be hours, damming up the stream with rocks and stones. How utterly dull and pointless.

'Ooh, there's another cricket!' shouted Mary and jumped up to try to catch it. I lay back in the sun and looked through the petals of a buttercup, twirling it, shining yellow on my skin.

All of a sudden there was a loud splashing and shouting from down by the stream. At first we thought nothing of it, but then Eric came scrambling up the bank.

'He's in. He's fallen in!'

Oh my God, I thought. Peter. He can't swim!

They'd wandered down to the bit where the stream gets suddenly deep; there's a spring and Mam told us never to play there. When we got to the edge of the water I could see him splashing about feebly, his little face poking out. Then he went strangely still and quiet. I started shouting and reached out across to see if I could grab him, but I couldn't reach, and I couldn't swim either.

'Help! Help!' we all shouted and started jumping up and down in the air for some reason. Peter began to splash again and then disappeared down into the water further.

'What's up? Lost your dog?'

Farmer Brian was checking on his cows in the next field and heard the shouts. He peered over the fence.

'Oh Lord, that's no dog,' he said, seeing Peter's arms flapping.

He leapt over, took off his hat and shoes and jumped into the water, disappearing for a while as he heaved my brother up out of the water. Eventually they both surfaced, their clothes blown up and full of water, Peter spluttering.

He lay on the bank with mud and silt all over him. Peter looked pale, almost green. Bill wrapped him up in his coat and carried him back to his truck nearby. We followed quietly. It seemed strange to be riding in the truck in this sombre, serious way when it was usually such fun.

'Will he die?' asked Eric nervously.

'The boy'll be all right. He's just had a shock, is all.'

I could see Peter through the window in the cab, slumped and shaking with the cold, curled up on the front seat.

Later that evening, when Peter was tucked up in bed, nearly asleep, Dad was sitting by his bed and telling him a story about a giant bird which saves a little boy who is all alone in the desert and takes him to a beautiful paradise city where everything's made of food.

'Even the walls and gates of the city are made of cheese and meat, and as you pass through the gates to the city, the most gorgeous drinks, fresh lemonade and ginger beer, are poured out whenever you want them. And the doors to all the houses are made of sweets that you can pick off and eat whenever you feel like it.'

My dad was always making up stories. Peter dozed off and I hovered by the door a moment but decided not to go in. I couldn't be sure but, as I turned to leave, I thought I saw a tear running down Dad's cheek. He never showed his emotions, it just wasn't the done thing in those days. But that night I'm sure I saw him shed a tear of relief that his little boy was safe.

After his accident, my brother stopped playing with Eric. Mam wouldn't let him, so Eric went back to teasing us both from across the road, but a little less often. Perhaps he felt a bit bad about what had happened that day.

I had a big important exam coming up to see if I would get a scholarship to the local grammar school. Dad had been the first in his village to get a scholarship and everyone was keen for me to continue the family tradition. I sat the exam and, the following week, two nuns came round to our house to let me know I had a place.

Mam and Dad were proud as punch when they sent me off to catch the bus. I would go on my own all the way to Bradford, and I felt very grown up as I paraded up the road in my smart new navy uniform, complete with hat and gold braid.

One morning the bus drivers were all on strike, so an army lorry came to take us to school instead. When it arrived it was khaki green with a big tarpaulin over the back; handsome soldiers helped us all into the back. Sister Joseph had told us not to fraternize with the boys from the other grammar school. But of course we did nothing *but* chat to them all the way there.

The first years of the war passed largely uneventfully for us. During the winter months, Mary and I played on the ice on the village pond, skittering round and round in circles, not caring when we fell over. We built a huge snowman, gave it a big turnip for a nose and said it was Mr Gordon. One summer we had two evacuees from Liverpool in the village, Beryl and Sara. Country life was new to them. We showed them how to build a little tent using Mam's clotheshorse, and we all pretended we were lost in the desert like wild explorers. In the autumn, we picked and ate crab apples, which looked like small cherries but were as sour as lemons. We even saw a cow jump over a fence once. We called it the Miracle Cow.

But, despite our games, the war was always there, a steady presence. We had an air raid shelter at school and a vegetable garden. The girls in our class knitted scarves for the troops and wrote letters to a battleship called HMS

Repulse. We got letters back from their captain about what they were up to, and they were read out in assembly. We all got quite attached to the ship and its adventures on the high seas, and looked forward to the letters immensely, imagining we were all on a voyage with them to far-off lands. It seemed much more exciting than arithmetic and French verbs.

One afternoon, Mother Superior called everyone into the big hall after lunch, which was unusual since assembly was in the morning. A few of the other girls and I were chattering away quietly when she stepped out onto the stage, looking very serious. We all shut up immediately.

'Girls, I regret to inform you . . .' she paused and cleared her throat. 'I regret to have to tell you that we have had a communication that the battleship *Repulse* was struck while on duty in the Straits of Malaysia, along with the battleship *The Prince of Wales*. It is believed they have suffered heavy casualties, with possibly many killed. We are awaiting more news.'

Her voice cracked. 'I am grieved to be the bearer of such tragedy. I know you have all got to know and love the ship and its brave men.' She sniffed and finally pulled herself together, inhaling deeply and folding her hands as if in prayer. 'But this is the nature of war. And I trust you will all take a moment to remember those sailors. Those boys.'

There followed the longest silence, as we girls sat there completely stunned. Those last words spun round and round in my head. Some of them were just boys, not much older than us. On the front row, Belinda Quinn let out a giant sob, but mostly you could hear a pin drop; that was the first time ever the hall had been so full and yet so deathly quiet, I'm sure.

Once the news had sunk in, we sang some hymns and said quiet prayers for the ship and all those men with it. Suddenly the war no longer seemed quite the adventure I had hoped. It wasn't just a game of Cowboys and Indians, after all.

When the war was over, not long after I'd finished school, Dad arranged a special holiday for us to Scarborough, the seaside town in North Riding. We watched Punch and Judy on the beach and ate fish and chips, or huddled from the rain in a little ice cream shop. For a few days, Peter and I stayed with a family friend during the afternoons, while Mam and Dad went off on mysterious trips around town.

One evening, after bacon and eggs, we were gulping down rice pudding when Dad made an announcement.

'Your mother and I have decided we'll be moving here, to Scarborough. We can get a bigger house, and you two can have bigger rooms.'

'But, Dad! What about my friends?'

I would have to leave Mary and our adventures. I even had a pang of regret at leaving old Mr Gordon.

'Your father and I will be setting up a guest house here. We've saved a bit of money together, and this is the time to get into the holiday market,' Mam said.

Peter seemed too absorbed in his rice pud to care. But I was stunned. In any case, it was all settled, we'd be moving to Scarborough. And now that I'd left school, I'd have to get a proper job and start paying my own way.

So what on earth is a young girl to do? Sixteen years old, with life before me. I knew a few people who worked at the mill but that wasn't for me, all day in the dust and grind. Others were already engaged to be married, working in the family trades, or training to be nurses and teachers even. But I hadn't a clue what to do.

'Why don't you get a job as a sales girl at Marshall & Snelgrove or Rowntrees?' suggested Mam one day as she stirred a giant tub of washing, froth overflowing onto the kitchen floor.

'I was a milliner, you know,' she said, stirring madly. 'In a big department store in Leeds. Matthias Robinson. Making hats for all kinds, even gentry. That was before I met your father. And there are just as good prospects, if not better, for a young one like you now.'

'I don't know the first thing about clothes!' I said.

But I didn't have a better answer than that. The next day she shooed me out of the door in the direction of the store to ask for an interview, and it turned out they were all too keen for new staff, so it was easy enough to get a job. And that was that. I would work as a sales girl in the huge department store on a three-year apprenticeship. I'd work for two years as a junior, and my wages would be five shillings (25p) a week, with one week's holiday a year.

Marshall & Snelgrove was a large, impressive Victorian stone building, which took up a good portion of the street it was on. As I approached the main doors on my first day, I was greeted by Albert, the doorman. He was an eager young chap who seemed to revel in wearing his official brown suit and hat with gold trim and buttons. He was always smiling and flattering the old ladies. But as I was about to march in through the front entrance that day, a skip in my step, he stopped me in my tracks.

'Staff come this way,' he said and pointed to a rather grubbier side entrance.

'Oh. How silly.' I blushed beetroot red.

'You're a new one, aren't you?'

'Yes. Sorry. I'm Pamela.'

'Well, pleased to meet you, Pamela. Look out for Mrs Preen, that's all I'll say,' he said in a low whisper. 'She eats the new girls for breakfast.'

Then he darted back to his position and greeted a very elderly lady, taking her arm as she walked through the main door. She was carrying a dog which kept biting his sleeve, but he smiled all the way.

I walked through the side door and found myself in a dingy corridor, which smelled slightly of fish. I could hear the sounds of hustle and bustle coming from a small flight of stairs that led up into the shop. There was a shrill voice and an apologetic voice, then the sounds of running feet.

When I got upstairs to my department, Separates, the department manager, Mrs Preen, stood waiting at the top of the stairs with her head to one side, a concentrated expression on her face.

'Ah, Miss Rhodes, there you are.' She looked over her specs. She was examining a long list of something on a very important-looking bit of paper.

'We like our girls to arrive at a quarter to the clock, so if you could keep good time in future.'

She didn't look up as she spoke.

'Yes, Mrs Preen,' I said, with a slight curtsy.

There was no messing with Mrs Preen. She ruled with an iron rod and was always turned out smartly, with neat grey hair in a pristine bob, nothing ever out of place. I was to spend many an hour arranging stacks of clothes into perfect order, ready for her keen inspection.

There were four sales girls in our department, and I was the fourth. Bottom of the rung. It was hard work, with little room for excitement. If jumpers came in too small and a larger size was required by a customer, I'd have to stretch them out and iron them to make them bigger. I marked off stock when it came in and marked up prices. Very occasionally, if we had four customers and all the other girls were busy, I served on the shopfloor, which broke up the monotony a bit. When customers paid, the money went into a long metal tube which was then put into a shoot up to the mythical-sounding 'counting house'.

Our department was on the mezzanine floor and the view from the window was straight out to sea, at times seemingly into infinity. Sometimes it took my breath away, until Mrs Preen screeched across the floor at me to stop daydreaming.

There was a hairdressing department and a restaurant on the first floor, and on the ground floor there were other departments with posh names like Model Gowns, Millinery and Furs.

Two of the other women on my floor, May and Fay, were in their thirties. I always got them muddled up. They were very competitive: May was second sales girl and Fay was third, but Fay thought she should be second and had her eye on the position.

Then there was Miss Fraser, who had been there for hundreds of years and was about 300 years old. She told me that when she had joined, back in the 1930s, she had actually lived in the shop, along with some of the other older employees, in a dormitory on the top floor. I couldn't imagine living here and never leaving. How awful!

For the first few weeks, I would have my lunch with Miss Fraser as I didn't know anyone else. She told me about her life during the First World War and about her son who had died. At first I was fascinated, then I got a bit bored of hearing the same stories over and over again. I suppose, on reflection, she was lonely, but at the time I longed to meet someone my own age who I could have a giggle with.

Just when I thought I might die of boredom, everyone was suddenly in a frenzy. Mr Richardson, the store manager, had caused a hoo-ha by announcing we were to be hosting a fashion show. When the big day finally arrived, Mrs Preen was running around, straightening displays and shepherding us girls to take armfuls of ladieswear to the restaurant on the top floor where it was all taking place. Just as I was rounding a particularly large pillar, carrying a pile of clothes, I banged smack-wallop into a girl coming the other way, carrying an equally enormous load.

We both said 'Sorry!' at the same time, and laughed.

'Mrs Smith will have my guts for garters if I tarry,' said the girl, who introduced herself as Jane. 'I've got to model children's wear. Can you imagine?' she said. 'Are you modelling too?'

'Oh no. I'm new.'

We walked together to the restaurant floor, where all the tables and chairs had been pushed aside to make an aisle for the models. In those days, they actually called the real live models mannequins, and it was a 'mannequin parade' rather than a fashion show. Some of the girls had come all the way from London, while others like Jane were from the store itself.

A local trio played a song from *Oklahoma!* and a very tall

young woman, who looked like a film star, came tottering up the aisle, swishing a fox fur. I was gobsmacked by how glamorous it all seemed, with this mannequin, all the way from London, in our shop.

Mrs Preen was flapping around next to the racks of clothes. She had just realized that Fay, who was supposed to be modelling for our department, was ill in bed with the flu and there was no way she could make it.

'Oh Lord, the pedal pushers! And we've got Andrea Maracci up from London. I so desperately wanted him to see them.'

I had no idea who that was but he sounded important.

'Pamela, don't just stand there gawping. You'll have to do it.'

Me? I thought. I've never modelled anything in my life!

But before I could protest, she thrust something into my hands, a pair of bright blue cut-off trousers, and waved me over to the dressing area.

'Come on, girl, don't be shy, get behind that screen now. Quick-chop. Remember – permanent smile!'

As I struggled with the pedal pushers, it was Jane's turn up the aisle. She looked really confident, carrying a big sign with the word 'Teenagers' across the front. Teenage fashion was becoming a whole new style in its own right.

As soon as the song finished, I'd be next. Hopping on one foot and then the next, I got my leg stuck, but managed to get the trousers on just in time. I smoothed down my hair, then walked as confidently as I could onto the catwalk. Jane gave me a wink as she passed, and I tried to keep Mrs Preen's 'permanent smile' on my face, head up, back straight.

'Here we have our latest in Women's Separates, for all those new gals about town.'

Mr Richardson had taken the microphone. He revelled in being the compere at any event.

As I turned at the other end of the aisle, I nearly tripped on a wayward shoe, but managed to keep my balance by grabbing onto a pillar and, with a little impromptu twirl, made it back in one piece.

When it was all over, the spectators actually clapped and I couldn't help feeling a glow of pride that I'd been a real live mannequin for the day.

However, despite the occasional glimmer of glamour, I soon began to tire of clothes and coupons, Miss Fraser's stories and Mrs Preen's sharp tongue. I wanted to see more of the world and I wasn't likely to find it here, ironing skirts.

Every time we had Saturday afternoon off work, Jane and I would have lunch at a little cafe on the seafront. It was a penny for Yorkshire pud and rice pudding and we gobbled it down, making all kinds of plans for the rest of our lives, planning our escape from Marshall's. As we tucked into our treats that day, Jane was pouring over an advert she'd seen in the local paper.

It said: *Assisted Passage. Start a New Life Across the World: New Zealand for only £10.*

'But what would we do there? It's so far.'

'I don't know. Be waitresses or something. Come on. Let's write to them and ask!' said Jane, her eyes shining.

So we shook on it that we'd write to the address listed and see if we could get a place on the next boat. I didn't know much about New Zealand except that it was miles and miles away, took weeks to get there and there were mountains, maybe even volcanoes. I'd seen an article in *National Geographic* once and I knew they had some strange animals, lizards with big heads and a bird called a kiwi that looked furry.

We drafted the letter the next day:

Dear Sir,

Please can we get an assisted passage to New Zealand so we can start a new life? We are very hard working and would be an asset to your country. We have saved up £3 and five shillings, between us.

Yours sincerely,
Pamela Rhodes and Jane Willow

PS We don't get seasick and would be no trouble at all on the boat either.

Actually I had no idea whether I got seasick since I'd never been on a boat, apart from the small ones in Scarborough, but I thought it should give us the best chance. We posted the letter, which needed seven stamps, and crossed our fingers for a swift reply. As the letter plopped into the post box, I realized I had been so caught up in the excitement I hadn't even discussed it with Mam and Dad and vowed to let them know my news over tea that evening.

When I got home I heard voices from the living room and peeped round the door. Dad's friend, Sergeant Baker, was sitting on the special chair that Granny always sat in, the one with the reclining back. We all called him 'Dad's billiard friend' on account of the fact that they played billiards together every Thursday. I noticed they had the good china out, and biscuits too. It must be something big then. But they were laughing, so it couldn't be serious.

Sergeant Baker was wearing his police uniform and his hat was on the table. He had a streak of silvery-white hair like a badger, and unnervingly wild, staring brown eyes. I was apprehensive of the whole situation and tried to creep past up the stairs.

'Is that you, Pamela?' called out Dad. 'We've got a visitor.'

I walked in reluctantly and the Sergeant shook my hand so firmly he nearly broke my fingers.

I was desperate to talk to Mam and Dad about my plans for New Zealand, but there he was, grinning back at me. Finally Dad spoke.

'Brian here says they have a vacancy at his station. For a woman. In the police. So what do you think about that then?'

A vacancy? The police? What's all this? I knew nothing about the police, apart from old PC Bennett, our village bobby, and that run-in from aeons ago with Mary. Would it mean arresting villains? Maybe I'd have to identify dead bodies. Eurgh.

'There are more women now joining the force, but still not enough. We have a female sergeant up at HQ, Freeman. Excellent specimen. But we're encouraging more. And with our towns and cities growing at such a pace, we need everyone to do their bit to protect the rule of law and order.' Sergeant Baker's eyes darted around the room with unsettling enthusiasm.

'So what do you think?' asked Dad eagerly. 'Do you want to give it a go?'

'I . . . I don't know. Maybe. It hadn't even occurred to me to consider . . .'

'Well. Think it over, lass. You've got until next week. And when you do decide to join, there's a round of interviews next week, so you can stay with me and the wife up in Northallerton.'

Dumbfounded by the whole thing, I made my excuses, said I'd think about it, and left. My head was spinning with the new possibilities my hitherto uneventful life had suddenly presented.

The next day, at work, I kept getting everything wrong and it seemed like the longest morning ever. First was ironing, and I managed to burn a huge hole in a really expensive cardigan. They came all the way from Ireland and I knew Mrs Preen would have a fit, so I tried to hide it under some skirts, hoping it might just miraculously disappear.

On the shopfloor wasn't any better. I had a nightmare customer who all us girls dreaded. We called her Dog Lady. She wore a huge hat, a different one each day with a different kind of fruit on it, and she carried her yappy dog, Snuffles, everywhere with her. She dressed the animal in clothes to match her own outfit and today they were both wearing peach-coloured jackets.

Dog Lady was renowned for trying on a hundred outfits in one go, then rejecting them one by one, for being too big or too small, too thin or too thick, too red or not red enough. As she preened and considered the clothes in front of the big mirror, Snuffles, with whom I had now been charged, kept trying to lick the inside of my nose. Meanwhile, she reeled off a list of questions.

'Is this hand-stitched? Where does this cloth come from? Is it silk? Are you using those terrible new synthetic fibres, made by *chemists*? Have you ever heard anything more ridiculous in your life?'

She even complained that one of the blouses she tried on smelled of cabbage and someone must have worn it before. I kept smiling until my mouth ached and tried to control the wretched Snuffles, who had wriggled away and was now nibbling his way along the clothes rail.

I was desperate for my lunch break too, so I could see Jane and tell her about Sergeant Baker and The Visit. Eventually Dog Lady decided she didn't have enough to buy anything anyway and she left, squeezing the breath out of the poor animal at her side.

I wasn't out of the woods just yet, though. Mrs Preen approached, holding up the offending cardigan.

'I found *this*,' she held up the article as though it were contaminated, 'stuffed – can you believe, stuffed? – under some skirts in the stock room. Pamela, do you know anything about this? Weren't you on ironing this morning?'

'I, umm, sorry, Mrs Preen. I was going to tell you but we got so busy and . . .'

'Do you know how much these cost? They should be treated with respect. And with rationing the way it is! Do you know what it's worth? Well?'

'I'm so sorry. It'll never happen again. But I've really got to go. I'm sorry.'

For once I didn't care about the consequences, and, totally out of character, I dashed off, leaving Mrs Preen stunned, still holding up the garment, while I went to meet Jane.

I told her in one long torrent all about the meeting I'd had with my dad's billiard friend, and she thought the whole thing sounded thrilling.

'It might be really exciting,' she said, 'all those handsome officers, and crimes and murders to solve.'

Apart from a few crime books, I really had no idea what being in the police force would be like, and I doubted it would be like it was in the novels, all jewel thieves and handsome rogues. But in the end, I decided what the heck, it could be fun, and anything to get me away from the dreaded Mrs Preen.

That evening, I told Mam and Dad that I had decided to give the police thing a go.

'Brian'll be chuffed,' said Dad as he flopped down on the chair after work. 'He's right keen to get more women in the force. Since the war they're up to all sorts.'

'Oh yes. Mabel from school made aeroplane parts and now she's a mechanic,' Mam said. 'She has to wear overalls and use a spanner and everything. And her friend Liza. She even flew planes during the war. You'll do as well as any of those lads, I know it.'

Mam's kind smile filled me to the brim with confidence.

'Pass the newspaper, would you?' asked Dad, and he started flicking through it. After a little while he remarked, 'Hmm, nothing much new. War in Korea. Isn't Fred's boy out there?'

'Yes. Awful business,' sighed Mam.

'More bad news. Who's dead then?'

'George, don't be so . . .'

'Never heard of him. Or him.' He continued to look through the obituaries. Then he said, 'Hey, isn't that that singer?'

'Isn't who that singer?' asked Mam.

'That Welsh singer. Who signed your photo in that beauty competition.'

'What beauty competition?' I asked.

'Oh that! That was years ago. Ivor Novello.'

'Yes, that's the badger. Well, he's dead.'

'Oh no! He was so handsome,' Mam said. 'Lovely eyes. How?'

'Coronary.'

'What beauty competition?' I asked again loudly.

'Before you were born. Before I met your father actually. In the twenties,' Mam told me.

'Go and get the picture,' said Dad, so I sat there intrigued as Mam went upstairs and rummaged about for a while. Eventually, she came back with a black and white photo and put it on the table in front of us. At the bottom was a large, curly signature in blue ink. Ivor Novello.

'You look so young. Like a film star,' I said, holding the photo up to the light.

'Well, I don't know about that,' she said and smiled, as her younger self looked back at her from all those years ago. 'I don't know why I did it really. I had this mad notion about being a mannequin and I went in for this competition. We all had to dress up swanky, like, and be photographed. And Ivor Novello was the judge. I got asked to go and do a screen test in Leeds. He signed my picture. I just can't believe he's gone.'

At that moment I realized this woman, my mother, had a life of her own. She wasn't just Mam. She had a past, youthful dreams, young larks, hopes and fears. And even now, all the time I was at work or out with friends, sorting out my own life, hers carried on minute by minute too. But I would never know what really went on in her mind, or who she really was.

I looked at the photo again, and the signature from Ivor Novello. I felt proud of her, but also a little sad. She still looked young now she was in her forties, but where once her skin had been clear and bright, now lines were starting to form round her eyes and there were shadows under her eyes.

'Innocent times. I'm not like that any more,' she said sadly and turned the photo over.

Dad looked up and smiled. 'You are to me.'

I applied to the police by letter, to Headquarters at Northallerton, and soon got a reply that there was to be an interview and a written exam for the course, which started that June.

I had the time off work already, so I didn't have to explain anything to Mrs Preen and Jane was sworn to secrecy.

I had to change trains a couple of times on my way to Northallerton. On the last train, I ended up in a carriage with a woman who was trying to control her small son. His sailor outfit was all covered in chocolate and he kept trying to stick his head out of the window to look at the 'choo-choo chimney'. She was fighting a losing battle to get him to sit still and gave me one of those defeated looks as if to say, what can you do? I told her I was off to be interviewed for the police.

'Ooh, they have ladies do that now, don't they?' she said. 'Sit down, Billy! You can't take him anywhere. So will you be working with the men, then? And doing what they do and arresting folks and so on? I'll have to be on my best behaviour then, won't I?'

I said I wasn't sure what I'd be doing yet, but that I had to meet the Chief Constable and do a written exam. As I said the words, it sounded very grand and official.

I looked out of the window as the Yorkshire countryside whizzed by, its landscapes half-familiar from childhood holidays. Huddles of cows and stone walls flashed by in a blur. A farmer hunched in his field eating a sandwich; a woman tried to control her washing in the wind. I wondered what we'd have for tea and whether the food would be good at the Bakers. I was starving. I looked up at the little boy, who had finally exhausted himself into sleep on his mother's lap. With the only sound the clattering of the train, I soon drifted off myself.

'Northallerton. This is Northallerton.'

I woke with a jolt as the guard shouted up and down the corridor. I grabbed my suitcase off the rack and made it out just in time. On the platform, Sergeant Baker and a woman I assumed was his wife were looking out for me, smiling as the train pulled away with shunt and a blast of the whistle.

Mrs Baker was tiny, only about four foot eleven, with a great pile of grey curly hair on her head, which threatened to unbalance her at any moment. She had a much louder voice than you would possibly have thought her tiny frame could produce.

'Miss Rhodes.' She embraced me with a huge hug for such a small woman. 'You must be as hungry as a boar. We'll have a nice cup of tea and some proper teacakes, baked only this morning by my sister, who's a baker in town, you know. Funny that, with me marrying Mr Baker, and all.'

She laughed extremely loudly at the thought of it. Sergeant Baker, his silver streak of hair flashing, shook my hand with vehemence and the grip of a vice, and took my suitcase.

The Bakers lived in a police house in a little brick terrace near the station. I was to sleep in their son's bedroom as he was away doing his National Service. I sat down on the bed and unpacked my suitcase: some books and a smart skirt and blouse for the interview. It felt funny to be in someone else's bedroom, and a boy's bedroom at that. It was nothing like my brother's, though. His was always full of toys and cars and soldiers in mid-battle. This was tidy and ordered to the extreme.

There was a neat little row of animal skulls on the mantlepiece, arranged in size order, neatly labelled in scratchy green ink. One said 'Dog. 1946. Devon', another 'Fox? 1949. Northallerton' and there was one which just said, ominously, 'Rodent', with no record of date or location. Next to this was a collection of beetles of all different colours: green, red, a brown spotted one and, in the centre, an enormous black stag beetle, its giant pincers pointing right at me. A shiver crept up my spine and I was relieved when Mrs Baker called up the stairs that tea was ready.

The next day I walked to the station with Sergeant Baker, who told me about the history of the town. As he droned away, I was distracted, trying to remember facts for my exam. I didn't know what questions to expect. What's the largest lake in the world? Lake Malawi, was it? And who's the Home Secretary again? Oh God, I thought, I can't remember it all.

Northallerton Police HQ was a large, imposing red-brick building with lampposts outside and a big 'Police' sign. Inside, officers walked past us urgently in all directions, essential cogs in the giant clockwork of official business. It felt overwhelmingly busy and important. I wondered what kinds of secret and heinous crimes were being solved and detected right then under that roof.

In a room someway up the corridor I heard the crackle of a police radio: 'Ten four. Over.' A sergeant sat me down outside the exam room; there were two young lads sitting there already. One was rather spotty with really thick glasses; as I sat down he picked his nose vigorously and flicked its contents across the room. The other was very tall with ginger wavy hair. After a while, the ginger-haired one said coolly, 'They didn't say there'd be lasses here. No one ever said anything about that.'

'They're quite common in the police now actually,' I lied, and vowed to make sure I passed that exam, just to prove to him that girls were just as good as boys, if not better.

A bored-looking sergeant yawned and ushered us into the exam room, where we sat at small tables. It felt like being back at school. The questions are a blur now in my mind, but I remember being asked to name the Home Secretary, and there was a geography section that asked us: 'How many counties are there on the east coast?' There was also a current affairs section, and a dictation test.

After that was over, I had to be interviewed by the Chief Constable. Lieutenant Colonel J. Moran was a very tall thin man, with a squeaky nasal voice and yellowy-white hair. He sat behind a big oak desk in an old-fashioned swivelling chair.

Above his head was a painting of a country scene in which a man on a horse, a general maybe, was trotting past a group of peasants lounging about in the sun. Next to that there was a photo of himself, receiving an award.

We shook hands. He gave me the distinct impression of a dead frog, which gave me a terrible sense of foreboding.

'Sit down, Miss, ah . . . Rhodes,' he said, peering down at his notes. 'I see you hail from Scarborough.'

'Yes, sir. Colonel. Chief Constable. Sir,' I said nervously, wondering if that was somehow a bad thing.

'I once had an aunt in Scarborough,' he said, taking a huge puff on his pipe. 'Renie. She fell under a horse and cart. Terrible, messy business.' He looked back at his notes then snapped, 'So why do you want to join the force then, hmmm?'

I had prepared a full and heartfelt answer, but my mind suddenly went completely blank.

'Because . . . umm . . .' I looked up at the painting, the man on the horse and the laughing country folk, hoping for some inspiration. 'Because I want to serve my country and do my bit to protect the law and order of the nation. And,' I added, 'I want to get on in the world and see more and do better and I'd love to ride in a Black Maria.' Oh god, why did I say that last bit? That was so stupid.

The Chief Constable let out a single burst of laugh, before assuming a seriousness more appropriate to the situation.

'Well, I think I have everything I need. We'll inform you

by letter presently. Thank you, Miss Rhodes. Sergeant Gaunt will see you to the medical room. Next.'

Sergeant Gaunt appeared out of the shadows and whisked me through to another room, where a balding, monocled doctor, who didn't say a single word except for 'Please lift your arm,' checked my blood pressure, noted my height and weight, and took a blood sample. And then, before I knew it, everything was over.

On the train home, I slept with exhaustion the whole way.

At work, I couldn't stop re-running the whole surreal experience, the interview and the exam, over and over in my mind. Had I answered the questions right, had I said the right things to the Chief Constable? I felt sure his tone of voice at the end meant I hadn't got in. I had also been trying to avoid Mrs Preen all morning, in case she tried to corner me again about the cardigan. But I hadn't seen her at all, which was strange.

On my way back from lunch, I was walking past Mr Richardson's office when I heard muffled raised voices from within. I stood on tiptoes and peered through the little glass window in the door. Sitting down was a policeman, looking very serious, with his hat on the desk in front of him. Mrs Preen was standing up, looking agitated. I strained to hear through the door but could only make out the odd sentence here and there.

'Well, she never said a *word* to me,' Mrs Preen said.

'But didn't you even suspect?' whined Mr Richardson.

The policeman then said, 'So what did she do here exactly?' and 'But is she a hard worker?'.

I couldn't quite catch the answer. It looked like the

officer was getting up to leave so as they shook hands, all smiles, I slunk away round the corner. I ran back to my department and pretended to fold some clothes. A few minutes later a voice cracked like Jupiter in the heavens.

'Pamela Rhodes. MISS RHODES! Mr Richardson wants to see you. Now. In his office.'

'Yes, Mrs Preen. Right away, Mrs Preen.'

When I sat down, Mr Richardson was smiling and being far too nice for my liking.

'You know how much we rely on you here, don't you, Pamela?' He smiled, fiddling with a paperweight in the shape of the Eiffel Tower. He never usually called me by my first name. 'All your years of hard work have not gone unnoticed, you know.'

'Did you think you could hide it from us? We're not stupid,' Mrs Preen burst in, unable to contain herself.

Although she was called Mrs Preen we had never heard hide nor hair of a Mr Preen. We all wondered whether she had murdered her husband and kept him hidden, maybe stuffed, in their house, so she could shout at him when the mood took her and he wouldn't answer back. Her screeching voice shook me back to reality.

'I put in all that time, training you how to count the coupons, how to fold and to iron, and to get the best sales figures. There are literally hundreds of girls, like you, who'd give their arms and teeth for this job. And you throw it right back in my face.'

'If it's the wages,' reasoned Mr Richardson, 'I'm sure there's some arrangement we can come to. There may well be an opening,' he declared grandly, 'in Furs! Now, what do you think about that?'

'Well, yes, the police wages are higher,' I said. 'But that's not the only thing.'

But before I could go on, Mrs Preen was right back in.

'Yes, but you know you have to spend half of that money on your lodgings. I mean, really, a woman joining the police. Whatever next? Women politicians? I don't object to women in the workplace as such, obviously, but fashion is so much more . . . suitable.'

'But money's not the only thing,' I said, surprised at my sudden confidence. 'And anyway there are more women doing it now and Sergeant Baker says . . . things are changing.'

After a short pause for consideration, Mrs Preen dropped her voice and changed tack.

'I have connections, you know, Pamela. In London. I could easily secure you a position as a top sales girl at one of the big department stores — a situation much more befitting a young lady.'

'You know policing can be dangerous work too,' added Mr Richardson.

'Exactly! You have to suffer such unsavoury characters. Thieves and beggars and . . .' Mrs Preen paused for effect and whispered, 'ladies of the night'.

After what seemed like hours of this unseemly joust, they let me leave. I managed to hold my ground, saying I was really very grateful for all their guidance but I had made up my mind. It had felt like another job interview all over again but, in the end, neither had managed to convince me to stay. In fact, everything they said made the police seem even more exciting than ever, and only stiffened my resolve.

But that evening, as I lay in bed and stared out of the

window at the wide open sky, I reflected on what they had said, the offer of work in London, and how dangerous police work would be. Maybe they were right after all, maybe I was making a terrible mistake.

A few days later I had sort of forgotten about the whole thing, and it seemed like a distant dream. Then an envelope arrived, blue with an official-looking stamp. I scooped it up and held on to it for ages, while I ate breakfast and then tidied my room. I carried it around with me all morning, not daring to open it.

Mam and Dad were in the garden, heads down in the vegetable patch. Eventually I ran upstairs and sat in my favourite spot, a window ledge on the landing, and pulled the letter from the envelope carefully to extract the neatly folded contents without tearing them. My stomach turned somersaults as I read the typed words.

Dear Miss Rhodes,

Further to your application to enrol on the training course with a view to becoming a probationary Police Constable, we regret to inform you . . .

Oh no!

. . . we regret to inform you that, although you have passed all the exams and were otherwise a highly suitable candidate, your medical tests have revealed that you have a condition called anaemia, which makes you unfit for service at this point. You will therefore need to attend a further medical. If you then meet the approved health standards, we will consider offering you a position.'

Anaemia? What on earth was it, I wondered. I hoped it was not serious. I rushed into the garden.

'It's something to do with the blood, isn't it?' said Dad. He was on his knees, pulling up a particularly stubborn weed.

'It's nothing to worry about. You just need to eat more iron,' said Mam.

'What does that mean?' I asked, my mind boggling at the thought.

'How about this for starters?' she said, and pulled up a great big handful of spinach.

So, for the next two weeks, Mam fed me up on as much liver and greens as she could get her hands on, even doing deals with some of the neighbours to get me more of the wretched stuff. It was liver every which way: fried, boiled and cooked in a big stew, liver mashed up on toast and liver casserole. I even dreamt of liver.

When the date for the medical check-up came, all I could do was cross my fingers and hope I was cured of the blessed illness.

I returned to Northallerton and the doctor took another blood sample and checked me for all the symptoms again, then tested my eyes and measured and weighed me. A few days later, the results came through: I was cured, fit as a fiddle.

So it was official. I would be going on the police training course in Lancashire the following week. I was later told that two boys I'd sat the exam with had failed to pass the test, and the other boy failed the medical because he wore glasses. But as for me, before long, I'd be a real live bobby on the beat.

2

'Right, Miss, if you just lift your head forward slightly. And . . . Ready.'

The camera flashed and I blinked in shock.

'Right, just one more. That's lovely! Eyes up. Beautiful.' *Click, flash.*

I wasn't sure whether I was supposed to smile or not, so I attempted a kind of half-hearted effort. Later I learnt you are definitely not supposed to smile.

I was having my official photo taken, for the records, at Northallerton Police HQ. It was the same place they photographed all the offenders. When I got my photo back I did look a bit like I had just committed mass murder myself, and hidden the bodies where no one would ever find them.

After the photo room, they took me to a corner of a big office where fingerprints were being taken. There was a large desk with ink-pads and piles of record books. The police had been using fingerprints to confirm identity in Britain since around the turn of the century and, in the early 1950s, it was still one of the few scientific methods we had at our disposal.

The same bored-looking sergeant who had shown me into the exam room for my interview now lifted my hand nonchalantly, and as he took my fingerprints he explained what he was doing.

'So you roll them this way,' he yawned. 'And then that way . . .'

I seriously thought he was about to fall asleep right there and then on the desk.

'. . . to get an even spread of ink.'

It felt funny to be 'on record'. My own unique identity, the prints of my fingertips, now preserved in black and white. When you leave the police, I had been assured, they destroy your fingerprints and return the photo.

After that, I got my uniform and all the pieces of police kit I needed from the storeroom, and I was given two large books, *Stone's Justices' Manual* and *Moriarty's Police Law*. These were given to all new police trainees, in order that we would learn about the law. Now I had everything I needed as a new recruit.

'Have you got everything? Your books, whistle? Have you got enough clothes?'

Mam fussed as she stood at the door to see me off. It was the first time I would be away from home for this long, thirteen weeks in total.

As I walked along the seafront, I looked at the two cliffs of Scarborough and felt a pang of regret at leaving its fresh sea air. That funny town, stuck out there on the edge of the world, or so it felt.

Up St Nicholas Street, as I went past Marshall & Snelgrove I saw Jane looking out of the window. We had arranged to say goodbye when I passed by and she ran out to meet me. She had another girl with her and they both looked excited.

'Here,' she said, handing me a small cloth packet.

'It's a "survival package". Open it on the train,' she grinned. 'This is Maureen, by the way. She's at Marshall's, in Furs.'

Maureen looked up shyly from under a small felt hat.

'She wants to be a policewoman too. Don't you, Maureen? Tell her.'

'Really?' I asked.

'Yes,' said Maureen quietly. 'Just wondered if you had any tips. You know, about exams or whatever you have to do.'

So I told her what I'd experienced and gave her a few hints. I said I'd put in a good word if I could.

Funny that, I thought. I had been the first woman I knew to think about joining the police, and now everyone wanted to.

'Anyway, make sure to write and tell me all your police adventures,' said Jane. 'We'd better get back in. I've got the dreaded Smith on my back again.'

I would be sad to say goodbye to the laughs we'd had together. Our dreams of escape to the other side of the world. We shook hands, and with that she was gone.

When I got to the station, there were only a few minutes before my train. I decided not to look back at Scarborough and I found myself holding back a few tears. Although it was a thrill to be going it was also a scary jump off into the unknown.

The only people in my carriage were a snoring man in a pork pie hat and a nun, who was knitting.

No one spoke and the journey seemed to take for ever. By the time we were out in the countryside I was too nervous and excited to read or do anything. Eventually, I opened up Jane's survival package. It contained a paper bag of my favourite sweets, Liquorice Allsorts, and some writing paper with rabbits up the side, with a little note on the first sheet from Jane saying 'Write to me!'

When I arrived at Warrington, a policeman stood leaning against the wall. I wandered over and said I was here for training and asked was I in the right place. He nodded and introduced himself as Sergeant Wooding. Two other lads, who had been on the same train, turned up and we all walked up the hill together.

One of the lads introduced himself as Ted; the other was Neville. As we wandered up the country lane, Wooding told us a little about the history of the training site.

'Bruche was originally built on open fields, in 1940, to provide temporary accommodation for workers at the nearby munitions factory at Risley.' He waved his hand vaguely and spoke as though he was reading from a guide book. 'It was never actually used for that purpose, though, and in the end the US Army took it over for a while as a transit camp. It opened as a Police Training Centre in 1946 . . .'

I was so tired from the journey, I was half in a doze as he spoke. Then I saw the site at the bottom of the hill: a collection of buildings and Nissen huts, and a large area like a school playground.

'That'll be where we parade, I'll bet,' whispered Ted as we passed by.

I wondered what that would involve. I had seen soldiers marching, during the war and at the pictures. But I had never done it myself.

47

When we arrived, Sergeant Wooding pointed the lads in one direction and then showed me over to the women's hut. Boys and girls were strictly separated, to avoid any 'unnecessary . . . distractions', as he put it.

Our sleeping quarters were old iron Nissen huts, where I supposed the soldiers from the US Army must have slept before us. They were divided up into little bedrooms; Sergeant Wooding opened a door to one and waved me in.

It was pretty stark and simple inside, with a small table and chair and a low metal bed with a single blanket. There was a little window, and the whole place smelled of dust and beeswax. A former resident had scratched something onto the desk: 'Jennie and Derek. 1949'. And there was a little love heart next to it. But I was happy: it was clean enough and it was all mine for the next thirteen weeks.

'You have a wardrobe and a sink and shared bathrooms there, at the end. And there's a shelf for your books here,' Wooding said. 'Wake up call is at six thirty a.m. sharp for Parade at seven a.m. Breakfast at eight a.m. and lectures from nine a.m. Schedule is typed up here.' He handed me a piece of light green paper with all the information for the week on it.

'Lights out at ten thirty p.m. but you're free to go into town before that. Just look out for Merriweather, he notices everything. So no funny business. Fridays we have a dance in the main hall. Any questions?'

My head was spinning and I couldn't think of anything useful to ask, so with a nod he left me to it. As I unpacked my case, I could hear two girls already in the bedroom next to mine talking and laughing. I laid out all my clothes and my official police equipment on the bed.

There was my tunic – the traditional police jacket – two crisp white shirts, one navy skirt, three pairs of stockings. I also had two sets of gloves – one white, one brown – and a large navy greatcoat.

Then there were my other bits and bobs. I was issued with a small leather bag. The lads would have a truncheon and a whistle, but we women only had a whistle. The police didn't carry radios at all in those days. We had a tape measure, for measuring distances in case of traffic accidents, and a torch for going on the beat in the dark, plus a little first-aid kit and a notebook and pencil.

I stood back and admired all the new items, then arranged them in size order, wondering if and when I might get to use them. A knock at the door made me jump. I peeped round and a strapping lass with freckles and a shock of blonde curly hair stood next to a smaller, slim girl with pale skin, her brown hair cut into a bob.

'I'm Sally,' said the taller girl, holding out her hand. 'And this is Marge,' she said, speaking for her companion. 'We're both from Durham, it turns out. Quite a coincidence. But we don't know each other. Well, we do now, but we didn't before,' she laughed. 'We got here last night. The rooms are quite small, and a bit chilly at night, but we've got enough to survive. I suppose it's a bit like camping.'

Marge peered into my room and looked desperate to come in, so I moved aside.

'Did you know these huts were used by American soldiers during the war, or so I was told. I could swear I heard the ghost of one whispering out last night, during the night. Didn't I, Marge?'

Marge nodded.

'How terrifying,' I answered. 'I'm Pam, from Scarborough, but I've only just got here. I suppose my room's much the same as yours, is it?'

'Yes. Pretty much. Ooh, you've laid all your things out. How efficient,' said Sally, peering about. 'Your bed's the other side to mine. I haven't even unpacked yet. Everything's still just spilling out of my case all over the floor.'

She paused, looked around and picked up one of my books, flicked through it, then put it back down again.

'Marge's room is that side of you and I'm on the other side. We wondered who would be in here. Anyway, we'll leave you to unpack and see you at dinner?'

'Yes, absolutely. Nice to meet you,' I answered, slightly stunned by Sally's confidence.

Marge, who had said nothing throughout the duration of the visit, flashed me a very pretty smile that revealed slightly crooked teeth and then they turned and left.

I packed my things away in the cupboard and made my way down to the canteen for dinner. Everyone filed along with trays past a lady called Mrs Bevell, who was dishing out what soon came to be known as 'slop'. Today, slop had been given the grand title of lamb stew, but when I sat down to eat I couldn't find a trace of lamb in it. It was 1951 and rationing was still in full swing, but I did, after some sifting, discover what might well have been a pea or possibly a piece of carrot, but then it could just as easily have been turnip.

Sally and Marge, who were already seated, waved me over to join them. They were with two lads, one was Ted, who I'd met on the walk up from the station. The other was a chap called Allan, from Liverpool, who had black wavy hair and intense brown eyes.

'The food's not much to write home about, is it?' Allan said, prodding warily at his plate. 'Did she say it was rat stew?'

For a moment I wasn't sure whether he was joking or not.

'I don't know. It's not bad,' said Ted, shovelling away, barely stopping to breathe. 'Besides, I'm starved to the brim.'

'Well, it's better than what me mam cooks, I suppose,' said Sally, somewhat siding with Ted on the issue. They looked at each other and smiled.

Marge said very little as she ate a mouse-sized portion, but when it came to the rice pudding for afters, she swallowed the lot practically in one mouthful. We all stopped talking, slightly shocked as she wiped her mouth and grinned.

After that first evening the real regime started. We were to be up at the crack of dawn for inspection on the parade ground. After breakfast, there would be an introductory talk from Inspector Merriweather, followed by self-defence and then lectures in the afternoon.

That night, I lay on my bed in the little hut, thinking of how different my life suddenly was. I wondered what Jane was up to, and Mam and Dad, and wrote them letters on my new notepaper, telling them all about the Nissen huts and the slop and all the new people I'd met.

When I looked at my little wind-up alarm clock it was still only nine o'clock, so I pulled the blanket round me and started to leaf through one the textbooks we'd been given, *Stone's Justices' Manual*. It sounded so grand. It was full to the brim with 'definitions', legal descriptions that we'd have to learn for our final exams, in order to identify whether a crime had been committed or not.

Today, you can look things up on a computer. But back then we had to remember every last legal detail, and I can still reel off dozens of the definitions at the drop of a hat:

A constable is a citizen, locally appointed but having authority under the Crown for the protection of life and property, the maintenance of order, the prevention and detection of crime and the prosecution of offenders against Peace.

A firearm is a lethal barrelled weapon of any description from which any shot, bullet or other missile can be discharged.

Theft. A person steals who, without authority of the owner and without a claim of right in good faith, takes and carries away anything capable of being stolen with the intention at the time of such taking to permanently deprive the owner thereof.

Assault. An attempt or offer by force or violence to do bodily injury to another.

As the words started to blur into one, I lay back, just about ready to doze off, when the book fell open on a page entitled 'Incest'.

Heavens. I had only read about this in the *News of the World* and I wasn't even entirely sure what it was. And now I'd have to be learning about it for real. What had I got myself into? I may have been about to embark on a new career, but I felt very unworldly indeed as I drifted off to sleep that night.

No sooner had I dozed off, or so it seemed, when my alarm clock rang loudly and dragged me back to reality. As the sun drifted in through the small window, I got up, stretched and reached out for my new uniform, hanging in the wardrobe. I checked my shoes were still shiny and gave them one last spit and polish. I grabbed my hat, which we were expected to wear at all times on site, and bumped into Marge and Sally in the corridor.

We headed out together onto the parade ground, an area about the size of a netball court, covered in tarmac and surrounded by small oak trees, with a front gate at the end leading out onto the lane.

We hadn't had breakfast yet and it was a chilly morning, with the sun just creeping out over the tops of the trees, mist hanging in the air. I hugged myself and stamped my feet to try to keep warm as the rest of the group made its way out. There were Ted and Allan, and other faces I'd never seen before. In total there were five girls and twenty-one boys on our course, and we all lined up for inspection.

'Do you actually know how to march?' whispered Sally, as we stood in line waiting for the Sergeant. 'My dad tried to teach me a bit.' She grimaced, demonstrating a moment of wild marching. 'It was a disaster. I kept tripping up all over the place and I couldn't take it seriously. He gave up in the end.'

'I'm so nervous my legs feel like jelly,' I said. 'I don't even know the proper way to salute. Is it the left or the right hand?'

Just then Sergeant Thompson came striding onto the

field. I expect we looked a right raggedy bunch. He walked up and down and checked our uniforms, pulled a few collars into line and made sure the lads were clean-shaven. He pulled one lad aside.

'You, boy. What's yer name?' he asked in a loud drawl.

'Carson, sir. Ted Carson.'

'Well, Ted Carson, learn how to use a razor!'

'Sorry, Sergeant; yes, Sergeant,' he answered.

'You're a slovenly lot and no mistake. But it's your first day, and we'll make an exception, this once. But from tomorrow Inspector Merriweather will be out, and if there's a stitch out of place, it'll be hell to pay for the lot of you. Atten—shun!'

'Parade, parade. Quick . . . march!'

And we were off, trying desperately to keep some kind of meaningful formation. We would have marching practice every day from now on, in preparation for the Passing Out parade which would come at the end of our course. Every year wanted to be the best and we were no exception.

The lads all seemed to know exactly what to do, having all just come fresh from their National Service. But we girls had no idea and got legs and arms in all kinds of disarray, veering off course in every direction and bumping into each other. Then, to my horror, Sergeant Thompson made us go right out of the front gates and up the road.

'About . . . turn! One, two, one, two.'

We marched past the village church and up the little lane towards the post office and on towards the Three Crowns public house. Marge, Sally and I were doing our best to desperately keep in rhythm, get our arms swinging to match our feet, and get everything to match the Ser-

54

geant. Marge seemed to be getting it all right in the end, but Sally and I were a lost cause.

When we got to the end of the lane we passed a pair of elderly ladies out walking their dogs. They stopped to stare and one of the dogs ran up to Sergeant Thompson and started biting at his trouser legs. That was it, it was too much to bear, and Sally, Marge and I only just managed to stave off a fit of hysterics. But this was a serious business and the Sergeant just carried on until the animal gave up. Nothing seemed to phase him.

When we finally arrived back at the parade ground Thompson dismissed everyone, but beckoned us three over before we could leave.

'Names!' he ordered.

'Rhodes.'

'Lyons.'

'Peters.'

We all spoke at once, staring straight ahead. My legs were shaking.

For a while he didn't say a word, just paced up and down, his top lip quivering, as though mourning the loss of a very large moustache.

'They said it was a good idea bringing women in. And I relented. In the end. And I'm not old-fashioned. I know times are changing. But this is not. I repeat NOT some village dance.'

Then he continued in a near whisper, with his face right up against ours. 'It's not a game. So you either buck up your ideas, or you'll be . . . there will be trouble. Understood?'

'Yes, Sergeant,' we said, and Sally bit her lip, just managing to suppress a smile. We gave our best attempt at standing to attention and were duly dismissed.

After breakfast, Inspector Merriweather met us all in the lecture hall for what he called his 'introductory speech'.

Along the wall was a row of pictures depicting jowly men in various authoritative poses. At the very end was a picture of a whiskered Victorian gentleman in a uniform, maybe one of the first policemen ever, I thought. I didn't see any pictures of women.

Merriweather walked out onto the stage. He had a fawn-coloured sprout of hair, rather like the top of a broomstick. There was a persistent rumour that it was a wig, but we never found out for sure. Merriweather was a fervent and heartfelt Evangelical Christian, and he assumed an enormous sense of propriety over the students, particularly the ladies. He clasped his hands together and emitted a high, squeaking voice.

'So, you think you've made it. You think you're going to be top dogs.'

What he lacked in depth of tone, he made up for with volume and zeal.

'Well, let me get one thing straight. Nothing is certain in this world. Least of all success. You have to earn it. Day by day, minute by minute.'

He cracked his fingers one by one. Ted scribbled something on a piece of paper and passed it to Allan, who stifled a smirk, then passed it on to Sally, who passed it to me where it stopped.

Inspector Merriweather eyed us all suspiciously.

I opened the note carefully. It was a cartoon sketch of Merriweather in the shape of a cartoon broomstick, resplendent in hat. I scrunched it up straight away and put it deep in my pocket for fear of being caught.

'Cursing,' he continued after a long pause, 'will not be tolerated under any circumstances. You ladies here –' he waved along the row with a flourish – 'I see it as my unparalleled duty to protect and uphold you all, in the name of virtue. And I will not suffer swearing or taking the Lord's name in vain from the men.'

He paused again and inhaled deeply.

'Not in the halls and corridors, not in your own rooms, not even in your dreams. And under no circumstances will you fraternize. We run a tight ship and there is no room for . . . personalities.'

He said that last word as though biting into a particularly bitter piece of fruit.

'I will be watching you. UNDERSTOOD?'

There was a mumble of 'yes, sirs', but I got the distinct feeling we weren't going to be able to take Merriweather entirely seriously.

The introductory talk now over, our first real class was self-defence. I had no idea what this would involve, but it was to be led by Sergeant Wooding, who had met us at the station.

Wooding never seemed to run out of energy, at any point, ever. He was limbering up in the main hall as we walked in. We all stood in a row as he explained that he would be showing us the basic methods to restrain without injury, as well as various holds and arm locks in case of need.

'OK. Who wants to be my first victim?' he asked, with an impish smile.

'How about you, young lad?' he leapt over and pointed at Ted, who was the tallest man in the room and, at a strapping six foot six inches, at least a head taller than Wooding.

Ted smiled awkwardly as he stood up, and we all, for one moment, genuinely feared for Wooding's safety.

'OK, lad. Now give me your best left hook.'

Ted poked at him flimsily with one finger on the arm.

'No! Not like that, man,' said Wooding, hopping from one leg to the other. 'Imagine we're in a tavern brawl. I've just nicked your pint, or your girl! And you're going to clobber me one. I'm your worst enemy. Now go!'

Ted swung at the officer with a wild left hook. And, in what I can only describe as a blur, in the flicker of an eye Sergeant Wooding turned on his feet, avoided the punch and twisted Ted's arm, pinning him to the floor and threatening at any moment to break his arm.

'Tap if it hurts, lad. That's how I know when to let it off,' he grinned joyfully.

Ted tapped the mat immediately and – after some time – Wooding released him.

We strained forward in excitement and fear as Ted stood up, released from his strange contortion and clutching his arm.

'Don't worry. We'll toughen you lot up. Right, who's next?'

We all tried to avoid eye contact with Wooding as he continued to demonstrate in a similar manner on a succession of students. They were asked to play crooks and villains being arrested or picking fights, and each time the sergeant produced a swift and efficient method of escape and capture, leaving the victim bewildered and clutching their limbs in pain.

Wooding explained that the techniques were based on a martial art called ju-jitsu; they would disarm and disable an attacker or a thief in an instant, and these basic moves would be invaluable 'on the ground', by which he meant once we were in the real world.

'Right. Who's next . . .' he looked up and down the row as we all tried to avoid his gaze.

'You, lass. What's your name?' He was staring right at me. I wanted the floor to dissolve so I could fall right through it, but there was no escape.

'Pam.'

'OK, pretend to walk down the street with your handbag. Hold it at your side, like this.'

He walked up and down, pretending to hold a handbag, eliciting a loud laugh from a few of the lads.

I stood up and walked up and down the hall with my pretend handbag, as if I was looking in shop windows. It all felt very silly.

'Right, Ted. Go up and try to snatch the bag.'

As Ted tried to creep up behind me, I pretended to be oblivious, but was waiting warily for the pounce. After a moment, he darted forward, went for the imaginary bag and then grabbed my real arm.

'So what do you do now?' shouted Wooding.

'I don't know!' I was wriggling to try to break his grip, but Ted clung on tighter to my arm.

'Give me that bag, missy!' said Ted, getting into the role a little too enthusiastically for my liking.

Then, out of the blue, I somehow managed to jump round his grip, get behind him and pull him down onto the floor by the back of his collar, pinning his arm as Wooding had shown us earlier.

Ted tapped loudly and I released him.

'Very good! You're a dark horse, aren't you?' Wooding said.

I was sort of starting to enjoy myself now. It was certainly a far cry from folding clothes. After that, he put us into pairs, so we could practise. At the end of the class, Wooding sat us all down, saying we'd done well and shown good spirit.

'I wouldn't want to be on the other side of you lot making an arrest, any road. I'll never forget one of my old instructors. He once disciplined a student severely for talking back.'

There was a gasp.

'And you'll never guess who that student was.' He paused and smiled as we realized he meant himself. 'I never answered back again. But I don't employ those methods. At least not yet.'

We were never sure whether he was joking or not, but either way, Wooding's classes turned out to be the most disciplined of the lot after that.

With all that exercise and excitement, I was ready for dinner. Allan and I walked over to the canteen with Sally and Ted, who were chatting together. They had found out that they shared a passion for road cycling. Ted wanted to ride from John O'Groats all the way to Penzance on his new racer one day, and Sally agreed it was a grand idea.

'Oh, Pam, you should have seen your face when Wooding picked on you!' Sally laughed, punching me on the arm lightly. 'But you showed a bit of spark with old Ted here, I should say.'

'What about Old Broomstick earlier? Did you see his "hair"!' Allan joked. 'It's not a wig, though. Really. I don't think it can be . . .'

'I swear he nearly caught me with that picture you drew . . .' But I stopped short as Sally gesticulated madly for me to shush. I turned round, and there was Old Broomstick, standing right behind me.

He nodded curtly and bowed towards us girls. We tried our hardest to suppress a giggle.

'Remember what I said.' He looked at Ted and Allan 'I've got my eye on you and don't ever forget it.'

He pointed at Ted and Allan and tapped the side of his head. We looked at each other in silence.

A good deal of our classes involved learning legal definitions with another instructor, Sergeant Baines, for the weekly exams which tested us for our knowledge.

Baines, a pleasant-looking chap with blond hair, took his role very seriously. The first thing he did, once we were all sat down, was to throw the two big textbooks we had all brought with us to one side.

'In my humble opinion,' he began, 'after fifteen years on the beat, the best method for successful policing is knowledge. But not legal knowledge. No. I'm talking about people. Understand people and they will respect you. Never set yourselves up as their enemy and they'll help you do the job. Remember, when you walk out on

61

the street in your uniform, you're not endowed with some special gift. A constable is a citizen. Just a capable one, with some extra powers of arrest.'

We all chuckled.

'You can learn all this legal mumbo jumbo,' he continued. 'And don't worry, you will. We'll get you through those exams. But essentially, to be a good bobby, you talk, and you talk to the people, you're turned out smart, you hold your head up high. And you get to know your beats like the veins in your own hand.'

All that said, we had no choice but to get our heads stuck into the two thick books of law and learn them by rote.

Life at Bruche was tough, and at times it felt like I'd signed up for the army. There was inspection every morning and we had to keep our uniforms in tip-top condition. There would be more marching practice before breakfast, and we were encouraged by Merriweather to march wherever we walked on site, as he said a good confident march made for excellent character and morals. You could, on occasion, be punished with extra inspections in the evening if you weren't turned out correctly.

The days were made up of a mix of lecture and practical sessions. Practicals were often outside in the grounds, where we would enact a variety of offences: larceny, drunk and disorderly. Despite awkward laughter all round at first, it wasn't long before we all started to enjoy the role-playing aspect of training.

Marge surprised everyone the most when she turned out to be a brilliant actress. Usually quiet as a mouse,

Baines would give her a prop and a scene to enact and she would morph into dozens of different characters. Her face would contort like an old music hall star, and her voice took on a vast array of accents and styles.

One day, when he asked us to create an imaginary scene in the street, Marge pulled off a particularly good drunken tramp accosting passers-by. Marge put on an old coat and pretended to brandish a whisky bottle, while Baines played the policeman and tried to calm her down.

We all pretended to be witnesses as she came staggering by, shouting and leering with unnerving accuracy, before rolling about on the floor and waving her arms and legs in the air. Some of us then had to become police officers and take her to the station without causing injury or making the situation worse. We then had to imagine it was some hours later, and take a statement from her and the other witnesses.

When she started singing 'Don't Put Your Daughter on the Stage, Mrs Worthington', in her best Dublin slur, we all collapsed with laughter. After we had finished, Marge stood up, transformed miraculously back to her old shy self, brushed herself down, and did a little curtsy.

Some nights we went off site in the evening and on those days we literally counted the hours before we could skip up the lane and into town. On the first occasion, Marge, Sally and I caught up with Ted, Allan and another lad from the course called Neville, who I had just noticed had a very handsome smile. Excited at being let out for the first time, we formed a long line, arm in arm as we made our way up the lane, putting one leg and then the other forward, trying to keep in step with each other and singing 'It's a Long Way to Tipperary' at the tops of our voices.

We found our way into town as the sun hung in the midsummer sky. Swifts flew overhead and the trees were in full leaf. We stopped off at a little pub on the High Street called The Bell. The landlord, Mr Jones, had a bizarre collection of naval memorabilia adorning the bar, including what he introduced proudly as 'a piece of Nelson's bloody stocking from the Battle of Waterloo'. I doubted the provenance of the article, but in any case kept as far away as possible from where it hung.

I'd never actually even been in a pub before or drunk any alcohol. Sally seemed to know what to do, though, as she marched up and ordered half a pint each of what she referred to confidently as 'milk stout' for me and herself. Mr Jones seemed to know what she meant as well, and started pouring the drinks from glass bottles. The lads ordered a pint each, and then Marge decided she wanted a stout too.

'That's my gal,' said Mr Barnet as he poured out the thick black liquid. 'I admire a lass who can hold her stout. My mother always swears by a pint of the black stuff, to keep the physician away. And she's got so many years to her name now she's lost track.'

I took a sip. 'Ooh, it's so bitter!' I scrunched up my face. 'What did you say was in it?'

'Roasted barley and malt,' said Sally. 'We drink it all the time in our house. And Da lets me have a whole glass on Saturday sometimes,' she said proudly.

Marge had already drunk half of hers by the time I

ordered an orange juice. I vowed at that point never to take up a career in stout.

In those days, women rarely went into pubs, and hardly ever into the bar, where we imagined men got up to all sorts. We left the lads in the bar playing darts and found a wood-panelled snug with green leather seats where we sat down to sip our drinks.

'So. What do you think of Ted then?' Sally asked.

'He's very . . . tall?' I suggested.

'No, I mean what do you *think* of him?'

'He's nice,' I replied. 'But hasn't Neville got lovely eyes? Have you noticed?'

But we didn't spend the whole time talking about the boys. Sally told me about her life in Durham where she had worked in the local laundry.

'It was absolute drudgery, you can't imagine. I came home every day exhausted, in a trance, seeing visions of froth and foam, even in my sleep. My dad, who's a police-man in Durham, he got so tired of me moping he suggested maybe I should give the police a go instead. And here I am.'

We tried to coax something out of Marge about her mysterious life but she revealed little, except that her mam had once been an actress in York, before she got ill. Then she went quiet at the memory of it and slurped back the last of her stout.

Later, on the way home, I told Marge about my life back in Scarborough: about Jane, the fashion show at the department store, and how, if it wasn't for the police, I may well have ended up in New Zealand. She was impressed by how adventurous it all sounded. As we walked, the sun gradually set, with streaks of orange and red across the skyline. Sally and Ted hung back a little, laughing lightly together.

We had to be back by ten p.m. sharp, and the clock in town was just chiming the hour, so we all legged it for the gates. As we approached, I caught sight of a dark figure lurking in the dusk. It was Merriweather, out on his evening stroll.

'Ah ha!' he said, leaping out into the light of the gas lamp, blocking our path. 'So you think you can get away with it, do you? Well, the Lord and I alone know what you're up to.'

'Evening, sir,' said Allan continuing as if to walk right past him.

'Don't you "evening, sir" me. I know your game.' He blocked Allan's path then swung round. 'You two.' He pointed at Ted and Sally, who were standing very close to one another at the back. 'What exactly are your intentions? I fear for your souls. I genuinely do.' He looked as though he might burst into tears at any moment. 'All I want is some peace of mind.'

He went quiet and thoughtful for a moment, as though called on by a higher being, then shooed us away distractedly.

'Move, move, move! You two, back to your quarters. You girls, to your beds. Not a peep. Lights out. Lights OUT!'

We slunk away and left Merriweather to accost the next group back from their night out, and collapsed into laughter as soon as we rounded the corner. Sally, Marge and I went one way and the lads the other. As we left, I noticed

Sally and Ted brush hands for a fleeting second and smile at one other.

One of the lessons I dreaded most was life-saving class. We were driven out to the nearby swimming baths at a local school. Sergeant Wooding taught life-saving and swimming with the same relentless energy as he did ju-jitsu, and he took no prisoners.

A few of our class were excellent swimmers, including Ted and Sally, who went immediately into the top group, splashing about and diving in like dolphins, even swimming proper front crawl, with their heads under and everything.

I was put in the beginners' corner, along with a few lads and a girl called Marion, where we sploshed about in the shallow end and tried for dear life to stay above water. Wooding would come past and shout instructions from the side at regular intervals as we tried our best to swim a width of the pool.

'Left arm forward, straight, kick and right arm, now keep it straight, full strokes. Pamela, keep your head under. It won't kill you.'

Just at that moment I swallowed a huge mouthful of the tepid water and nearly choked.

'Well, it might, but . . .'

This swimming lark was going to take a while.

Just then, from nearby, there was splashing and a shout, then a few bubbles as Marion disappeared under the water. Ted, who was limbering up for a dive, caught sight of her, jumped straight in like a giant heron and swam an arc under water, lifting her up to the surface of the pool.

When they got to the side, Marion was choking and spluttering, with her eyes streaming and hair flat against her head. But she looked quite dreamily at Ted as he patted her on the back and put her in the recovery position.

It turned out Marion's leg had cramped up and she hadn't been able to keep afloat. Wooding came running over and called it a day. We all agreed later that Ted should have got his life-saving certificate there and then for his heroic actions.

Later that night, I was learning my definitions for the first of our weekly exams. We had a written exam every week, and if we failed too many we were in danger of being kicked off the course. Some of the more diligent students would wander around in a zombie-like state all week, mumbling to themselves in preparation, trying to memorize the difference between felonies and misdemeanours, or the Road Traffic Act.

I was trying to remember a particular definition when I heard a scratching and scraping from Sally's room next door. I thought nothing of it. Then, a couple of hours later, as I was about to turn my light out, I heard another commotion, some giggling, and then a loud thud and heavy footsteps outside, running towards the lads' block. A moment later there was a soft knock on my door.

'Pam. Pam! It's me. Can I come in?'

It was nearly lights out, but I opened the door and Sally stood there in a pink blouse, her hair all curled, with lipstick on. I had no idea where she had got hold of haircurlers.

'We snuck out! To town. Ted and I! I had a snowball! Oh, you should have been there. It was so exciting. At one

68

point Old Broomstick nearly caught us. Ted was walking me back to the hut. But we slipped behind a bush, and I swear I'm sure Old Broomstick could almost hear us breathing. He stopped and actually sniffed the air. Can you believe it? I think he's got a super sixth sense for misdemeanors. Anyway . . .' She paused for breath. 'I had to tell someone!'

I had to admit it did sound quite exciting.

'How did you get back in?'

'Through the window! Ted gave me a bunk-up. Oh life!' she said, sighing. 'It can't get much better than this.'

With that she said good night. Before sleep took its weary hold, the page of my book fell open at the definition of breaking and entering, and I dreamt that I caught a burglar climbing in through through the kitchen window of our house in Scarborough. When I pulled off the burglar's mask it was Inspector Merriweather. I had an unsettled night.

After morning parade we recited definitions to one another over breakfast, winding each other up about how many we could remember. Marion, who had a photographic memory, it turned out, said she could already recite most of them off by heart. She looked at Ted for approval; he was watching Sally, who was peeling an apple.

Later that afternoon we were taken to one of the rooms on the site, which had been made into a mock courtroom, where we had court practice with Sergeant Baines. We had to take an oath.

'I swear by Almighty God . . .' We each took our turn,

nervously, at the front. And we learnt about how different religions and cultures swear an oath.

Some of the class would then act out being defendants and we would cross-examine them. Then there would be a turn giving evidence, or acting out all the other characters in court, to get used to it. Baines would advise about what to say and what not to say.

'So . . .' Baines stalked up and down the mock courtroom, cross-examining me. 'Can you explain how the twenty cans of Spam made their way into your bag, Miss . . . Lilliput, if you didn't put them there? Did they fly in of their own accord?'

'Well,' I stumbled, trying to get into character. 'I did put them there. But if I hadn't put them there my ten children would starve to death.'

'Ten children!' barked Baines. 'Are you a woman of loose morals? Why doesn't your husband provide for you?'

'I . . .' I tried to think on my feet. 'My husbands, all five of them, umm . . . died. Of the smallpox. Most unfortunate.'

'OR!' Baines paused for effect. 'Did you murder them?'

Baines stopped the act at that point, saying we were going a little off point. He explained what else would happen and how we'd have to go and give evidence as police officers, if we'd found the defendant shoplifting.

'PC Rhodes,' said Baines, beginning again. 'You say the woman in question,' he pretended to look at his notes, 'had ten cans of Spam in her handbag, but how can you be sure she didn't come into the shop with them, having purchased them at another shop?'

'Well, I . . . I suppose . . . I did see her putting the cans into her bag.'

'You suppose you saw her? Well, *did* you see her or did you *not* see her put the ten cans of Spam into her bag?'

'I did see her.'

'Yes, you see. You must be sure about what you say,' Baines said. 'Nothing vague or uncertain. These people are trained to seize on any hesitation, as I did.'

Court role-play could be quite fun, and involved a lot of thinking on your feet. At times, I almost felt like we were in a real court, and it certainly did prepare me for later in my police career.

Every week, on a Friday, there was a dance at the training centre. Nurses from a local hospital were invited to make up the numbers because we had so many men on the course and hardly any women.

We all got dressed up, as far as we could with the small suitcase of clothes we'd been able to bring with us. The boys put on smart suits and ties, and I had a lovely blue silk blouse and a cotton skirt to match. Sally, it transpired, also had this neat trick of putting pipe-cleaners in your hair to curl them, in place of haircurlers; we all sat there, crammed into her little room, tying up each other's hair into tight curls. We scrabbled together the bits of make-up we could find – Sally had a bit of lipstick and Marge had some blusher and an eye pencil – and we made our way out, as glamorous we could manage under the circumstances, to the hall.

I had learnt to dance in Scarborough, where I'd had

lessons above an old shop with Miss Trent, a teacher from a dance school. I was quite confident with the military two-step, the waltz and the foxtrot and was looking forward to the evening. I wondered who I'd end up dancing with.

As we all walked in, Ted, Allan and Neville were hanging around by the bar. We wandered over. My hair had turned out such a shock of tight curls that night, the lads all christened me Bubbles.

Sergeant Thompson had his gramophone at the front. First he played a waltz, and Allan whisked me onto the floor. Ted and Sally glided past us, and Marion and Neville followed. Allan was a bit of a clumsy dancer – he kept treading on my feet and scraping my ankles – but we had a laugh anyway, capering about the floor together. Inspector Merriweather kept a beady eye on proceedings from the side.

Next was a military two-step, which is a bit like a Scottish country dance. I paired up with Neville for this one, which involved us holding hands and turning, stepping with one foot forward then the other, walking with held hands back and forth, all followed by a boisterous polka around the room. Neville turned out to be quite a good dancer and he knew this dance well. At the end of the evening, Neville offered to walk me back to my hut. We just escaped the eye of Inspector Merriweather, who was questioning another pair about their 'intentions' as they left.

I hardly knew anything about Neville. We'd only chatted once or twice, passing the time of day, but he seemed a nice lad. And I now knew he was a good dancer. He had a lovely, well-defined nose, with thick black hair.

'What's it like in Liverpool, then?' I asked, filling the silence as we strolled across the parade ground.

'Oh, it's grand. Especially the docks. That's where me da works. I go down there and help him out most weekends. I love all the ropes and chains, and the hustle and bustle. The noise can be tremendous.'

It sounded wonderfully exciting.

'So you didn't want to work the docks, then?' I asked.

'Me da didn't want me to. He said he wanted more for me. You know.'

Just then, Sally and Ted came running up after us, laughing.

'Allan's gone off with a nurse!' Ted said.

'He hasn't "gone off" with her,' said Sally. 'He's being a proper gent and seeing her to the bus stop.'

'Yeah, and I bet that's all he's doing,' Ted teased.

'Ted!' gasped Sally. 'You little . . .' and she punched him affectionately in the stomach as they walked off, arm in arm, giggling. ''Night, you two,' she called back at us.

'Yeah, 'night both.'

I was just about to say goodbye to Neville when I saw Inspector Merriweather coming over. We hadn't escaped his all-seeing eye after all.

'And where do you think you're off?' he shouted across the grounds.

'Nowhere, sir. Only to our very separate quarters,' said Neville, flashing his most innocent smile. 'I was just warning the lady, Miss Rhodes, here, about keeping her wits about her, with all these young men about. You know, keep her guard up at all times, sir.'

'Yes, well, I couldn't have put it better myself, lad. You're a man who speaks after my own heart. Well, as you were. Good night.'

I almost thought he was going to doff his cap at that point. But he turned away and barked at another passing couple.

'We got out of that one!' I giggled.

'Good night, then,' said Neville softly, and then he was gone.

That night my heart was all aflutter. I imagined strolling somewhere, up a country lane in midsummer. Perhaps it was with Neville, but I couldn't quite see his face. We've packed a hamper, and are going down to a little river, stepping onto a boat. He takes my hand, the music playing . . . it's a waltz. But then Inspector Merriweather's big face comes into view, barking about the sanctity of youth . . .

As I drifted into sleep, strange visions forming in my mind, I wondered what the next ten weeks would really hold.

3

'Have any of you ever seen a dead body?' asked Sergeant Wooding, right out of the blue, after first-aid practice. 'Because when you're out there, on the streets, it's going to happen. And you need to be prepared.'

A few people put up their hands, and Marion announced grandly that she'd seen no less than three.

'My grandmother. I found her actually. Her tongue was quite blue and her eyes were sort of, well, squinting, and she kind of breathed, even though she was definitely dead . . .' She paused for further recollection. 'And one of my mother's friends from pottery class, Mrs Evans, she'd been dead for about two weeks before anyone knew. We found her, just sitting in front of the wireless. Cat on her lap, licking its paws. And there was such a stench, you wouldn't believe. Maggots crawling in and out of her ears and all over . . .'

'OK, Marion.' He didn't wait to hear the third item in her ghoulish repertoire. 'Thanks for that . . . fulsome account. Anyone else?'

Ted said that one of his old school chums had died suddenly in a maths class, of a heart attack, which was quite a shock. We all looked grave for a moment at the thought of the young lad.

A few other people had seen grandparents, or elderly relatives, in coffins at their wakes. But neither I, Sally, Marge nor Allan had ever seen a dead body, so Sergeant Wooding said he'd arrange a trip for us to the local morgue. It was to be the strangest outing I had ever been on, that's for sure. I wondered whether it would be appropriate to pack a lunch.

'Do you think it'll be very gruesome?' said Sally, over dinner. It was the day before what we were calling the Death Trip and we were all a bit apprehensive. 'I mean, they will have cleaned him or her up, sort of thing, won't they?'

'I should think so. I suppose it depends on how he died,' I replied.

'Well, if this . . . whoever it is . . . if their neck is cut, or something, that would be quite hard to clean, wouldn't it? Or would it?' pondered Sally, before Marion joined in a little too gleefully.

'Maybe the person isn't actually dead yet!'

I got the feeling she was actually a little envious that she wasn't allowed to come on the trip with us.

'Maybe it's a poor man, dying right now!' she said. 'In a horrific car accident, or the victim of a crime of passion!'

'In any event, we need to be respectful. It's not a joke,' said Allan.

I had to admit I was somewhat losing my appetite already at the thought of it.

The next day, we took the local bus into town with Sergeant Wooding. Any initial enthusiasm was wearing off by the second, as we became increasingly apprehensive at the prospect of an actual real-live dead body.

'Do you think it'll be cold in there? Like a larder? So the body doesn't rot so quickly?' Sally asked.

'We don't have to . . . touch it, do we? Or cut it up?'

'It's not a post mortem!' said Allan. 'We're just looking round the morgue and seeing a dead body, that's all. Calm down, will you?'

He sat back and stared out of the window but I could tell he was quite anxious too.

When we arrived at the morgue we were met by a breezy young woman in a kind of reception area. It was surprisingly pleasant, with a potted plant and a rather posh red leather sofa in the corner, all set against a backdrop of William Morris-like flowery wallpaper. The only thing to remind you it was a morgue was a frail-looking elderly woman sitting on the sofa, clutching a handkerchief. I wondered if she had come to visit the body of someone she'd loved. The sofa looked as though it might swallow her up at any minute.

'So. Is this your first time then, is it? You get used to it,' chirruped the receptionist as she led us down a narrow staircase and into the basement.

'You're from the police, aren't you?' she continued, despite the somewhat obvious clue that we were all wearing our uniforms. 'I always feel a bit nervous when I see the police. I don't know why. You know, like I've done something wrong or something. I haven't though!' she quickly assured us.

'So. Here we are. This is the store where we keep them before the funeral. The gentleman you're to see is just this way, if you'll all follow me.' She clacked down the corridor.

By that point we were all completely silent as the smell of death seemed to rise up in the air. It wasn't a smell as such, more a lack of smell. A lack of air or any kind of vitality.

As we approached the body, the first thing I saw was a foot. Then another foot and the legs.

'This gentleman,' continued the woman, 'has been very carefully presented for you personally, by our excellent director, Mr Pringle.'

I was quite relieved to see that the gentleman in question wasn't covered in blood after all. In fact there wasn't a hint of the injury that had killed him. I thought for a moment he had a sort of odd half smile across his greying face. But when I looked back, there wasn't a trace of it. He was lying next to three other covered bodies; I could just see a foot sticking out from one of them. The room we were in was like a cross between a hospital ward and a church crypt, quite cold and damp, with a red tiled floor and thick echoey walls.

'This gentleman,' she went on, 'was, in life, a window cleaner.' She took on the air of a slightly supercilious vicar as she stood near the head of the body. 'We know that he fell, tragically, through a glass conservatory roof, whilst engaged in that most dangerous of jobs.'

She paused and clasped her hands. 'And he was only fifty-three years of age. Such a waste.'

We all stood at the foot of the little bed, or slab, or whatever it is most appropriate to call it, for a good ten minutes. We didn't say a word. It was hard to stop looking at his face, maybe for a clue as to the person he once was, or for a last vestige of life.

But there was nothing and, as we walked away, I realized it hadn't been that strange at all really. It was just a body.

When we got back on site, Marion was hovering about by the canteen, keen to know all the gory details.

We all kept quiet, though, pensive with our own thoughts. The experience had been both liberating and a little sad, as though we had been given an extra glimpse of reality but lost something of our innocence too. It would be the first of many such moments in my police career.

In those first few weeks at Bruche, I learnt more legal terms than I ever thought it would be possible to squeeze into one human brain. But I was shocked to learn one afternoon that Sally had failed two of her exams. She had kept quiet about it until now, but Baines had taken her to one side, and told her she was on borrowed time.

'Why didn't you tell us?' I asked her.

'I don't know. I was embarrassed, I suppose. You're all so good at remembering it all and it just goes in one ear and falls out the other with me. What should I do?' she asked me and Marion, as we were making our way onto the parade ground one morning.

There was an ominous-looking cloud on the horizon, as if a gigantic black inkwell had spilled its contents across the sky, and it was heading straight for us.

'If I don't get through my da will kill me. I can't go back to working in that laundry. I can't.'

'Why don't we all work together on it?' I suggested. 'We could meet in my room and help each other memorize the stuff.'

'Maybe,' she said sadly. 'Thanks.'

'Well, you'll have to stop all those late-night escapades then, won't you?' said Marion slyly. 'You and Ted.'

'What do you know about that?' Sally quickly turned on her.

'Oh, everyone knows. Even Inspector Merriweather, I think. And certainly Baines.'

Whether or not it was true that Merriweather and Baines were watching her, which I somehow doubted, Sally would have to keep her head down for a few weeks.

As we took our formation, ready for inspection, it started to rain. I was so hungry my stomach was clawing back at me. Sergeant Thompson came stalking over, his arms clasped behind his back.

'Right, you lot. The party's over. This is where the real show begins. We've got six weeks 'til Passing Out, and I want to see proper marching from now on. Not this mothers' meeting stuff.'

By now the rain was so heavy we could barely see each other, let alone Sergeant Thompson, and the ground was filling up with muddy water at our feet. Seemingly oblivious to the inclement conditions, Thompson surveyed the line, up and down, and we all tried to keep perfectly still, squinting as water poured down our faces and backs.

'You!' he shouted. 'Carson, isn't it? Ted Carson.'

Ted stood up as straight as possible.

'Your shoes are an absolute disgrace.' Thompson continued along the line. 'And you, Miss . . . ?'

'Rhodes, Sergeant.'

'Have you never heard of polish? Or is it just too . . . difficult?'

I didn't dare point out that we were standing in a near monsoon, and that any effort we had put into polishing had gone right out the window the minute we stepped across the parade ground. He seemed to hear my thoughts.

'You think a bit of rain ever stopped me turning out properly? In my day it was nothing BUT mud and rain. And we never had a stitch out of place. Stand at EASE. Parade, parade. ATTEN . . . SHUN. Quick-MARCH!'

And we were off. Amazingly, we girls all managed to keep in step in spite of the downpour, and in a strange way it was actually quite exhilarating, even with mad Sergeant Thompson at the helm.

We made our way right out of the gates, past the old ladies with their dogs again, who seemed to stop and stare in wonderment this time as they peered out through their headscarves. I think I even saw a flicker of a proud smile on Thompson's face as he watched us march up the lane that day.

Since she'd confessed to failing her exams, Sally had been avoiding Ted in order to concentrate on revising. Marion seemed to be taking every available opportunity to fill her place in Ted's thoughts, and Sergeant Wooding's Life-saving and First Aid class was a prime opportunity.

We had finished our swimming lessons for the day, during which time I had managed to swim two whole lengths, when Wooding announced that we would be doing artificial resuscitation and first aid.

'If someone collapses, passes out and stops breathing, we use what's called the Holger Nielsen method to revive them,' he said, passing round a small pamphlet with diagrams of two men demonstrating the technique, one wearing swimming trunks and the other somewhat incongruously dressed in a pinstriped suit.

Referred to as a 'back pressure arm lift,' the Holger Nielsen method involved putting the victim on his or her stomach to stimulate breathing, instead of lying them on their back like we do with CPR today. The technique was invented by a Danish army officer and used well into the 1950s.

'Right everyone, pair up,' shouted Wooding as we lined up awkwardly alongside the pool in our swimsuits. 'I want one of the pair to lie down, as though you've collapsed or passed out and stopped breathing.'

Marion darted to Ted, quick as a kingfisher, and paired up. Sally had paired up with Marge and I was just looking around for someone when Wooding shouted my name.

'Rhodes, you'll do. I need someone to demonstrate on. Just lie here on this towel.'

So I had to lie down in front of everyone as he pulled my limbs this way and that to show the technique.

'Now if the victim is lying face up, put him or her in the prone position, that is on the front, as soon as possible. Remember every second counts. But before placing the victim on the stomach, remember to check to make sure there is nothing blocking the airways of the nose and mouth in this manner.'

He indicated something around my face and nose and then turned me onto my stomach like a piece of meat on a slab. The floor felt wet and cold through the towel and I began to shiver.

'Place the victim face down, bending the elbows and putting the hands, one under the other, like this, underneath the head.'

I could see Sally and Marge stifling giggles as Wooding yanked me this way and that.

'Turn the victim's head to one side, on his or her hands. Try to extend the victim's head out as far as possible, with the chin jutting out.'

I honestly thought he was about to pull my head off.

'Then, kneeling at the victim's side, place your hands in the middle of the back just below an imaginary line here, above the waist. Lean forward, with your bodyweight on the middle of the victim's back, and then release.'

I breathed in deeply, expecting the worst, but Wooding showed mercy and only indicated the remainder of the technique.

How anyone would show signs of life after this I couldn't imagine. Fortunately I never had to employ the Holger Nielsen method in real life; it didn't look much fun for either party.

As I stood up and brushed myself down, the others were already practising on one another. Marion was giggling with Ted as she lifted his arms and knelt down by his head. I could see Sally distractedly keeping an eye on the pair, pulling roughly at Marge's elbows.

'Careful!' said Marge. 'You'll break something.'

'Sorry,' Sally said, but she was in a world of her own.

After that we learnt other first-aid basics, such as the recovery position, tying a sling and bandaging up wounds. I saw Marion chattering away and making a joke to Ted as she wound a bandage round his head. He laughed loudly, and Sally, who was watching from the other side, jabbed Marge with a safety pin in the ear.

'Watch it!' said Marge. 'You'll have my eye out in a minute. Really, Sally, I don't know what's wrong with you today.'

'Sorry! It's just . . . oh, I'm sure it's nothing.'

'Right. Let's have a look at what we've got here,' said Wooding, arms folded, surveying our various efforts. We must have looked like the walking wounded as we stood there, arms, legs and heads tied up in all that bandage.

'What's this?' he said to Sally as he passed. 'This won't do,' and, as he reached out, the bandage unravelled in a coil and fell at Marge's feet. 'You'll have to do better than that. It needs to be much tighter,' he said, tutting.

He continued along the line.

'Ah, now, Marion. This is excellent work. Neat, secure,' he said, pointing to Ted's carefully bandaged head.

'I had to do my dad's arm once,' she began. 'He had an accident with the firewood. The axe slipped and . . . oh, there was so much blood. And then another time, our neighbour, Mr Quill, his toe came almost clean off when a hammer fell on it and I . . .'

'Thank you, Marion,' Sergeant Wooding said and promptly dismissed the class.

That night, at dinner, Marion and Ted sat on a different table from the rest of us, and poor Sally was completely distracted.

'I just don't know what to do. I've got my exam at the end of the week and if I fail I'm out. But I can't think about anything else but Ted. I'm not normally the jealous type but . . .'

'I'm sure it's nothing,' I tried to reassure her. 'Marion's like that with everyone.'

'She's not his style anyway. He likes blondes,' said Allan. 'She's just got her claws in, that's all.'

84

'He's probably just too polite to say anything,' said Marge.

'Or maybe he's trying to get your attention?' I suggested.

'Maybe,' Sally said, and she pushed her plate away, the food almost untouched.

When I stood up with my tray to leave, Ted and Marion were nowhere to be seen.

That Wednesday, a few people had gone into town, to the pub, or for a late tea of egg and chips. We quite often had an extra dinner if we were in town, since the food on site was not so good. But Sally and I decided to stay in and revise for the exam on Friday. We looked at definitions and tested each other's answers, doing a pretty good job of remembering them. I reassured Sally about the exam and said she'd fly through it.

When she left, I sat up in bed and read some of the letters I'd received during the week.

One was from Granny and was written in her beautiful copperplate. It told me how she had left home as a girl at ten and started work. She wrote too about how my dad was the first boy in the area where they lived who had won a scholarship to the Grammar School; then her second and third sons, my uncles, all got in too. What an achievement, I thought, that she had managed to afford to send them all on the five-mile train journey to school.

The other letter was from Mam, the envelope bearing her immaculate tiny handwriting. She always took great care over writing, as if each word was a work of art. She had been given a beautiful ink pen for Christmas from my dad, which she loved and used with great ceremony.

Dear Pamela,

I hope everything is going well for you at Bruche. Do take care in those self-defence classes. I hope it's not too dangerous. And congratulations in your exams. You seem to be doing very well.

We're off on our own little adventure next week. We've hired a coach and your father has organized the whole thing himself. It's a pilgrimage to Fatima in Portugal.

The Misses Fairfaxes across the road are coming, and Father Michael, and I have even packed a sun hat!

Peter has met a lovely girl called Tina who works at the theatre as an usherette.

Write back to us and tell us how it goes.

God bless and take care,
Mam

There was another envelope, this time in Jane's wild handwriting, with little drawings of rabbits all over the back. She said she had met a sailor out dancing one night and she was spending a lot of time with him. He even had a tattoo, but he was very romantic and would pick wild flowers for her and leave them on her doorstep with little love notes.

I thought back to when Jane and I used to go dancing, at a big dance hall on the seafront. I used to leave my dancing shoes hidden in a bush in the garden so my dad wouldn't know where I was going. He didn't like me going dancing, so I'd say I was off to the pictures and then skip out, collect the shoes and run all the way there, the sea wind in my hair. It seemed like so much time had passed since I had left that life behind.

I wrote a letter to Jane about seeing the dead body, and

the Holger Nielsen technique, and was just starting to feel sleepy when I heard a noise outside our hut. There was scratching and scraping and the sound of stones being thrown, followed by some loud whispering.

I put down my pen and paper, wrapped my dressing gown round me and peeped out of the window. I could just make out Ted, standing beneath Sally's window. They were talking urgently to one another. Sally looked quite cross and Ted seemed to be pleading. Then she slammed the window shut and I returned to my bed without seeing what happened next.

The next day, we had a lesson with Inspector Merri-weather, grandly entitled 'war duties'. He saw this section of training as his area of ultimate expertise and insisted on taking these lessons himself. He said he was preparing us in case we faced another war. As we shuffled into one of the old Nissen huts, he waved us over to a pile of tatty-looking tin hats and a heap of boiler suits in a corner.

'Take your pick,' he said, and we sifted through, jostling for position.

At first, I couldn't find anything to fit. The hats were all ginormous, and nearly covered my eyes, while the boiler suits were huge too, hanging loosely round the shoulders, obviously originally worn by men. In the end, I found something that almost fitted; on the inside a name was scribbled on the collar: Private Tilsley. I wondered who he was and how his clothes had ended up here.

'The war may be over,' said Inspector Merriweather, as we stood in a huddle in our costumes. 'But the war spirit lives on. Believe me.' He breathed deeply and put on his own tin hat, patting it firmly on the top. 'What we learnt in those six long years you couldn't learn in a lifetime of peace. You lot don't know you're born, living in these times.'

With that, he trooped out onto a grassy area, next to a huddle of derelict-looking huts, and we followed, slightly bemused, wondering what was next.

Inspector Merriweather had a young PC with him and they disappeared for a while. They came back carrying a kind of pump, with a handle shaped like a big horse-riding stirrup and a long hosepipe at one end for squirting water out at high pressure.

'Imagine this is a house, on fire, just hit by an incendiary bomb. The flames are raging like the devil himself! Your entire family is trapped within. Including your grandma and your dog.'

We all looked at the hut, doing our best to imagine Inspector Merriweather's bizarre scenario; when we looked back, he was carrying a big tin bucket, water sploshing out all over the place.

'You place the pump here and put your back into it.' Merriweather pumped away vigorously, his face going redder and redder, before he stopped and bent over, his hand on his back. 'I'm not as young as I was. Here, lad, you take over,' he said to the young PC.

'And you, you take this.' He handed Allan the long hose, but before he could properly get hold of it the water came gushing out, and it began flinging about wildly everywhere. Allan finally got it under control, though not before getting us all thoroughly soaked.

We all had a go on the stirrup pump and it was quite

fun, but I wondered whether it would really put out a fire, and save a whole family, with just one small bucket.

Merriweather, by now getting quite carried away with his role, marched us over to another hut, where there was a pile of gas masks on a table. We had all carried these during the war so they were a familiar sight from our childhoods; although we'd never used them, we'd played many a youthful game wearing them, their big round eyes and scary noses making us look like extra-terrestrial giant insects.

'I want you all to enter the building, here, when I do this,' said Merriweather, lifting his arm. 'Crawl through the building and exit . . . here.' He jogged, panting, to the other side of the hut, where there was a little hatch in the door. 'In the meantime, I'm going to fill the hut with poisonous gas, and you're all to escape it.'

I looked at Sally and gasped. 'Is he serious?' I whispered.

'I don't know. We'll soon find out! Let's hope these gas masks work, anyway!'

Still unsure whether he was joking or not, we lined up at the front of the hut in our masks, waiting for the signal. On his command, we ran in one by one and crawled along on our hands and knees, aiming for the exit.

Merriweather called through the window that he was pouring the poisonous gas, so we all ducked down. I could just make out Ted's head above everyone else's, he was crawling on all fours towards the exit. I imagined I could see the gas, but then it disappeared. I could hear people shouting with relief when they reached the end, while others banged into table legs and into each other.

'Where are you?'

'I don't know. Can you see the way out?

'No. Ouch! What was that?

'My foot!'

'Sorry, my fault.'

It was chaos and confusion. The gas mask was hot and sticky and my face was dripping with sweat as I felt my way along the floor with my hands. I was starting to panic and get a little breathless; as we were all crammed so tightly into that little hut, one behind the other, it was impossible to see where we were going. At one point I got stuck under a chair but managed to wriggle my way through.

Eventually, after what seemed like eternity, I caught sight of a glimmer of light through the open hatch. I saw Sally's beaming face; she grabbed me by the arms and pulled me through.

'Come on, you. You took your time. We've all grown beards, we've been here for so long.'

'Got stuck. Under a chair.' I panted as I rolled onto the grass, exhausted, the remaining few students piling out around me.

We were so relieved to be back in daylight we all started laughing into our gas masks, and stretched out on the grass. Merriweather shouted at the top of his voice.

'What's all this? It's not laughing gas. This is serious! Life and death. Now, on your feet. Quick-march.'

With that, he marched us all the way back to the main building, right round the site, still wearing our gas masks.

I still, to this day, don't know whether he poured a poisonous gas into that hut or not.

Everyone was in a state of nervous anticipation of the week ahead. We had been told by Baines that most of our lessons would be covering subjects of a somewhat . . . delicate nature. It was basically the part of the course on which we would learn about all the different sexual crimes, and any other uncomfortable situations we might find ourselves in on the job. It came to be known among us students simply as 'Dirty Week'.

First lesson of the week was First Aid with Sergeant Wooding, but instead of the usual bandaging up of wounds, putting people in the recovery position and artificial resuscitation, the lesson was, to our horror, entitled 'Emergency Childbirth'.

'So, who's ever seen a baby being born?' asked Wooding, pacing up and down at the front of the class.

Of course Marion had seen several. Three of her siblings, and a neighbour's triplets, who she claimed to have actually delivered herself. Not to mention her cat Matilda and its sixteen kittens. 'We thought it was all over, and then they just kept coming!'

But most of us girls hadn't seen a live human birth, and certainly none of the lads had.

On the wall in front of us, Wooding had pinned a large scientific diagram of a woman's uterus with a baby in it, head about to pop out of the exit.

'The child emerges from . . .' he pointed with his pencil, 'this area here, head first. We hope. The child will emerge in this manner, still connected to the mother here.' He pointed again.

'Putting the science aside for a moment,' he said, stepping towards us and lowering his voice, 'we're here to talk about real life. When you're out there, on the streets, it could happen at any moment. You might be strolling along on your beat, checking shop doors, when you see a woman collapse in the street. She's gone into labour. Or you're on traffic patrol and you see a broken-down car by the side of a road. A woman inside, about to give birth. What do you do?'

Silence.

'Well, if you're near a phone box all's well, and you can call for a local doctor or midwife. But you might be on a country lane, on a rural beat, with no passers-by for hours . . . what then?'

'Deliver the baby?' suggested Marion.

'Well . . . yes and no. First, you find out if there is any way to get the mother to a doctor or to a hospital. Someone with a motor car, a convenient bus route. Is she able to walk to the police station and get a lift there?'

'But what if we can't get her to a doctor or a midwife?' asked Allan, looking quite perplexed.

'Yes, exactly. What then? Well, if she seems close to birth, you can help the mother deliver the baby. By relaxing her and in a sense "receiving" the baby as it's born.'

Everyone looked quite shocked at the prospect.

'Now, the last thing you should do is panic. People have been known to pass out at the sight of a woman in labour. Not to mention what follows. And we can't have that from our constables. No, indeed. You need to be prepared for every eventuality. Questions?'

'What . . . position should the mother be in?' asked Ted.

'Ted!' gasped Sally.

'Well, you know. There must be a correct . . . angle.'

'No, it's a valid question. You lay the mother on her

back, legs open, and make her as comfortable as possible. You may have to ask her to remove her underclothes.'

There was a flurry of stifled laughter from the back.

'If possible, you should get her indoors. Perhaps there's a farmhouse on your beat, which might have a telephone. You might be able to walk the mother there. Or a nearby local shop or residence. Flag down a passing vehicle, even.'

'But what if we have to deliver it right there and then? The baby?' I asked. I was, by now, quite concerned. 'How do we know what to do?'

'In that case, you make the mother as relaxed as possible and just let nature takes its course. Don't, above all, stress the situation by panicking. You might see some things that will turn you right off your breakfast. It's a messy business, but we were all born and it's perfectly natural. It happens every minute of every day, all over the world, and it's nothing to be shocked by.'

Sergeant Wooding, seemingly quite proud of his openness on the subject, produced some more graphic diagrams, some depicting newborn babies emerging, attached by umbilical cords, and one of a woman, with the baby lying on her stomach. We passed them around the room to a few quiet gasps.

'I was there for the births of all three of my children,' Wooding went on. 'And I can tell you it's a miracle to behold. Above all, don't try to rush things, or pull on the baby's head. And don't attempt to cut the umbilical cord. That should be left to a doctor or midwife. But you can gently clear out the baby's mouth of all the muck and . . .'

'Eurgh. Really, this is too much,' whispered Ted to Allan.

'. . . blood and so on from the uterus,' continued Wooding, as though describing how to make an oil change on a motor car. 'Anyway, I hope you all now feel more capable of facing this situation should it occur. And remember, above all, let nature take its course.'

As one of the few girls in the room, the lesson had been a bit embarrassing to say the least. And it made me more than a little anxious about what the rest of 'Dirty Week' might hold. But perhaps the prospect of assisting with childbirth wouldn't seem quite so daunting, if I was ever to come across that particular little emergency in my police career.

As it turned out, emergency childbirth was the least shocking of the things we learnt that week. The next few classes included examining the definition of indecency, and how we would recognize it, followed by incest and bigamy. We also learnt about prostitution, rape and sexual offences against minors; other crimes we studied then aren't offences now, including abortion and homosexuality.

The more Baines revealed in these classes, about what the law was and what we might come across, the more naive and innocent I felt. Even Sally, who always seemed so confident, was quite horrified by details of bestiality, and when it came to crimes committed against minors, I think we were all shocked into silence.

It's not that we hadn't heard about some of this stuff before, in the tabloid papers and through local gossip, it's just that imagining actual cases, and then the thought of having to deal with them ourselves, made it all seem so much more real.

Marge showed a surprising degree of unshockability, and asked some of the questions we were probably all thinking but were too shy to say. When it came to bestiality, she wanted a detailed list of all the animals we might be likely to encounter sexual acts being committed with; and she was the most vociferous in her questioning of how we would recognize the signs of crimes such as indecency, and what they involved.

By the end of 'Dirty Week', no one bothered to giggle in class. We were all just a little less shockable or embarrassed by the more 'delicate' subjects, and perhaps just a bit more grown-up. However, Baines warned us that we had by no means covered everything, and we should expect plenty more shocks on the job.

We were nearing the end of our thirteen weeks at the training centre. It was blazing hot and we were desperate to be outside enjoying the sun, but before we were free for the weekend we had to sit one of our final exams, and we all wanted to do well.

A big white clock ticked in the corner of a classroom as we sat hunched over exam papers. Allan had already finished; Ted was scratching his chin, looking concerned.

When Sergeant Wooding finally called time and collected our papers, Sally had a big smile on her face. The extra revision had paid off, and we had all managed to remember our definitions. We decided to go for a celebratory egg and chips in town.

It felt like we were on holiday as we sauntered along to

the little cafe. Along the road, wild flowers and hedgerows were in full bloom, dripping with insects and birds. All the rain had given everything an extraordinary lushness that filled us with optimism.

After lunch, we had an ice cream on a little bench outside the church. I had been looking for a chance to ask Sally what all that commotion was about, outside the hut the other night with Ted, but before I could ask she blurted it out.

'He asked me to marry him! I've been bursting at the seams to tell you. I didn't know what to do.'

'Wow! That was fast work indeed,' laughed Marge.

'He was a bit drunk, though, I think,' said Sally. 'Does that count? He'd been to The Bell and Allan says they drank two whisky and gingers each.'

'I'm sure he meant it,' I smiled. 'It's obvious he's crazy about you.'

'I said I'd think about it and tell him tonight,' she continued, then paused, obviously thinking about how much she should tell us. 'I did ask him why he's been spending so much time with Marion, though. I had to. He said it was nothing, they're just friends. But I don't know . . .'

'I'm sure it's true. He'd hardly ask you to marry him if there's anything else going on.'

'I suppose. But I hardly know him really. I do think he's the one, though! And I couldn't bear the thought of anyone else . . . Don't mention it to anyone. Please! I swore I'd keep it secret but I was just absolutely bursting to tell you.'

By the time we got up to leave, Sally's ice cream had melted all down her arm and onto the floor.

*

That afternoon, we sat around the Nissen huts in our swimming costumes, pretending to be on holiday on the beach. Sally was in a kind of dreamworld, lying back in the sun with her sunglasses on. Marge and I pretended to be mannequins, walking up and down on an imaginary cat-walk, with our beach towels wrapped round us.

As were we doing a silly trick with our towels, making it look as though we were naked, and taking photographs, some of the lads came walking past. Ted was there, and Neville.

I had been a bit anxious, as I hadn't really seen Neville properly since we'd danced together and he'd walked me to my hut that night. But now, when I looked at him, I wasn't sure he was the one. I certainly wasn't sure, like Sally and Ted. The other lads all whistled as they walked past, and we carried on up and down with our towels, and Marge and I collapsed into laughter. Neville didn't look back.

'Give us a twirl,' said Allan, but just as we dropped our beach towels to reveal that we were, in fact, wearing swim-suits, Inspector Merriweather, with his impeccable nose for impropriety, appeared from nowhere.

'Girls!' He shielded his eyes in shock. 'This is not the place for such a display! And as for you,' he turned to face the lads, whose faces were deadpan as they stood up straight and saluted, 'have I taught you nothing over these past weeks? Everywhere I look, I see the nation's morals collapsing at my feet. An unstoppable tide of filth.'

As he walked away, I could hear Merriweather mutter-ing about broken moral fibres, the world heading for destruction. When I looked back at Sally, she was talking in urgent tones again with Ted, who had his hands clasped round her bare arms.

Neville was nowhere to be seen.

I yawned, stretched and looked around my little room. It was the last week, and we were all quite nervous about our final Passing Out parade. At marching practice, Sergeant Thompson was more than ever on the lookout for anyone stepping out of time. Marge had been made a marker, which meant she had to stand out in front of us and lead.

With the morning's marching over, the first lesson was Traffic Control with Sergeant Baines. We stayed outside and he came out to show us how to direct traffic. I wondered how on earth we'd learn to direct traffic when there wasn't a road or a car in sight.

Eventually, Baines began running up and down the parade ground, allocating us vehicles to enact.

'Carson, Rhodes, you come and stand here. You're traffic coming this way. Peters, Owen, you're a bicycle and a bus coming this way. There's an accident . . . here.'

So we all chugged along pretending to be cars, lorries and buses, or acted as pedestrians waiting to cross the road, as he showed us the correct traffic signals. The stance to assume was left arm out to the side at shoulder height, while the right arm was out in front, waving the traffic forward.

The rest of the week we spent brushing up on all the basics: how to make an arrest, how to take a statement, court procedures, and how to make points at a telephone box in order to communicate with the station. We also did our first-aid and life-saving practical exams, bandaging each other up in slings.

After thirteen weeks, the final day had almost arrived. First thing in the morning it would be our Passing Out parade. The night before we all made sure we were as smart as possible. I spent hours checking the shine on my shoes, and making sure my hair was regulation length, well above the collar. Sally, Marge and I even practised our marching, up and down the corridor in the Nissen hut.

At the final parade, there was a real marching band, and all our instructors were standing alongside as we showed off what we'd learnt. When it was over, we trooped into the big hall and were awarded our First Aid certificates. But what we were all really waiting to hear was the news from Inspector Merriweather about where we were going to be posted. In those days you had no choice; you could be sent anywhere in the north of England.

Merriweather stood at the front and began reading the list of names from a piece of paper.

'Carson, Ted – Liverpool. Peters, Marjorie – Darlington. Rhodes, Pamela – Richmond.'

Richmond? Where on earth is that, I wondered. I had no idea. I had been waiting all day to find out, and I was still none the wiser.

'I'm going to Darlington!' whispered Marge. 'That's quite close to Richmond.'

'What's it like then? Richmond?' I asked.

'Well, I know it's got a castle. And a lovely market. I

used to have a great-aunt lived there. I'm sure it'll be grand.'

As well as the formalities, at the end of our course there was a little performance too, in the main hall, at which we sang songs from *The Student Prince* and the boys even did a ballet, dressed up in real ballet costumes, which made us girls all laugh.

After the festivities were over, we were so excited about the start of our new careers we were hardly sad all about leaving Bruche. There were no long goodbyes, except of course for Ted and Sally; though we now wondered whether Sally would join the police, given that she and Ted had decided to get married that autumn. He'd been posted to Liverpool, and she would most likely join him there as a housewife.

We certainly wouldn't miss the food, or the early morning marching, but as I looked around the Nissen hut for the final time, picked up my suitcase from the bed, turned out the light and shut the door behind me, I couldn't help feeling a little sad that this part of my life, and all the laughs we'd had, were now over. From here on in, there would be no pretend arrests and mock court procedures. It was time now for the real world.

Everything looked exactly the same on my parents' road in Scarborough, although the flowers were all in bloom and the trees in full and vibrant leaf.

It felt like this little town, and everyone in it, had been stuck in a time warp while I was away. There was Mr Murphy, our neighbour, out watering his roses as usual, almost exactly where I had left him, I'm sure. And as I stood outside our front door, I could hear Radio Luxembourg drifting through an open window, just as it had been when I left thirteen weeks earlier.

I could see the top of Dad's head over the newspaper he was reading in the front room, and I could hear Mam lightly humming in the kitchen. It was like their lives were exactly the same, but I had grown up. I almost felt scared to go in, in case they didn't recognize me. Perhaps I had changed beyond all recognition; I felt like I'd seen and learnt so much these past months.

When Mam answered the door, of course she did recognize me, and gave me a big hug.

Over a cup of tea, I was happy to listen to their stories and glad to be home.

'Your father organized the whole thing so well!' said Mam, as she dunked a custard cream into her tea. They were excited, having just come back from their pilgrimage to Portugal with church-goers and friends. 'Mrs Crouch came, and even Mr Jolly, who hasn't left Scarborough in over forty-five years. In one town we saw them do this procession, all in their finery through the streets. But the funniest thing of all was when were got lost one day and the coach broke down on the way. In Spain, wasn't it, love?'

She looked at Dad, who was stuffing tobacco firmly into his pipe.

'Yes. None of us spoke a word of Spanish either,' he said.

'And all the ladies of the village were in these black dresses, sat in chairs by the road, and watching as Mr Ridley, who hasn't got a mechanical bone in his body, tried to fix the carburetor.' Mam was getting animated as she told the story. 'Anyway, eventually Father Parry found their local priest and managed to speak to him. And you'll never guess what he did. He spoke to him in Latin. To make himself understood that we were lost, and did he know where we could find a local garage? In the end they sent a coach all the way from Madrid.'

'Lord only knows what he said to get that message across. I don't think the Romans had cars, did they?' said Dad, laughing.

'But anyway. Enough about us. What about you? Are you a fully-fledged officer of the law now?'

'Not quite,' I said, kicking off my shoes and curling up on the sofa next to our large German Shepherd dog, Laddy. 'I'm a probationer now. For two years. Then I'll become a proper officer.' Laddy gave my face an enormous lick on the face so I pushed him off.

'Well, we don't care what the neighbours say about your being a lady police, and everything. We're proud as punch,' Mam said.

When I relayed the story of seeing the corpse, Mam then told me about when she'd seen her first dead body, her great-auntie Kay just after she had died.

'They had an open casket and we all walked past. Quiet, like. She looked . . . grey. I was a bit nervous at first, you know, expecting blood and gore, I suppose. But it was a kind of . . . release. Because she wasn't there. It wasn't her at all. Just a sort of shell. And after that we all got on with remembering Auntie Kay as she was in life.'

'I kept thinking he was going to smile,' I said, nuzzling up against Laddy and ruffling his thick fur.

'So where are you off now, then? Did they station you, or whatever you call it?' asked Dad.

'Yes. Richmond. Do you know it?'

'I think your mother and I stopped by the castle once when we were courting. We had an ice cream. Didn't we, love?'

'No, that was Bridlington. Ooh, by the way. We've been waiting to tell you too. Your brother proposed. It was very romantic, he said. By the seafront. He got down on one knee and everything. He's so grown up now,' she paused and looked down into her tea for a moment, as though reading some kind of far-off future in the leaves. 'So both my little chicks'll be flying the nest,' she whispered, almost to herself, as the last of her custard cream dissolved and sank to the bottom of the cup.

On my final day in Scarborough I wandered into town, taking in the sights. The dance hall on the seafront, the Spa Theatre, where I had performed in plays at the drama festival as a teenager, and the windswept sea crashing in against the shore. I'd arranged to meet Jane, from Marshall & Snelgrove, and a few of her new friends, at the Italian ice-cream shop nearby.

'Pam!' she called out, as I walked in. For a moment I hadn't recognized her. She looked all glamorous in a new dress and with short curly hair. 'It's so lovely to see you,' she said. 'You look, older. In a good way, I mean. Come and meet everyone.'

Jane was sitting with two other girls and three lads, who were eating knickerbocker glories and smoking cigarettes.

'This is Philip,' she said, and held onto the arm of a sailor in uniform. He looked a few years older than us; he had a small scar on his left cheek and a tattoo of a swallow on his arm. 'He's on leave,' Jane said, and looked up at him, smiling. 'And look!' She showed me a glimmering engagement ring on her left hand.

'Congratulations,' I said as she held up the ring for us all to see.

'This is Pam, a dear friend,' she said to the others. 'How many hours we must have spent on that shopfloor I don't know.'

We were quiet for a moment as I sat down. I smiled at everyone. There were a couple of new girls from the department store I'd never met, and their boyfriends, two lads in civvies, who were both motor mechanics.

They had all met at a dance at the Spa Ballroom, and become a bit of a gang, hanging out together, going to dances over the summer. They were excited because they had just been to London on the train, to the Festival of Britain.

'Oh, Pam, you should have seen this thing, they call it "telecinema". It's like the pictures, but more real. I don't know what they did, but it was amazing. Everything looked like real life.'

'I don't know. Everything I wanted to see was broken. New technology, my foot. You had to queue for hours, we missed half of it and kept going round in circles.' One of the lads in civvies spoke with a loud Liverpudlian accent. 'I've seen more interesting stuff down at the docks on a Friday night than I saw there. I don't know what all the fuss is about.'

'Oh, you misery guts,' said one of the girls. 'What about the Pleasure Gardens? You can't deny that. There was a foaming fountain!'

'What's the point?'

'I did find it quite boring, if I'm honest,' said the other girl quietly. 'It was like being back at school again. Trains and engines and stuff my dad likes.'

'Too many steps, not enough chairs, too many people,' said the lad from Liverpool again, stubbing out a cigarette and lighting another one immediately. 'And do you know how many houses and workshops they had to clear away to build all that stuff? People lost their homes, you know.'

'Well, I enjoyed it. But Mrs Preen says it's all a Labour conspiracy,' said Jane. 'So it probably won't last, now that it's gone all political. Nothing good ever lasts.' She looked down at her ring, then up again, and smiled. 'Almost nothing, anyway. Gosh. All this negativity, all of a sudden. Anyway. How about you? How was your course?'

As I started to tell them about my time at Bruche, I found it suddenly hard to articulate what I had seen over the past few weeks. How do you explain seeing a dead body, and all the changes which take place in you in such a short space of time when you're thrown together with other people, learning about the law, sexual crime, emergency childbirth . . .

In the end, I just told them about the Holger Nielsen technique, which made them laugh, especially when I demonstrated on poor Jane.

After the laughter and the milkshakes were finished, and we said our goodbyes, I realized that life had gone on for both of us since we had last met. We had drifted apart a little, and the ties that bound us, our youthful adventures in the department store, our plans to go to New Zealand, these things were all firmly in the past.

4

'You must be our new policewoman,' said a tall officer wearing sergeant stripes. I was all done up in my smartest civvies, with a hat and coat. My uniform was in a little leather suitcase.

I had imagined Richmond police station to be much bigger and grander, after my visits to Northallerton HQ with Dad's billiard friend. But the two cottages knocked into one did have a certain rustic charm. I stood there nervously, looking around. There was wooden bench seating round the walls and an open fireplace.

'I'm Sergeant Hardcastle,' he said. 'Pleased to meet you. Now, that door there leads to the washrooms and, through there, the cells,' said the Sergeant, waving around the room proprietorially.

I'd forgotten there'd be cells. I looked along the stone corridor, wondering what they were like and whether there were any villains in there right now. Just then, a young PC came in with another sergeant, helping through a soldier in uniform, who could barely stand up.

'We found him lying in the road, by Castle Street. Fast asleep. Drunk and incapable, blocking the pavement. So we thought we'd better bring him in and let the Red Caps deal with it. Let's get him through to the cells.'

I was to encounter a few more of these, soldiers from the nearby Catterick Garrison who were often brought in after a night out in Richmond. They'd drink one too many beers and miss the last bus back. The Red Caps were the army police; they'd come and take them away to dish out their own punishments.

As the young soldier and the two officers disappeared round the corner, I peered into the next office, where an attractive young woman with dark hair sat at a desk with a typewriter. She was in civvies not uniform, and she was typing very fast, never looking at the keys, just peering over her glasses at what she was copying.

'Come through to the office and meet Doris, our clerk,' said Sergeant Shaw, the office sergeant. He worked alongside Doris from nine to five. 'She's the only other female here, so hopefully you'll have lots to talk about.'

Inside the office was a small radio for receiving police messages from HQ, but no computers or photocopiers like you'll find today. Just some filing cabinets and files, lots of paper and two typewriters.

'That passage there leads into the Inspector's house. He lives on site. You'll meet him tomorrow. So don't be late! But you must be exhausted from your travels. Take Miss Rhodes to her digs, Carter,' said Sergeant Hardcastle to a young PC who was filling out some notes at a large desk by the door.

Carter leapt to the task, eager to get out of the office, so I followed him back out onto the street into the bright sunlight. As we walked, PC Ben Carter explained to me who everyone was at the station.

'There's Doris, who you met. She's the clerk, and a right cracker of a lass. Then Sergeant Shaw, who you also met. He's pretty amiable. Only works office hours. One to go to with your questions first, perhaps. Sergeant Cleese does the night shift. Then Sergeant Hardcastle, who you saw briefly. He's a bit of a tough nut. Nothing gets past him. Then there's the Inspector, who lives on site. You call him sir, and he comes round to check we're all where we should be, making our points. The Super – who's very much of the old school and works all the hours God sends – he's the top dog, so you stand and salute the first time he comes in every day. Then there's us PCs: myself, you, George and Bill, and a few more who you'll meet. We also make contact with the village bobbies by telephone and Traffic Patrol drop by every now and then. And that's Richmond.'

By the time we got to my digs, a small terraced house, my head was so full of all these new names, I didn't know how I'd remember them all, or who was in charge and what to say to who. I just hoped I would get it all right. Ben left me at the house and I rang the doorbell on my own.

A young woman of about twenty-eight answered the door, and introduced herself as Janet Marshall. Her husband, Don, did something on the buses, though I could never work out quite what. Her children were Michael, a thoughtful seven-year-old, wise beyond his years, and his older sister, Fiona, aged nine, who was the bossier of the pair. When Janet answered the door that first time, Fiona was plonking away on a small out-of-tune piano and Michael was on the floor, grimacing in dismay at the piece of broken railway track impeding the journey of a stately green engine.

'You must be Pamela. Come in. Come in. You'll have to excuse the mess,' she shouted over the sounds of the piano, picking her way through a complex network of railway lines. 'These two think they own the place. Cup of tea? Come on through here and sit down.'

I wasn't sure how I'd fit into this tiny house, which only seemed to have two rooms downstairs. Janet pulled things from chairs and tables and cleared away a space for us to sit. Although she seemed to do nothing but housework, the place was always in a state of perpetual chaos.

'So tell me about yourself. You're to be a policewoman, are you?' she said, rinsing out two cups. 'Sorry about these. Michael broke the best ones. All of them. Poor lad. He didn't mean to. He was being such a good boy and carrying them for me. Cried for hours, poor lamb. Can't bear to see things broken. Anyway. I do hope you'll feel at home here.'

My room was to be a tiny box room at the back, which just about fitted a bed in it; I supposed the poor children had to bunk up together. It was a squeeze, but it was to be home for now at least. As well as squeezing an extra person in to their home, the other thing Janet and her household had to put up with after my arrival were occasional late-night calls from the station. An officer would come by and knock on the door if they needed me. If they had a woman in the station, no matter what time of day or night, a female officer had to be present.

And that's what happened in my first week, when the PC came knocking at three a.m. and I was called in to deal with Pearl, the 'lady of the night'.

Apart from the occasional late-night call-out, what I mostly had to get used to at first was the geography of the new town and the Richmond police beats. We would make 'points' at all the different phone boxes, that is, we'd stand and wait for a phone call, in case the station needed you to go anywhere in particular or deal with anything specific.

PC Ben Carter took me round Richmond on my first day; after that I'd be on my own.

'Every half hour you stop at a phone box and wait for a call from the station, in case they need to get in touch with an officer,' he said, as we strolled towards the market place. 'Watch out for the Super, though, he drives past sometimes to check up on us. So don't be late for a point, whatever you do.'

As we walked up the street, past rows of old stone cottages and stately Georgian redbricks, on the skyline I saw the imposing outline of Richmond Castle with its ragged Norman fortress. Ben made his first point outside the grand-looking King's Head Hotel, but no one rang through, so we wandered on, up King Street, towards the cinema.

A large part of the job seemed to be chatting to the locals, and I remembered what Sergeant Baines had said to us about getting to know the people on our beats, so I tried to take in all their names as we walked along.

'Mrs Tibbs. How's Eric? And the boys?'

'Oh, you wouldn't believe. Poor James has got the measles, and Timothy is at that age. You know, no help to anyone and eats like a horse. And with this rationing set to carry on for ever. And Eric losing his job at the mine. I don't know what we'll do, I'm sure.'

'Well, chin up. I'm sure it'll all come good,' Ben said, before continuing up the road.

A bit further on, we saw a very elderly lady with a shock of grey curled hair, a sharp nose and thick blue eye shadow cracking round her eyes. She had the look of someone who used to be very beautiful, but whose formerly thickly lashed eyes have now taken on a look of heavy sadness. She was standing almost at the very edge of the road and gently swaying back and forth, staring into the distance.

'Mrs Colbert,' said Ben to me, in a low whisper. 'Since her husband died she's become a little, how shall I say, unstable. She lives with her daughter now. But there's only so much she can do – she's on her own, and she works full time and has a family too.'

Mrs Colbert stepped out into the road as a motor car came whizzing round the corner, swerved to avoid her and tooted its horn. She continued on, oblivious, as a few more cars and a bus narrowly missed hitting her, their angry yells fading into the distance.

'Mrs Colbert. You must be more careful. These roads are a lot busier these days,' said Ben, running over to prevent any further motoring chaos.

We took an arm each and guided her safely to the other side of the road, but she didn't say a word as we crossed. When we reached the pavement she looked up with a sad smile of thanks, and I saw she was wearing a pair of light pink slippers, while underneath her coat, just visible, was the edge of a patchwork dressing gown.

As we walked her back to her house, Mrs Colbert lightly sang a little hymn to herself and seemed quite happy shuffling along the street. When we arrived, a plump woman of about forty-five, red in the face and holding a tea towel, answered the door.

'We found someone for you,' Ben said to her.

'Oh, Mam! How did you get out? I thought you were listening to your music. I'm so sorry, constable. I don't know how she got out. She loves Mozart so I put it on the gramophone for her while I baked, but I thought I'd locked the door. I'm making a cake for little Patrick's birthday. He's eight now, would you believe?'

'Let's bring her in and sit her down. This is PC Rhodes, a new addition to the station.'

'Pleased to meet you,' I said, and we took Mrs Colbert into her daughter's tiny living room and sat her down on a wingback chair in front of the fireplace. As she sank back, she looked small and frail and sad that her little adventure was over.

'We'd better be off. Take care now.'

And off we were up the road again, on to the next telephone box. This time the phone rang and Ben answered.

'Yes, yes, righto, Sergeant.' He turned to me. 'It's Hardcastle. He's got a job for you. You'd better get going.'

I just about remembered my way back to the station, and as I went in through the door, breathless from fast walking, I almost bumped into Sergeant Hardcastle, the other duty sergeant at the station. He was putting on his hat.

'Ah, Rhodes. Good, you're here. Get your things. I'll explain on the way.'

It was all I could do to keep up with Sergeant Hardcastle, who always walked as though he was pursuing someone just around the next corner.

'We've to visit a young woman, a teacher, Miss Binns. She's not from round here, down south, a new lass at the primary school. Now, I have good sources who say the young lady in question has carried out, or attempted to carry out . . .' He hesitated, perhaps trying not to shock me. 'an offence against an unborn child.'

Abortion in those days was illegal, and a big taboo socially. In the early 1800s it had even been punishable by death in Britain. Although they had long got rid of that by the time I was in the police, you could still get a hefty prison sentence.

In 'Dirty Week' at Bruche, with Baines, we'd learnt that abortions took place either through 'back-street' abortionists or via a variety of self-administered herbs, drugs or poisons which could flush out the foetus. Some women carried out dramatic and vigorous exercises, or pulled risky stunts, occasionally even launching themselves down flights of stairs in order to try to get rid of an unborn baby. These unregulated attempts often resulted in injury or even death for the women.

'One of the other teachers at the school, a Mrs . . .' he looked at his notebook, 'Verity, has passed on some information, saying that she suspects a colleague, a Miss Binns, has been administering something in order to destroy an unwanted baby, got with the caretaker of the school. A married man, no less.'

'How will you know?' I asked. 'What the truth is, I mean?'

'Well, that is the question. We'll just have to see what the young lady says, shan't we? And anyway, I have a knack of . . . knowing . . . when it comes to such matters.'

Miss Binns lived in a flat above a small newsagent's shop, on the way out of town. We walked up a rickety wooden staircase to get there, and a pretty young woman of about twenty-five, wearing a floral print dress and with a neat straight blonde bob, opened the door to us.

'Miss Binns?'

'Yes. What . . . I mean, can I help with anything, officer?'

'May we come in? It's a matter of some . . .'

'Of course. Is it the school? Has something happened to one of the children? Would you like something? Water? Some tea?'

'No, that won't be necessary. Though I wouldn't mind using your lavatory, if you don't mind.'

Hardcastle disappeared, and I stood awkwardly with Miss Binns, who stared up at the ceiling, picking at her fingernails. She looked a little nervous, but not anxious or guilty that I could sense.

The flat was quite bare, with wooden floorboards full of gaps and draughty cracks. In one corner was a simple metal bedstead, with a red crocheted blanket, and next to it was a small kitchen table and a cupboard. In another corner was a gas stove and a little sink. The wallpaper was a damp yellow colour and a small blue curtain fluttered in the wind next to a cracked window.

I wondered why a teacher would live in such poverty, but didn't like to ask.

A slender glass vase on the table, with some freshly picked flowers in it, and a row of books on a little shelf were the only signs I could see of Miss Binns's own possessions.

'Jane Austen. Do you know her?' she said quietly, breaking the silence as I looked at the books.

'Can't say I do much reading,' I answered. 'Sergeant said you were a teacher. English?'

'I was. But I'm teaching the young ones now. Five to tens, up at St Martin's. I'm from Rugby originally. I do want to teach English. Well, actually I wanted to be a writer. But I had to get a job here because of . . .' She stopped abruptly as Sergeant Hardcastle came back into the room, wiping his hands on his trousers.

'So, Miss, er, Binns. We'd like to talk to you about some rumours. Shall we sit down?'

There were only two chairs, so they sat down and I stood up nearby.

'Ugly rumours.' Hardcastle shook his head as he spoke and flicked through his notebook, but watched out of the corners of his eyes, to observe her reaction. 'Rumours that you've been engaged in . . . Well, we might as well get to the matter in hand. Illegal abortion.'

As the words hung in the air, Miss Binns looked down at the table and then back up at Hardcastle. She looked at me and I tried to look neutral.

'Now, you don't have to say anything at this stage. We'll just listen at this stage to what you have to say and take it from there. OK?'

'Yes, but . . . how? I mean . . . I didn't . . .'

'So I'll ask you, Miss Binns, have you or have you not been involved with an illegal abortion or other attempt to abort an unborn child?'

'No!' she said, just a little too quickly, perhaps.

'Because if you try to cover things up, it will only get worse for you and the other . . . person involved.'

'Other person? I swear. I hardly know anyone here. How could I . . . ?'

She was starting to panic a little, breathing quickly; even to me the room suddenly felt very hot and stifling.

'All right, all right. Take your time. A moment to consider the question. I'm giving you a chance to tell it your own way. Did you perhaps purchase something . . . something to hurt the unborn child? To kill it?'

'NO! I didn't kill anything. I didn't . . .' she stopped, and wiped away some tears that were now flowing quite freely down her cheeks.

'Because before you deny anything, I have to tell you I found this – quite by accident, of course – in your bathroom.'

Sergeant Hardcastle produced from his pocket a small blue glass bottle, with a handwritten label saying simply 'Penny Royal'.

'Are you familiar with this bottle, Miss Binns? This herbal concoction, most commonly used for that very purpose.'

'How did you . . . ? You can't do that! Go searching! That wasn't for that.'

'Then what was it for?' said Hardcastle, placing the half-empty bottle firmly on the table.

Penny Royal was among the herbs often used by women who wanted to get rid of a baby in those days, and could be bought in the form of an oil quite easily for the purpose from a herbalist or anyone who knew about plants. It rarely actually worked, and often made the woman ill.

'Now you can talk to us. We're not after anything but the truth.' I smiled and tried to put her at ease. Then she started to talk.

'I was worried because I hadn't had my . . . time of the month for a while. I thought it might be because I wasn't eating right. I wasn't feeling right. And this woman, this herbal woman, my friend recommended her. She said this would encourage . . . it back. The menstruation. So I tried it. And it worked. But I wasn't . . .'

'So you weren't with child? Can you be sure of that?'

'Yes! Well . . . I think. I'm sure. I think. Oh God . . . I don't know!'

'Right. Good. We're getting somewhere. So you might then have aborted a child?'

As I sat there I couldn't help thinking how intrusive it all felt. I tried to be professional and dispassionate, to think about the law, how that was the backbone of society. Hardcastle was doing his job, and abortion was illegal. He needed proof, and he thought he had it with the bottle of Penny Royal. I tried to think of it like any other crime, a simple shoplifting or traffic offence. But seeing that woman there, struggling to tell the Sergeant about her most private moments, I suddenly felt very uncomfortable and sorry for her.

'There was no child. We were . . . oh God!' Miss Binns put her head in her hands on the table and started to cry. Sergeant Hardcastle shifted in his seat slightly uncomfortably.

'Look, we are duty bound to investigate a suspected crime. You do understand that?'

She looked up with red eyes. 'You can't prove anything. I bet it was that spiteful Mrs Verity who's reported me. She's been out to get me from day one. She can't bear that I . . . we might be happy. But you can't prove anything.'

'You might be right. On the other hand we may well have enough evidence. We'll just have to see.'

By the end of my first week, I had already encountered prostitution, a suspected abortion and nearly been killed by an escaped bullock. But it wasn't always that dramatic at Richmond police station.

If I was on an early shift, I had to be in at five forty-five a.m. and when I arrived at the station I'd first have to dust the Superintendent's office. Not a very glamorous job, but it was a bit of thinking time. The office wasn't large but it was certainly the grandest room in the station. I tried not to knock anything over as I dusted his large wooden desk, with the photo of his wife along with some very posh-looking writing paper and a large inkwell. There was a big black telephone on his desk, and a large painting of a horse on the wall, which stared back at me with its long nose wherever I was in the room.

After dusting duties, I'd have to type up reports and statements that might have come in through the night. I was slow, a two-finger typist, but I got through it steadily enough. After that, I wrote reports of a jewellery theft and a runaway girl in the occurrence book.

At about nine a.m. the Superintendent arrived. Walter William never had much to say for himself, but he had a very commanding presence. The Super, as we called him, though not to his face, seemed to be on duty all the time, staying until about ten o'clock at night, going home only for dinner and tea. The only evening he would ever take off was once in a blue moon, to go to meetings with the

Freemasons. He had a wife, but we never met her; I don't think she can have seen much of him, so dedicated was he to the job.

I was nervous of meeting the Super for the first time, and stood up straight when he came in. We always had to stand up the first time he came in in the morning.

'Morning,' he nodded to Sergeant Hardcastle, myself and another PC called Bill. 'I hear we have our new female officer,' he said, looking me up and down and inhaling. 'Good. Just remember, we run a tight ship here.'

'Yes, sir,' I said. And that was my introduction to the Super.

When he left, we all relaxed again but, before long, Sergeant Hardcastle had a job for me.

'Ah, Rhodes. You'll do,' he said, waving a list of typed names and addresses on a sheet of paper.

'Visit these addresses, and check these aliens are where they should be,' he said, thrusting it into my hand.

Aliens? My mind boggled at the thought.

'Foreigners, aliens, who are living in Richmond – non-British citizens,' he said, in response to my stunned expression. 'We're to check on a regular basis they are where they say they are.'

'Yes, Sergeant. Should I say anything to them?'

'You can remind Mr Leonie we need to interview him next week. He knows about it. Just remind him.'

And off I went, on an official mission, to check on all the aliens in Richmond.

The first address on the paper was Maria Campanella, 7, Willow Street. That was what PC Carter had called the posh end of town when he showed me the beats. It was a row of big Georgian houses all set back from the road, some with imposing shrubbery and trees hiding the house from the street.

In the garden of number 7 there was a big fountain, with statues of Pan and Neptune spouting water and laughing. There was even a palm tree, which seemed extraordinarily exotic for Yorkshire. The front door was set between two Roman-style pillars and there was a huge red knocker in the shape of an eagle. I knocked, but I was so nervous and tentative it hardly made a sound. I knocked again, louder, but then this time it was so loud it set some dogs to barking in the house.

'All right, all right, I'm coming,' said a woman's voice from within. 'Pascale, Benedict, do shut up,' she said to the dogs who were whining at the door.

A sixty-something woman opened up, quite glamorous-looking, in a peacock blue jumper and pearls, her hair set in a pristine bowl of red curls.

'Yes,' she said rather curtly, holding two giant Red Setters by the collars.

'Morning. I'm here to enquire about . . .' I looked down at the list, 'Maria Campanella? Is she here? We're just checking on . . . and she's . . .'

'I'm too busy for all this. We're having a dinner here tonight. The mayor. Lord Tranton will be home any minute and I don't want to attract attention with the police. So if you don't mind . . .'

She went to close the door, but I persisted.

'Please. If *you* don't mind, I have got a job to do. Please. Just confirm that Maria is still here.'

I wasn't sure where this unexpected burst of confidence came from, but it seemed to work.

'Fine. She's here.'

At that moment, Maria herself came to the door, concerned by the noise.

'Lady Tranton, is everything . . . ?'

'Yes, girl. You just get back to work. Never mind all this.'

Maria was a very thin, pretty young girl of about twenty-two. I wondered how she had ended up in Richmond working for Lady Tranton. I knew there were some Italian families who had been prisoners of war and stayed on. Perhaps her father had been a POW.

Maria hardly said a word, she just half smiled and confirmed to me that yes, that was her name. It was clear she was where she was supposed to be, so I said goodbye, to deter any further trouble from her boss.

The next location couldn't have been more different. At the other end of town, by the train station, was a small garage, run by a couple of brothers, Max and Fred Dent. Max was incredibly tall and thin and never spoke but seemed to do most of the work, and Fred was short, stout and talked all the time, as fast as a moving train, but seemed to do very little.

Max, the taller, silent brother, was meticulously polishing the wing mirrors of a large silver Bentley when I arrived, while Fred was barking into the telephone.

'Well, it could take several days, weeks even, to get those parts, sir. Yes, she's in fine shape,' he went on. 'All I'm saying is, we want to do the best job possible. It might cost . . . a little more, is all. I know you need the vehicle.

I am aware of that fact. But this is hard times, sir. Since the war it's been damn nigh impossible to get hold of parts. All I can say is we'll do our utmost. Now I have to go. I have a visitor. Yes, sir. Goodbye, sir.' An angry voice could be heard on the other end of the line as he slammed the phone down.

'Blessed politicians, think they own the place! He doesn't even live in Richmond. Holiday home, would you believe? Ooh, sorry, miss, didn't see you there. What can I do you for?'

'Mr ... Dent?' I deduced, looking up at the Dent Brothers sign above his head.

The garage forecourt had a small petrol pump and a little shed, where another man was at work on the Bentley, and next to that was the little office where the telephone was situated.

'I'm here to check on one of your employees, a Mr Leonie? Is he present?'

'FRANK!' he shouted, and made me jump almost out of my shoes. 'A young lady to see you. A police lady.' He put a knowing emphasis on the word lady both times.

A man emerged from underneath the Bentley, put down the spanner he was holding and wiped his hands on a rag in his pocket. He was wearing blue overalls, and had a large grease smear across his face, and a shock of black hair and deep brown eyes.

'Francesco Leonie?' I asked, holding my notebook to make it all seem a little more official.

'Yes. But they call me Frank. But then what can you do, eh?' His English was good, but he had a strong Italian accent.

Again, I wondered how and why he had chosen to stay in Yorkshire. He was older than Maria, about twenty-eight, so perhaps he had been a young prisoner of war himself. He was very handsome and seemed quite exotic and dashing compared to the lads I was familiar with in Scarborough.

'I just need you to confirm your name, and I'll tick you off as all present and correct,' I said, attempting a bit of lighthearted banter. 'Oh, and Sergeant Hardcastle says not to forget you're to be interrogated next week. But he says you know about it.'

'Interviewed,' he said, the smile vanishing from his face. 'Not interrogated. I think is the word you're looking for.'

'Yes, so sorry. I don't know what I meant. I mean, yes, interviewed. Of course, sorry!'

Perhaps the war had done funny things to our perception of these so-called aliens.

'Don't panic. I don't hold the resentments for long. Not for young lady police ladies anyway,' he smiled again and I hoped I was forgiven for my mistake.

I wanted to ask Francesco all about his life in Italy. How he felt about ending up here in Richmond, and what his family did back home. But for now I just said, 'Good. Well, I'll let you get back to your job. Thanks again. Thanks, Mr Dent, and Mr Dent.'

I practically ran down the lane back to the station, quite relieved it was all over.

Being in rural North Riding meant my duties as an officer were many and varied. One minute I might be helping someone across the road, and the next sitting in on an interview with a lady of the night, or going down to check on someone in the cells. You never knew what would come round the corner.

One of my first encounters with farming life in Richmond had been being chased by Bertie the bullock into a phone box on my first day. Once we had recovered from our shock, Farmer Joe had managed to get the beast tethered. I was in a hurry to get to work for inspection, so he led the animal back up the hill to his farm alone; I hadn't seen him since. After a few weeks, that first day had begun to seem like a distant dream, until one morning when the Inspector came in with a job for me.

'You've heard of swine fever?'

'I think so, sir. A kind of animal flu, isn't it? Affecting pigs.'

'Yes. And it's on the increase so we need to be vigilant. Farmer ... what's his name? ... McGregor? He's got some new animals, and I need you to go and check he's keeping the pigs separate. That's so if there is any illness it won't spread through the whole lot of them.'

'Yes, sir,' I replied and put on my greatcoat. There was an autumnal chill in the air and the leaves were starting to fall. I was actually looking forward to a nice walk out of town and being able to take in some more of the local scenery.

The great, swirling River Swale curved round the edge of the town, and in pride of place on the hill sat the castle, as it had for hundreds of years, watching over Richmond. I walked out of town, up the lane towards the farm, past a herd of cows grazing. And next to them, in his own field, was Bertie the bullock, nostrils flaring, pacing up and down like a sentinel. He looked even bigger than I remembered and I shivered slightly at the memory of our last encounter.

The ground was wet as I trudged up the lane to the farmhouse and my lace-up police shoes, soon thick with mud, seemed woefully inadequate. Over the brow of the hill I saw Farmer Joe, strategically carrying two buckets of water that swished from side to side, miraculously without spilling a drop. He was a thin, wiry man with wispy, grey hair and a pointy nose, but strong-looking arms and the rough and ready skin of someone who has spent a lifetime outside.

I wasn't sure he recognized me at first and I felt quite out of place in my smart uniform, tunic, skirt and coat, slushing about in the mud against this rural backdrop. As I approached, a gaggle of geese marched past, followed by some chickens who seemed to think they were also geese, all being surreptitiously followed by a raggedy black cat in stealthy pursuit.

'Joe!' I shouted up the lane, as he shuffled along with his buckets. 'How's Bertie? Has he recovered from his ordeal?'

'You again? What are you doing up here? I remember you. That animal is twice the size and ten times as heavy at least. How he didn't knock you over flat I'll never know.' Joe spoke with a smile as he put the buckets down. 'Are you here to check on him then?' he asked, his grey whiskers twitching. 'For he's back there, in that field. You just passed him. He's right as rain now. Fine animal. Best few pounds I ever spent that was.'

'No. I'm not here about Bertie, though he is looking lovely. I hear you've some new pigs. And I need to check you're keeping them all separate.'

'Oh, the pigs, is it? Yes, we've got some new 'uns. Beauties. Pink as the soles of a bairn's feet and healthy too. No need to check on them. They're right all right,' he said proudly.

'I'm sure they're wonderful, but I do need to check all the same. You know, regulations,' I said.

'Well. I suppose a job's a job. That's what the police seems to do these days. Check on this and that. No offence. But that's the way it is now, I suppose. Not like in my day, when we was left to get on with it. Well, you might as well come in. The wife'll make some tea, if you're lucky.'

So I followed Joe up the track and to the little stone cottage where the pair lived and we reminisced about the day with Bertie and the phone box. Joe and his wife had never had any children, so they had to run the farm on their own, with some seasonal help from some of the local lads.

There was an air of sad decay about the place as we walked past the old cowshed and up to the little stone cottage, which had most of the slates missing from the roof and several cracked windows. There were a variety of farming tools scattered about the place and some old rusting tractors in varying states of disrepair.

'I don't have a moment to fix anything these days. And what with the arthritis, and the wife's hernia . . . We'll probably be the last generation to run a farm here, before some rich banker buys it up as his holiday home, I don't wonder.'

We went into the cottage through a tiny wooden door; we both had to duck to get in. Three mongrel dogs came bounding over, their tongues lolling out. One only had three legs but had worked out a miraculous way of running even faster than the other two.

'We rescued that one. Well, the wife did. She's soft for puppies. Abandoned in the river. She came home with him one day. Didn't you, love?'

As we entered the little kitchen, Mrs McGregor was at the sink, sleeves rolled up, peeling potatoes.

'Didn't I what?'

'Found our Caspar. In the river.'

'Oh, such a sorry-looking thing. All pink like a little squashed piglet. Hardly any fur on him at all. Now look at him. You can't hold him back.'

Caspar ran round and round in circles, trying to catch his tail. I wondered what he'd do with it if he ever did.

'What can we do for you, anyway?' asked Mrs McGregor.

'She's come to check on the pigs. But I think she'd much prefer a nice cuppa. Don't you?'

I felt bad for noticing, but I almost had to hold my breath to avoid being sick as I sat at the table. There was a distinctly sour smell, possibly emanating from the several dead rabbits and the pheasant hanging from the doorway to the larder. Then again, I also noticed quite a gathering of flies were congregating around a hollow sheep's head on the table, the wool still on it.

'Dinner, that is. Joe can't get enough of a bit of sheep's head.'

A fly settled on my arm and rubbed its legs together.

I brushed it away, but then another two immediately took its place, so I soon gave up and let them go about their business.

'Do you take sugar, love?' asked Mrs McGregor, waddling over with a tray, some cups and the teapot. 'We haven't got much but you'd be welcome. And you must try one of these jam tarts. Joe loves them. Don't you?'

'Oh, aye, she makes the best jam tarts this side of the Great North Road, and no denying that. Damsons fresh from up the woods.'

'I'm not as nimble as I used to be, though,' she said. 'Hernia. Like a couple of old cart horses, almost beyond their working life, aren't we?'

'Oh, I don't know. We've got a few years in us yet.'

Mrs McGregor placed a plate on the table in front of me, and several flies swooped down gleefully from all directions towards the glistening confectionery.

'Oh, thank you. But really I couldn't eat a thing.' I was actually starving hungry, but the sight of all those flies had quite turned my stomach.

When I think back now I feel bad, because they were probably living close to the bread line on that farm, and their hospitality was generous and kindly meant. Farming was becoming increasingly difficult, especially for a family with no children to help out.

After the tea, which I had to admit was tasty, Joe showed me down to the shed and his new pigs.

'Aren't they beauties?' he said, leaning on the fence. 'I got them at market, for a song,' he explained as we looked over into the pig pen.

The animals came grunting over to him and rubbed

their prickly pink backs against the side of the fence. I leant over and stroked one on the nose.

'They look like they're smiling, don't they? I never name them, though. Only Bertie. Otherwise you'd get too attached to let 'em go. If you know what I mean.'

As I ruffled the pig's snout it rolled over onto its back and looked as though it was about to burst out laughing.

'She likes you,' Joe said, and looked around affectionately at the animals on his farm. 'So you see, these girls are kept quite separate from the others.' He pointed next door to another pen, where some much larger pigs were lounging about, caked in mud, flies buzzing around their faces. A small sparrow had even sat on one of the pigs' heads; it didn't move an inch, even when the pig stretched and rolled over.

I made a note in my pocketbook that I'd seen the pigs, with the time and date, and, satisfied, I bade my goodbyes to the farmer and his wife. As I walked away, they stood arm in arm and waved me off down the hill. I had a sense that they didn't see many visitors and were a little sad to see me go. They carried on waving until I had rounded the corner, out of sight. The last thing I heard Farmer Joe say to his wife, as I departed, was: 'She's no' but a lass'.

I may have been 'no' but a lass', but the next case I was to encounter would be a lot more shocking than some pigs on a farm and a few flies.

5

When I had first got my *Stone's Justices' Manual* as a trainee, all those months before, I remember the page falling open on the definition of 'incest', but I never thought I'd encounter it for real. It turned out life was never boring for long in Richmond, and just when I thought I'd be stuck in the station all day, Sergeant Hardcastle came in with the Inspector. They had been in deep and serious discussions in the office all morning and, when they emerged, the Sergeant called me over.

'You've been here a few weeks now, and you've shown you've got your wits about you, Rhodes. I need you to accompany me on something of a sensitive matter. A suspected case of incest. With a young girl. Twelve years old.'

'Right,' I said, trying not to sound too shocked.

'Yes. It's not a pretty story, by any means. The Inspector's just been filling me in on the details. Her father, it looks like. So we're to interview the mother. Not sure where he is, but we're trying to trace him now. She's a Mrs Taylor, but no sign of a Mr Taylor at that address.'

We took the station car. We only had one car so it was a bonus if we got to use it and didn't have to take the bus or train. There were no seatbelts in those days, so we slid about in the seats as we went round all the windy country lanes. I was struck by the contrast between the beauty of the fields and hills around us and the possible severity of the case we were about to investigate.

The address the Sergeant had scribbled on a piece of paper turned out to be in a neighbouring village, among a huddle of neat cottages. As we walked to the door I noticed a gnome in the garden, holding a wheelbarrow. A woman answered the door. She had long black hair, and a flowing skirt made of a kind of exotic satin, with a swirling print across the front; quite different from the fashion of the time.

'Mrs Taylor? Do you know why we're here?'

'Yes. I think so,' said the woman, reluctant to open the door fully.

'It's in relation to your husband. May we come in?'

'Of course. Sorry. I'm all over the place today.'

Mrs Taylor showed us through into the living room, where two young girls sat together on the sofa, darning some socks. They were softly chattering to one another and didn't look up when we came in. Mrs Taylor signalled for them to leave the room, which they did only after some persuading. When the girls had gone, Mrs Taylor looked us both full in the face.

'I don't know anything about anything, you know. They rang and told me you were coming, but we're just getting on with our lives. We don't need anyone poking their noses in.'

'Let's start at the beginning then, shall we?' said Hardcastle gently. 'Get a few things clear?'

As we sat down, I noticed that the room was adorned with all kind of exotic ornaments, such as carved elephants and statues.

'We're here because someone . . . at the school . . .'

'I know who it is and she's a liar,' Mrs Taylor inter-rupted. 'She never stops . . .'

'I'm afraid I can't say who it is. But what I can say is that we have had some very serious allegations, concerning your daughter, Elizabeth Jane. Can you tell me where your husband is, Mrs Taylor?'

'He's not here. We haven't seen him in years. I don't know what these "allegations" are, but we haven't seen him . . . the girls wouldn't know him from Adam.'

'Well our – person – says they've heard a very serious rumour at the girls' school that he – that is your husband – and Elizabeth Jane, here, have been involved in acts of a . . . sexual nature. Do you have anything to say about that, Mrs Taylor? Might the girls have been talking about something like that at school? Were you aware of any-thing like that going on in your house?'

'He was so kind to us all, me and the girls. When we were in India. I owed him a . . . favour and . . .'

'India?'

'My husband was in the army out there. Hadn't been home for years. We thought he was dead. You can't imagine what it was like. The waiting. I spent months looking for him. Asking everywhere I could. And those mosquitos . . .' She shivered and looked around distract-edly for a moment. 'Big grey hulking things that would bite the flesh off you soon as look at you . . .' She broke off.

After a while she looked down at her lap. 'I was lonely . . .'

'Very well. So, your husband and your family moved to India, then?'

'No, well not exactly, we went to look for him, as I say. But we hadn't heard from him for years. His regiment hadn't seen him either. Thought he must have gone AWOL. Said he went on a trip into the mountains and never came back. That's when I met Clive.'

'Clive?' asked Hardcastle, raising an eyebrow.

'Jessica's father. They're only half-sisters . . .'

She paused for a moment and then commenced with a torrent of explanation, almost as if she was quite relieved to have someone to tell.

'We got this boat, don't know what it was carrying, big boxes everywhere. Clive managed to get us a place. He said he would help us find Derek. Through the Embassy. I know it's mad, now. But we all got terribly sick. For weeks Elizabeth Jane had a fever. At one point I thought we'd lose her, she was that grey. Eyes all sunken. Clive never left her side. He was good . . .'

The woman looked like she might break down then managed to pull herself together again.

'I was so grateful for all he'd done for me. For us. And I was . . . pregnant by then. There was no going back. He asked me to marry him, didn't he? Well, he had to. Then little Jessie was born. She looked so like him. It was fine for a while. Five years, it was fine. Then last month he left a note: "It's gone too far. I can't go on," it said. And when I came back from work that day, he was gone.'

At this, the woman finally did start to cry, a sort of silent sob, but Hardcastle continued, unmoved.

'So you married this . . . Clive. But did you get a divorce from your husband, Mr Taylor?'

'Well, we thought he was dead, didn't we? But then I got

a letter. I hid it from Clive. I burnt it in the end. Why shouldn't I? He'd left us. Turned out he'd been found half-starved up a mountain or something, living with some monks. So skinny they hardly recognized him.'

In that moment it dawned on me that this had suddenly gone from a case of incest to indecent assault, because the man wasn't the child's father after all, and now there was bigamy too.

'Well, I'm afraid this takes us into some very awkward territory indeed,' said Hardcastle, also clearly a little flustered by this sudden turn of events.

'Clive loved that girl like a daughter. He wouldn't hurt her. He cared for us. All of us.'

Just then there was a creak and we all looked round. The two girls stood in the doorway. I wondered if they had been listening the whole time. There was a mix of what I can only describe as fear and pity on their faces as they looked back at their mother. Had Clive really been just a doting stepfather?

Mrs Taylor went over to the girls and knelt down, clasping both their hands. Then Elizabeth Jane started to speak directly to her mother.

'He would come into my bedroom, Mam. Didn't you know? Sometimes if we was in the bath . . . at first it was friendly . . . he'd play ducks with us. But then . . . Did I do wrong? I didn't know what to do, Mam. I'm sorry . . .'

For a good few minutes, although it felt like longer, nobody spoke, and I sat slightly awkwardly on the sofa not sure what to do. The investigation suddenly seemed to have taken on a life of its own. Finally, Sergeant Hardcastle coughed.

'This is very serious, Mrs Taylor. Young Elizabeth may have to testify in court. And this bigamy situation throws everything up in the air, of course.'

I took down a statement from Mrs Taylor when the questioning was finished, but after that she didn't move, just sat there and held onto her daughters. We seemed to have disappeared from their world at that moment, become insignificant as the horrible realization of what had happened to their family finally sunk in.

When I got home that night, my landlady, Janet, was stirring a huge pot of chicken stew for us all. I gave her my ration coupons for food every week so there would be enough food for all of us. Her husband, Don, came in from work, and the two children, Michael and Fiona, scrubbed their hands for dinner. As we sat together eating, Janet asked the children what they'd been doing at school and they chattered away excitedly. I was quiet about my day; inside I was thinking how lucky they were to be able to do the simplest of things like sit round and eat dinner together.

I worked hard at Richmond, but I did have some time off. I worked seven days and would then have the eighth day off. And if I worked the early shift, from five forty-five a.m. until two p.m. I had the afternoon off. I could also take time off for church. 'Standing Orders' said that PCs were to be allowed to go to services. It was hoped that senior officers would set the example. I'd stay an hour later on those Sundays to make up the time.

St Francis's Roman Catholic church was a tiny medieval building, with a beautiful carved wooden altarpiece. The whole place seemed very ancient and mystical, and there was always a strong smell of incense.

Father Reilly, the priest, was a quiet man with a small pointy face and round spectacles. His voice barely rose above a whisper and his sermons were often more philosophical than religious, rambling on in all different directions.

'Each second has equal weight. As a bird flutters from branch to branch, beak darting for the next insect . . .' He raised his hands, as if offering the birds some food, and pursed his lips thoughtfully, looking up into the rafters for inspiration, 'so as Man's thoughts on earth flutter from moment to moment. But, hear this. No moment is worth more than the next.'

He paused again and looked up at the stained-glass window, which depicted some scenes from the New Testament. Someone coughed and then a baby began to cry.

'Heaven is here on earth. We are not waiting for the next life. The next life is with us already, in each second. Look outwards, as does the bird, and see Heaven in all things. HEAVEN IN ALL THINGS!' he shouted suddenly, staring out at the congregation.

The front row of ladies, who had nodded off at various angles onto each other's shoulders, all woke simultaneously with a start. One even let out a small snort.

'If you can actually follow what he says it can be quite enlightening,' whispered a woman to me after the service had ended. I had never seen her before and we were walking towards the door, out into the morning sunlight.

'Yes. Very different from our priest at home, who was much more straight down the line, if you know what I mean,' I said.

'Oh, where's home?'

'Scarborough. Are you from Richmond?' I asked.

'Yes. I grew up here. I'm a teacher. We both are, actually, at the convent school. This is Eleanor,' she said, introducing another woman walking beside her. 'And I'm Gertie.'

Father Reilly was outside the church, shaking hands and saying soft, holy things to the congregation, which was mostly made up of elderly ladies who wanted a bit of comfort and conversation.

'What brings you to Richmond, then? I haven't seen you in church before.'

'I'm over at the station. Police station. This is my first posting.'

'Gosh. How exciting! I didn't know they had girls in the police now. Times *are* changing, aren't they?'

'I suppose they are,' I said.

As I watched Father Reilly shaking all those hands, I wondered whether times would change so much that one day we might have women priests too. Before we left, I arranged to meet up with Gertie and Eleanor again, for a cup of tea at Philpot's Tea Rooms in town. It would be nice to make some friends since I didn't have all that much opportunity for socializing with people at the station.

As I made my way back from work to my digs that evening, Ben Carter and George, another PC, were standing opposite the gents public toilets. They were dressed in civvies, chatting together and looking about to see who walked past. I didn't recognize them at first in their normal clothes.

I waved hello to them and nipped quickly into the ladies on the other side. On my beats I would occasionally come in and check under the toilet doors there were no dead bodies or anything so I thought I might as well check now too. When I came out I wandered over to the lads to say hello properly.

'We've got a sink in our toilets now,' I said. 'I think they should do that everywhere.' This public convenience was the only one in town with a sink to wash your hands in.

'Don't be ridiculous,' said George. 'What do you want sinks everywhere for?'

'What are you doing hanging around here, anyway?' I asked.

'Checking the gents,' said Ben, nodding towards the door. 'You get all sorts here now. Up to all sorts an' all.'

'What kind of all sorts? Drunks?'

'Not exactly,' laughed Ben and he looked at George conspiratorially.

'Well, the gents is a favourite place to meet other . . . you know, gents of that . . . persuasion, isn't it?' said George cryptically.

Just then, a tall man in a brown suit, carrying a brief-case, walked past us and into the toilets. He looked this way and that before entering.

'Keep an eye on him. He's got that look about him,' Ben said.

Another man walked in quickly afterwards. He had a neat moustache and slicked back hair in the style of Ivor Novello.

'Ah, here we go,' said Ben, standing upright and making as if to enter the toilets after them. But before they would have had time to do anything, the man in the brown suit was already out.

1. When the buses went on strike for a few days during the war, army lorries took us to school in Bradford.

3. Some of the other boys from the youth club competing in the cycle race. A friend and I waved them on at the corner of Seamer Road.

2. My brother, Peter, being presented with the prize for winning a cycle race at the youth club in Scarborough.

4. First trip away from home on my own, aged seventeen. With the girls down in London, in Trafalgar Square with all the pigeons.

5. Me in *Maritana* at Scarborough open-air theatre. My friend and I were in the chorus.

6. One of the lads at the Scarborough youth club had a motorbike. We were 'trying it out'!

7. Early days at the Bruche police training centre.

8. Me with a couple of the lads.

9. War Duties course – having a giggle in our gas masks.

10. Putting out a blaze
with stirrup pumps and
buckets of water. Hope it
was a small fire – there's
not much water!

11. All bandaged up,
practising our First Aid.

12. All smiles after Physical Training – mustn't have been too tiring!

13. This is what we got up to on sunny weekends. You can see the Nissen huts in the background.

14. Relaxing after class.

15. At the end of the course, we entertained in our concert with songs from *The Student Prince*.

16. Don't they look a treat? The lads in their ballet outfits!

17. Me in my new hat.

18. Leading a parade in Richmond.

19. On the beat in Redcar. Maureen and I met up on our separate beats along the seafront and a friend took this picture. We were 'hamming it up' for the benefit of the camera, I think.

'Maybe not,' said George. 'But you never know. They're everywhere these days. Got to be on guard.'

I never did knowingly encounter any gay people in Richmond. In those days it was a criminal offence to have any hanky-panky, so I'm sure if there were any in town they took good care to hide it from the likes of us.

One of the most popular forms of entertainment in Richmond was the pictures. I often walked past the little cinema after finishing my shift at ten p.m. I would hear the strains of 'God Save the King', as the anthem was played at the end of the picture. The audience all stood up while it played, then the crowds would come streaming out, chattering about the latest cowboy film, or who was the new heartthrob in Hollywood.

There were a few pubs in town as well, which were frequented by the troops from Catterick Garrison at the weekends and locals during the week. One evening, Sergeant Cleese, who was the duty sergeant when Hardcastle was off-duty, asked me to go with him to check for underage drinkers. As we walked into The Golden Lion the place was thick with smoke. In the bar, some local traders, Mr Parry the butcher and Welsh Bob the shoemaker, were discussing the news over pints of thick stout.

'Good evening, officers,' said Welsh Bob. 'Have you seen anything tonight then?'

'Evening, lads,' said Cleese. 'No, it's been a quiet night, thank the Lord.'

'And who's this, then? Have we a lady constable at the station now?'

'Yes. This is WPC Rhodes.'

'Pleased to meet you,' I said.

We continued on round the pub and went over to the landlord, Mr Groat, who was cleaning some glasses.

'No trouble tonight then?' asked Cleese.

'Not at all,' he said. 'Well, only if you count being bored to tears by this lot.' He motioned towards Welsh Bob and Mr Parry, busy setting the world to rights as they tucked into their pints.

Over in the corner, a group of elderly men sat playing dominoes, serious expressions on their faces. I checked to see whether they were playing for money, as gambling in pubs was illegal, but they didn't seem to be. Satisfied there were no underage drinkers – in fact, there was no one under the age of about sixty – we left the pub and walked back towards the station.

Although there wasn't much in the way of entertainment in Richmond itself, at nearby Catterick Garrison there was a dance every Friday night, in the main hall of the barracks. After the week I'd had, I needed a break. I wouldn't dream of going on my own, but I met up with Gertie and Eleanor, the teachers I had met at church, and they invited me to go along with them.

All the lads in the station were either engaged or married, so I hadn't come across many eligible bachelors. To be honest, I wasn't that bothered for the time being, as I was so absorbed in my new job. But it would have been pleasant to have a nice young man to go to the cinema with once in a while, or just to have a laugh with. It would be exciting going to the dance, anyway, and a bit more lively than staying in at my landlady's house and watching her darn her husband's socks, which she seemed to do most evenings.

I was on earlies that week, so Gertie, Eleanor and I decided to meet when they had finished school. We got dolled up for the evening ahead in my little box room.

'Better to conceal than reveal, they always say,' said Gertie, as we got ready. Then she laughed and pulled out a lovely long cotton dress, with sleeves, but which fluttered around elegantly.

'Ooh, you'll look lovely in that,' I said.

'A man only respects a woman as much as she respects herself,' said Eleanor.

I had two dresses with me, one turquoise and one royal blue. I went for the turquoise, which had a nice close cut. We curled our hair and put on some new sheer stockings that Eleanor had got hold of, through her mam who worked in a clothes shop. We didn't wear much make-up, but Gertie did have a bit of pale pink lipstick, which added the final touches.

'Have you been up here much then?' I asked the girls as the bus clattered out of town.

'A few times. It's always a good laugh. And besides, I'm keen to find myself a nice lad before anyone can call me an old maid,' laughed Gertie. 'And this is the best chance around here.'

'I've been once before,' said Eleanor. 'An oaf of a man trod on my foot and then another one spilled his drink over me. So I'm hoping it's third time lucky tonight, and I might meet a nice one this time!'

It was dark by the time we reached the lane up to the barracks. Autumn leaves had scattered and settled across the road, making everything quite slippery, and chestnuts had begun to fall. I caught sight of my reflection in the bus window, light brown hair in a burst of curls, blue eyes and light pink lipstick. I hoped I might catch someone's eye at least. But I wasn't too bothered really. It was just nice to get out.

As we walked up to the path there was a guard at the gate, and men in uniform walking all around, all with their regulation short haircuts. The atmosphere reminded me in a funny way of Bruche, except that it was a lot bigger, and there were military vehicles and tanks parked along the main road and barbed wire everywhere.

When we got to the hall, there was an actual band, playing a military two-step. On stage, the band leader, in a suit and dickie-bow, was conducting some brass and strings, a drummer at the back. He was very short, with huge glasses and thick black hair like one of the Marx Brothers. At intervals, he would take the microphone and make some jokes, which got the crowd onside. As he conducted, his hair rose higher and higher with enthusiasm; at times, the music got so fast the dancers struggled to keep up and just broke down laughing.

The next number was a high-energy jitterbug. I was about to turn to the girls, thinking about getting a drink first, when a tall young soldier appeared out of nowhere and took my arm.

'You look like you need a dance,' he said, grinning. He had a southern accent.

'Well . . . I . . . I only just got here . . .' I said, and looked back for Gertie and Eleanor. But they were already chatting to two other lads, so I thought what the heck, and, before I could say another word, I was whizzing around the floor.

The brass band was playing a strong dance rhythm and the lad was a wonderful mover. I hardly had to think as he guided me this way and that, every now and again throwing in a twirl. I flung my head back and saw the other dancers in a blur around me. Then the band went very quiet, and all the dancers crouched low and close to the ground. As the music got louder and louder, we all rose up gradually and moved our arms about in time to the music, until the brass kicked in again and we twirled around in pairs again, laughing. The whole thing was quite different from the more formal, restrained dances at Bruche, with Inspector Merriweather and Sergeant Thompson keeping their eagle eyes on us.

When the music finished we all clapped, and I realized I had completely lost Gertie and Eleanor. I was now on the other side of the hall among lots of soldiers and women I didn't recognize.

'You're a great little dancer,' said the soldier who had swept me up.

'Thanks. We used to have dancing lessons back home in Scarborough. But what about you? You're not so bad yourself!'

'My sisters taught me. Four of them, all absolutely barking mad for dancing. We used to practise for hours in the front room. And being the only boy among all those girls, I was everyone's favourite dance partner.'

'Well, they certainly taught you well.'

'I'm Jim, by the way,' said the young soldier, holding out his hand. He had the short-cropped hair of someone on National Service, but I could see it was thick and a reddish colour. He had a wide, beaming face, a bit like a kindly, giant frog.

We chatted for a while about where we were from, and he told me he grew up in Luton, down south, near Bedford.

'Bit of a grim old place,' he said. 'I was relieved when they posted me up here, despite the training. See a bit more of the country, I suppose.'

'Have you been anywhere? On duty or something?'

'We haven't yet but we're going to Germany in a few months. There's still a lot to do there. Some of the lads I know, who've been there already, they had to do all sorts. Dig up bodies even. Not nice. But enough of that. Another dance?'

This time it was a waltz, so we twirled along the floor and Jim put his arm round my waist. As we whizzed along we passed Gertie, who was dancing with another soldier. She flashed me a smile and then disappeared. Just then, another pair of dancers came hurtling towards us, and I wasn't quick enough on my feet to stop. They crashed into us, and I managed to half hang on to Jim, before we both went toppling over in a heap on the floor.

There was much tutting from other couples who whizzed on past us as we scrambled to our feet.

'Are you all right?' asked Jim, as he stood up. He was bending down and looking at his ankle, which he had twisted in the fall.

'Are *you* all right?' I asked. 'That looked painful. I'm so sorry. I think that may have been my fault.'

'They came from nowhere, didn't they? The brutes.'

We got up, but Jim winced when he put his foot down. I put my arm in his arm, and we walked to the edge of the dance floor.

'Who thought dancing was such a dangerous sport?' he said, laughing, as we sat on the wooden chairs along the wall and got our breath back.

'Get something cold on that when you can,' I said, remembering my first-aid course.

Next to us, a young couple were arguing in strained tones under their breath. The lad, who couldn't have been much older than eighteen, had his hands on the girl's shoulders. She looked up at him, and I could see the make-up had run down her face and a thin strand of hair was covering her eyes.

'I did write to you. I don't know what the problem is. This place . . . they read our letters. I lose track of time. You can't stay here, anyway. How did you get here?'

'I told you. Bus. But you said you'd write every day. It's been weeks. I'm not going.'

'You'll get me into big trouble, you will, Jen.'

'And who was that woman you were talking to? You're always ignoring me. I might as well be a ghost. I feel like a dead, pointless ghost.'

'Well, I don't know what I can say. Whatever I say is wrong with you. I didn't ask to be sent to this blasted place.'

They paused for a while and stared ahead. Then the young lad took a parcel out from inside his pocket.

'Anyway. I bought you this.'

He stood up, threw the small package down into her lap, and walked away. The young girl, who did look very young to be out dancing, opened the paper and took out a thin blue box. Inside, there was a delicate, silver bracelet. She ran it through her fingers for a while, sadly, then put it back in the box and wrapped it in the paper. She stared ahead, and the music thumped away in the background, as tears dripped down her cheeks and onto her dress.

'I hope she's OK,' I said, then looked back at Jim. 'How's your ankle?'

'Not too bad, but I don't think there'll be any more dancing for me tonight.'

'I'd better get going anyway. All this excitement has worn me out,' I said.

'Are you getting the bus into town? I'll come with you. I could do with some fresh air.'

We found Gertie and Eleanor, who were at the bar with a group of lads who had already been on active service. They were describing how they'd all nearly been killed in a motor accident in the desert. We left them to it.

After saying our goodbyes, Jim and I stepped outside into the dark November evening. As we stood by the side of the road, I could hear two foxes wailing in the fields behind the garrison and a motor car humming in the distance. A young lad was striding up the road towards us. I soon realized it was the one who had walked away from the girl in the dance hall. He was smoking a cigarette vigorously and kicking at some stones on the pavement. A few minutes later, the girl came running out of the gate too, and called after him.

'Robert! Robert! Stop.'

'What?' He didn't turn round but just kept walking up the road past us as she chased after him.

'It's beautiful,' she said quietly. 'The bracelet. I love it.'

They stopped and stood for a while, not speaking.

Then the bus came up the hill and stopped right in front of them, blocking my view. As we stepped on, I could see them out of the window as they hugged under the light of the lamppost. As the bus drove off they were walking back towards the camp, arm in arm and laughing.

'Young love,' said Jim, staring out of the window.

I wondered whether he was speaking from experience.

'What do your parents do? In Luton?' I asked after a while, as we bumped along the dark country lane, branches from overhanging trees scraping along the windows.

'My father works at a car factory. My mother . . . she died when I was eleven.'

'Oh. I'm sorry.'

'Peritonitis. Appendix. We called the nurse and she said it was nothing. She refused to come out. The dragon! Mother died in the night. I nearly bit her finger off.'

'Your mother?'

'The nurse. She was also the dentist's assistant in town. She had two jobs, see. I was there having something done a year or so later. I gave it a good chomp too. I never forgave her for what she did.'

He looked out of the window for a while into the darkness.

'My dad wanted to give us up. Said he couldn't cope with all five. So my eldest sister, Margaret, left school aged fourteen to look after all of us younger ones. Anna was only five.'

He stopped talking, realizing perhaps he'd already revealed too much of himself to a complete stranger on a bus.

147

'How long have you been up here then?' I asked, quickly changing the subject.

'Oh, a few weeks. We train here and then we're off to Germany. Beer and women. That's what they say to expect, anyway.'

I found it very easy to talk to Jim after that, and we compared notes about training, me in the police and him in the army. We talked about the parade ground and marching practice and some of his sadistic officers, who he thought seemed to enjoy seeing new recruits suffer. It turned out Jim hadn't wanted to join up, but he had failed at failing his medical, which was really the only way out of National Service.

'We wanted to fail, a whole bunch of us from school. We had a plan, to raise up our temperatures by lying in a hot bath. We had this woman doctor come in and ask us all to drop our trousers and cough. She was having none of it. Just too healthy, I suppose. We come here human and we'll all leave machines. Can't tell one from the other after a while. Still, it's only two years, I suppose.'

'What'll you do after, do you think?'

'When I was younger I had this idea about being an inventor, or an engineer. But before I came here I was working with my Uncle Brian in a car showroom. So when I get back who knows . . .'

'This is my stop,' I said, surprised at how quickly the journey had gone.

'I'll walk you to your digs, if you like.'

'Thanks. That's kind. But I'll be fine.'

But as I stepped off the bus, to my horror, I caught sight of Sergeant Hardcastle on duty with PC Carter, right at the bus stop. They were standing about six yards away and looked as though they were checking the passengers, perhaps looking for someone.

'Oh my goodness! Quick. It's my boss,' I said, putting my head down and walking up the road as quickly as I could, trying to hide behind Jim who had got off after all. 'Do you think he saw us?'

'I don't know. Why? Is he funny about that stuff?'

'I don't know. Just feels a bit strange. It's such a small town. Like he'll be keeping an eye on me or something. Silly really.'

The town was quiet, just the odd group of soldiers from Catterick coming in and out of the pubs, a few couples out for an evening walk and a collection of town cats prowling about, stalking their territories.

'Here we are,' I whispered, trying not to wake the children as we approached the house. Jim had ended up walking me back after all.

The light was on in the front room, so Janet would still be up, darning and chatting with her husband in front of the wireless.

'Sleep tight, don't let the bedbugs bite. That's what my sisters always used to say.'

'You too. How's your leg, by the way? I forgot all about it.'

'So did I. So it can't be that bad.'

He leant forward for a moment and I thought he was going to try to kiss me, but in the end we just shook hands. I felt a flutter of excitement, though, as I was hit by his overwhelming smell of cleanness and coal tar soap. I stood for a while, swaying a bit, then, without another word, Jim turned back down the hill towards the bus stop and disappeared.

As I lay in bed that night I should have been happy but I found I was nervous. I could hear a pair of crows on a rooftop, perhaps calling out to one another. A dog barked in the distance. Even the wind seemed to be saying something as it whipped up the trees. All of nature, it seemed, was engaged in some incomprehensible conversation from which I had been completely excluded.

'Rhodes. Do you have a minute?'

I was startled out of a reverie by the piercing tones of Sergeant Hardcastle, calling round the door of the Super's office. I was standing on tiptoe, dusting down one of his particularly difficult to reach light fittings, and thinking about the events of Friday night.

'I wanted to have a quick word with you about a small something.'

I turned round to look at him and could feel my face flushing bright red.

'I know you know I saw you with a young gentleman in town. From the garrison, I presume? On Friday night? Coming off the bus.'

'Yes, Sergeant. I had been to the dance with my friends and he offered to . . .'

'I'm only looking out for your best interests. Those young men up there – we see all sorts, of an evening. Drinking and fights and things not fit for young ladies' eyes. You have to be careful, is all I'm saying. Do you know where he's from? Anything about him? You walked off up the road together, I saw, and . . .'

As Hardcastle was about to try to extract more information, the Super came in. We both stopped. I stood to attention and put down the feather duster.

'Morning, sir,' said Hardcastle.

'Ah. Just the man.' The Super put down some papers on his desk, and raised his eyebrows at us, perhaps wondering whether he had interrupted something suspicious he ought to know about. 'I need to talk to you about this . . . business with the Taylor woman. Thank you, Miss Rhodes.'

I practically ran out of there, relieved to have escaped the third degree. I knew Hardcastle was only being protective, but sometimes I got the feeling that he felt the need to look after me in some way more than he did the lads, just because I was a woman.

On my way out I passed a young girl, aged about sixteen, sat in the parade room, eating a plate of sandwiches. I thought she looked familiar and then realized I knew her from the Catterick dance on Friday, the girl who'd been arguing with her boyfriend. She looked different, quite tired and wearing a plain cotton dress, no make-up on, her long black hair tied back in a ponytail. She had with her a small green canvas bag and sat hunched up quietly on the bench.

Having finished his business with the Super, Sergeant Hardcastle came out of the office.

'Ah yes. This young lady, Jennifer, isn't it?' he said and she nodded. 'She was picked up at Catterick. You know the place,' he said knowingly to me.

'Yes, Sergeant,' I answered, relieved that his previous cross-examination of me seemed to be over.

'Well, she's going home. Aren't you, my girl? Parents on the phone to us, sick with worry. But they thought as much what was going on. She'd come down to see some lad up there.'

Jennifer looked down and fiddled with the string on the canvas bag without saying a word.

'Take her to the station and see she gets on that train home, will you?'

It was a bright autumn day, crisp and sunny, and perfectly still. Chestnut shells crunched under our feet.

'I forgot to ask where you're getting the train to,' I said to Jennifer, as we walked down Newbiggin towards Market Place.

'York,' she said quietly.

I looked up at the clock tower. 'Well, in that case we've got nearly an hour to the next train. Fancy a cup of tea first? I know I could do with one.'

I took her to my favourite café, Philpot's Tea Rooms. Mrs Philpot had run a teahouse here for ever, or so it seemed. My landlady's husband, Don, said he remembered her when he was a young boy, and that was at least forty years ago. She'd had a husband once but he had died long ago. My landlady had a theory that she had taken some elixir of immortality and was actually about 200 years old. Mrs Philpot was remarkably vital, at any rate, with a pile of bright white hair, which apparently used to be jet black. She wore a green pinny and was only about four foot tall, and was a bundle of ceaseless energy. Every day, she got up at five a.m. on the dot and baked all the cakes in the shop, then laid them out on a collection of silver cake tiers she said she had mysteriously 'inherited' as a young girl. She seemed to have had a kind of mythical, glamorous past that we could find out little about but that involved the Russians. She was a master at piping and cake decorating.

'Morning, Pam,' she said as I came in, 'and who's this pretty little thing?'

'She's on her way home to York. But first how about one of your finest fairy cakes? And a nice cup of tea?'

I sat down in the corner by the window with Jennifer, who hadn't said a word all the way. I decided not to mention seeing her at the Catterick dance, but I noticed she was wearing the bracelet that the young lad had bought her.

'So what brought you up to Catterick, then?'

'Robert. He never wrote to me,' she said glumly, and took a huge slurp of tea. 'He said he would write every day. But then I didn't hear a word for weeks. So I got on the bus. I had it all planned. I knew they had a dance and I even brought my dress and everything.' She held up the green bag. 'It's in here. I made it myself,' she said, and smiled a little at the memory of her adventure.

After a little while her face dropped again.

'It was supposed to be a surprise. But when I got in, he was talking to this other girl. Really tall, and they were laughing. Anyway. He saw me and . . . I thought he'd be happy.'

She looked down at the bracelet, and for a moment I wondered whether it had been meant for her at all.

'I hid for a while. Would have got away with it too, but that other man, he came and got me. Brought me to the station. And now I have to go back to that house, like a prisoner. While he's out with other . . .'

'It's a cruel world,' I said. 'But I'm sure he'll come back and it'll all be fine. Or you'll meet another lad who's just as nice. If not nicer.'

But I wasn't sure of course.

When we had finished the tea, we walked down towards the train station, past the river, where a group of cormorants had come inland and were diving for fish, their slick, oily backs disappearing into the water. In the distance, I heard the level crossing and knew we only had a few minutes left before the train arrived, so we ran the rest of the way and got there just as it pulled in.

As Jennifer walked up the steps, clouds of steam puffing around her, she turned round and waved back at me sadly. I had a feeling this wouldn't be the last time I'd be putting a reluctant young 'camp follower' back on the train for home.

6

In 1951 there was only one female sergeant in the whole of the North Riding Constabulary. Sergeant Maureen Freeman was in charge of the nine WPCs located across the region, and though I'd never met her, I reckoned she must be a force of nature to have got that far in this male-dominated world. I knew she would come and check periodically that the female officers were doing OK and conduct a kit inspection.

After a few months at Richmond, Inspector Armstrong informed me that Sergeant Freeman would be visiting me. She would go to the station first and have a chat about my progress, while I was to prepare for inspection at my digs.

It was early December, and a drizzly damp Saturday. My landlady's children were playing dressing up in the next room and kept creeping in, dressed in all kinds of different costumes. First they came in dressed as a shepherd and a sheep, though the sheep costume consisted of a pair of grey shorts on Michael's head, while Fiona wore a straw hat and a stripy dressing gown to be the shepherd. Then, a while later, they came back in dressed as a cowboy and cowgirl, and kept attempting to lasso things in my room.

'What's it like being a police lady?' asked Fiona, when they had tired of that game. 'Do you arrest people and find . . . burglars and things? What if they run away or attack you?'

'Not much like that happens in Richmond,' I said, as I straightened a row of clothes out on the bed. 'But I did once see a man stealing some daffodils on Gallowgate. That was funny. He ran away when he saw me and disappeared over a wall. I thought about chasing him for a while, but I would probably never have caught him, he was gone that quickly. I suppose he wanted the daffodils for his garden, maybe.'

'Hmm,' said Fiona, unconvinced. 'I think I want to be a police lady when I grow up. But real villains not just boring stuff. Or maybe I'll be a mole catcher. We saw one once, with a real live dead mole!'

'Well, whatever you do, I'm sure you'll be great at it.'

I was distracted, hoping I'd kept everything neat enough for Sergeant Freeman. Two pairs of gloves, white for summer, brown for winter, as well as a shirt, a tie and shoes, which, in the cold light of day, were now looking a little tired from all the walking I'd been doing on my beats.

A loud knock at the door made the children run downstairs. On the front doorstep, underneath the familiar women's police hat, was a lady I assumed must be Sergeant Freeman, gloved hands clasped together. When I got downstairs, Janet had let the Sergeant in and they were standing in the hall together, talking about the weather.

'I know, it hasn't stopped. Ah, here she is,' smiled Janet.

'Pleased to meet you,' said Sergeant Freeman, nodding her head at me.

I was slightly nervous, and wasn't sure what to say.

A weak-sounding 'Hello' came out. For some reason I had lost my usual confidence.

'Why don't we all have a nice cup of tea in the kitchen?' suggested Janet helpfully. 'I wouldn't normally say it, but I think poor Pam's been a little nervous about your visit,' she said as she put down some Jammie Dodgers next to the pot. I blushed, wishing she wouldn't say any more, as I wanted to give a good impression.

Sergeant Freeman scooped up her skirt as she sat down at the head of the table. 'Don't you worry. I take good care of all my girls,' she said to me.

'Well. I'll leave you two to it, then. I've some bits to buy. Come on, you two rascals!' Janet called up the stairs to the children. 'What are you wearing? You can't go out in that! Oh, it's too late now . . .' I heard her voice trailing off and out of the door.

When Janet had left, I topped up the teapot and sat quietly as Sergeant Freeman dipped a biscuit in her cup and looked around.

'So how are you finding it?' she said after a while. 'At the station?'

'It's been a big jump from training,' I said. 'A few surprises and some funny things, I suppose. But interesting too.'

'And the lads are all right?'

'Oh yes, they're all smashing.'

'Any tricky cases?'

'Well, there was one . . . it was abortion. Suspected anyway. I never found out what happened. That was a bit sad actually. Sergeant found some Penny Royal in a bottle.'

I realized I found it very easy to talk to Sergeant Freeman. She had a kind way of really listening as you spoke.

'Yes. He told me about that. Case dropped. Impossible to prove in the end, apparently.'

I was quietly relieved.

She looked around the small kitchen, which Janet had spent much of the evening before scrubbing in preparation for the visit.

'And you're getting on well here?'

'Oh yes. It's convenient and they are lovely. The children and everything.'

'Let's get down to real business then, shall we?' she said, clapping her hands and standing up.

I was pleased that there had been no mention of my going to the dance, and Sergeant Hardcastle's little 'cross-examination'. I lead the way upstairs to my bedroom.

'Neat and tidy. Very nice,' she said, her eyes darting about the little box room noting every detail. 'Hmm. Shoes are a bit shabby, though, aren't they? Well, you'll be able to buy a pair of police boots now. For the winter. Much more suitable than these old things.'

I had grown quite tired of walking around in the rain with wet feet, so that was some good news.

'Oh, and soon you'll be visiting me up at HQ, by the way. You can stay with us and I'll show you where all the important stuff happens. By the way, have you been to a post mortem yet?' she asked out of the blue, as we walked back towards the front door.

'I haven't. Fortunately all the ladies in our division have been very considerate,' I said, risking a joke, 'and decided not to die when I was on duty.'

She smiled. 'Let's hope it stays that way, eh?'

But in the police, you never know what's round the corner.

There were only about three million cars in the UK in 1951, so the Richmond streets were nowhere near as busy as today's roads. But traffic was sometimes a problem even then.

As a policewoman, part of my job was to do the School Crossing Patrol (I was like today's lollipop ladies but without the lollipop) in the mornings and afternoons, as the local infants were crossing opposite the Lower School. I would stand and direct the traffic, allowing the children to cross at intervals; they all trooped across, some holding hands, some skipping and chattering away to each other. As they came past they would call me 'police lady', and on the way out of school they would trot by again, and show me pictures of all manner of strange animals and scenes they had drawn that day.

One morning, one of those winter mornings which seem to never really get light, I stood by the crossing in my greatcoat and new fur-lined police boots. The morning traffic filtered through the mist and, like clockwork, the schoolchildren started to wander over from the streets and houses. Two boys were engaged in a little fight on one side of the road, so I went over to see what was going on. One said that the other had tried to take his lunch, so I scolded them both and sent them on their way.

In the meantime, quite a crowd of children had built up waiting to cross, so I stopped the traffic and waved them over again. Just as they were all nearly across, there was a loud car horn and a scream from further up the road. I waved the stragglers across quickly and ran over to see what had happened.

One of the little boys who had been fighting was sitting in the road, staring ahead, with his lunchbox next to him. Cars were building up in a queue, and one had stopped right in front of him, just in time by the look of it. The driver got out, and at the same time a woman in an apron came over, waving her arms.

'Billy!' she shouted. 'My baby! What's happened?'

'I fell over. I don't know. Tom told me he'd get me and tried to take my lunch or something, so I crossed here instead. It doesn't matter,' the little boy told his mother.

'You silly boy! Don't you know what these roads are like now? It's not safe.'

'I just slipped. I'm all right, Mam.'

'And you?' said the woman, pointing at me. 'How could you let this happen? You're supposed to be helping them cross safely.'

'With all due respect . . .' I hesitated, summoning up some confidence. 'He didn't cross at the crossing. And I had all the other children to keep an eye on.'

'Well, you'll be hearing from me,' she said, and scooped her little Billy into her arms, though he looked thoroughly embarrassed by the whole affair.

'I didn't see the child, officer. He came from nowhere,' said the driver of the car, looking quite shaken.

'Well, no harm done. He wasn't hurt. You'd better be on your way, before this traffic blocks the whole town.'

In the distance I could see Billy's mother, staring back at me. I wondered if she would carry out her threat and try to report me to the station. I kept my eye on her before allowing the last of the children to cross; when I looked back, she was gone.

After my dance at Catterick Garrison, with Jim, I had been being a bit careful; I didn't want the Sergeant on my back again. But I was keen to see Jim again, so when he sent me a note, asking if I wanted to go to the pictures in Richmond on Friday evening, I was quietly delighted. They were showing *Scrooge*, based on the Charles Dickens story, with Alastair Sim as the old miser. I was nervous about seeing Jim again, and I found I had almost forgotten what he looked like as I walked down into town. Did he have blue eyes or green? I couldn't even remember that.

When I arrived he was already standing there, leaning against the wall, wearing a nice blue shirt and tie, coat over his arm. He was smoking a cigarette, his eyes closed, face tilted upwards. The film was about to start so we didn't have long for small talk, just walked to our seats and sat down. I could smell coal tar soap on his skin again.

At one point, when loads of bells started ringing and a huge growling noise made me jump, Jim put his hand on my arm. I tensed up slightly, unsure what this meant, but left it where it was. At the end of the picture the National Anthem was played, and Jim and I chatted about the film.

'Oh, he was so wonderfully horrible. As Scrooge. Don't you think?' I said as we walked into the chilly night.

'Why don't men wear top hats like that any more?' Jim wondered out loud.

'I don't know. Too tall? You should bring them back.'

'When I get out, anyway. Not sure it would go down so well at my uncle's showroom,' he joked.

'You'd better not walk me home tonight,' I said suddenly, back in the real world again.

'Why not? Will you be all right?'

'It's just . . . you know, the Sergeant. He looks out for me and . . . it could get difficult. It's such a small town. People talk.'

But instead of parting, we continued to walk in silence for a while, past the school and the empty playground.

'We've been told we'll be out of here before Christmas now,' he said after a while. 'Possibly next week even. So this is kind of goodbye. Before we've really said hello.'

'Better make the most of it then, hadn't we?' I said.

We turned and walked towards the castle, as though there was nothing else we could possibly have done at that moment.

'Lovely night,' I said after a while, as we walked round past the river and up towards the great Norman fortress. 'Funny to think of all those kings and queens and knights and people who used to live here, in all their chainmail and dresses probably.'

I ran my fingers across the cold stone breathing it in.

'My mum took us to a castle once. In Dorset.' Jim lit up a cigarette and looked up at the sky. 'Before she . . . went. She used to pack a little picnic in a basket, all wrapped up. Even during the war she was a master at rustling up something out of nothing. Scotch eggs somehow . . . apricot flan made with carrots!'

'She sounds nice.'

'She would have liked you.'

There was a calm silence; it seemed unlike any other I'd experienced. Not even the owl I sometimes heard up there, on my beat, was around. Perhaps he was off catching voles. Or maybe they hibernate? I wasn't sure.

A cloud moved across the sky, and the sliver of a crescent moon came into view. Jim put his hand on mine and I breathed in the sharp, clean air. I had never kissed a man for real. How did it work? Who 'started' it? We both just stared up at the sky, breathtakingly clear and infinite.

'What time's your bus?' I asked in the end.

'I should get the ten-thirty, really. So I suppose we should get going.'

I had forgotten all about the Sergeant and the possibility of being seen out with a man. I didn't care any more. Jim was here and all was right with the world. But the bus was already coming down the hill as we approached the stop, its headlights spreading out into the road ahead.

'You'd better run. Or you'll miss it.'

'I'm sorry. To go.'

'Don't drink too much German beer.'

He got on the bus and I watched as it moved away: two specks getting smaller and smaller, blinking, then gone.

That night I had a dream that I lived in Richmond Castle. I was a cook in a big Norman kitchen, roasting huge hogs on spits. Jim was a prisoner there. I took him some food in the cells and he was all starved and thin, tied up with a big ball and chain. Suddenly, a lamb came running up to me and jumped into my arms. Its coat was thick and oily like a real lamb, but it had a human face. Then there was a loud knocking on the cell door . . . someone whispering my name . . .

But it was a real knocking on the door. I managed to wake up, and looked at my clock. It was just past two thirty a.m. PC Carter was downstairs in the cold. I was needed down at the station again.

'Pearl, that woman they picked up on the Great North Road before, well, she's back in the cells. She looks awful. They found her up there again. Her and one of the soldiers up at Catterick, apparently. Doing it. If you know what I mean.'

When we walked into the station, Sergeant Cleese was filling out some forms.

'Good, Rhodes. Sorry to drag you out, but you know the drill. She's down in the cell. We've told her she's being reported for being drunk and incapable, but if you wouldn't mind going to check on her.'

'Yes, Sergeant.'

'Not a pretty sight. Not a pretty sight at all,' he sighed to himself.

Pearl lay on the bed and had thrown her blanket off, her legs hanging over the edge. She looked very thin; where her eyes had been bright and clear before they now looked dull, with dark rings under them. She was wearing a silk dress but it had a large tear on one sleeve, and there was a big bruise on her arm.

'Pearl,' I whispered. 'It's WPC Rhodes. Do you remember?'

'I remember you. Little police girl. So innocent.'

She was drunk, but a deep drunk, not like before, when she had been quite lively. It was as though a spark in her had been dulled, almost extinguished. I turned on my torch rather than fill the room with the main light and looked over at her on the bed.

'He left me,' she said, sitting up and grabbing on to my arm.

'I'm sorry.'

'I'm better off without him anyway,' she said with sudden bitterness 'He ruined me. Ruined everything.'

'Get some sleep. If you can. It'll be all right.'

'It won't be all right,' she said, but she drifted off to sleep.

The next day, Reggie didn't come and collect her and she was sent home. We said we would notify her later when she would have to appear in the magistrate's court. As she walked out of the station alone, blinking in the sunlight, she was silent, as though she had given up on a previously all-pervading dream. I had the saddest feeling I would never see Pearl again.

Market day in Richmond was a sight to behold. Farmers and food producers from across North Riding came to sell their wares in the market. Crowds flocked in from the villages all around, and, with the proliferation of the motor car, the traffic did too. One of my duties was controlling the traffic for three hours, taking my turn with the lads on the corner of King Street, so that cars and lorries, and army trucks from the garrison, could pass through without hitting shoppers.

That day, I took over from PC Carter, who had been there for three hours already and whose fingers were turning blue. I watched as the market holders called out their wares: cabbage and carrots, fruits, cheese on another stall from a local farm, even fish fresh from the coast.

A long train of lorries from the garrison came down the road, so I waved them through. The trail of vehicles was seemingly endless, lorry after lorry in army khaki, like the ones I had seen the night of the dance. Lads were hanging out of the back, all piled in together, all alike with their cropped hair and kits bags. I wondered where they were off to. Then a voice shouted out.

'Pam! Pam! We're leaving.'

I looked round. There was Jim, by now quite a way off in the distance, hanging out the back of a lorry, waving wildly.

'I'll write to you!' he shouted.

I lifted my arm slowly, half waving, but in an instant he was out of sight.

Towards the end of my shift, as I looked back at the last lorries, the dark clouds above me opened up, and rain poured out of them in torrents. Water beat against my legs. I didn't even have my mac with me, only my coat. But I had to get back to the station to let Doris leave early. Sarge had said. I swallowed rain and rain went in my ears. My hair was stuck to my head, even with my hat on, and my coat was drenched through.

When I finally got back to the station, I was relieved that someone had lit the fire. I could see the smoke twirling up out of the chimney. As I trudged in, and shook my feet, there was no sign of Sergeant Cleese. But the Inspector (the 'Spec', as we often called him) was standing in the hallway. He looked me up and down. Then he looked at the pool of water collecting at my feet.

'You been swimming?'

'No, sir. It's just . . . you know, raining.'

I was always a little nervous of the Spec. He was hard

to predict. He folded his arms and disappeared. I continued to remove my wet coat and was just working out where to put it without getting everything else wet when the Inspector reappeared.

'Here. Put these on.'

He didn't smile, just handed over a pair of brown girls' shoes. His daughter's, I supposed. He had two daughters. One was training to be a nurse.

'Put yours in front of the fire. If you like.' This time he did smile and I finally relaxed.

'Thank you, sir.'

'I tell you, you do look like a little drowned rat, and no getting away from it.'

I had to laugh. But there was no rest. No sooner had I put on the new footwear when Sergeant Cleese came in.

'Ah, Rhodes, can you go and deliver some summonses? On Bargate.'

Bargate was a steep hill towards the green. And I wasn't looking forward to walking back out in the rain again. I walked down and delivered the summonses. One was for a young man, who looked like a small ferret, and hardly opened the door wide enough to let me hand the paper over. His house smelled of rotting cabbage, I noted. The other was for an elderly lady, and I couldn't imagine what she had done. She looked quite frail and confused, but took the summons all the same.

On my way back I saw a car with its engine running, but with not a soul in sight. I waited for quite a while, unsure what to do. Then a woman came out of a nearby house. She was flustered, putting something into her handbag, and seemed in a hurry.

'Is this your car?' I asked, pointing at the vehicle.

'Yes . . . but I'm a nurse. State registered.' She continued to fumble in her bag. 'I've been visiting Mr Farthing there. Can't leave the house, you see.'

'Sorry, but I have to take your details. Leaving a car unattended with the engine running is an offence.'

Her face dropped. 'Is there nothing you can . . . ?'

'You will be reported.'

I took her name, address, occupation and age, and looked at her documents, entering the details into my notebook. The poor woman looked quite devastated by the whole thing, since she was only doing her job and would be late for her next appointment, she said.

The rain continued to pour down. As I walked home, the shoes the Inspector had given me filled up with water too. Perhaps, I thought, it was some kind of divine retribution for stopping nurses who leave their engines running while on the job.

It was three days before Christmas and the whole town was in a festive mood. I was passing through the town centre on my beat and soaking it all up. A small girl in a little red coat pointed at a shop window where a lifesize talking doll was being demonstrated. When you pulled a cord at its back it appeared to have a spectacular variety of words and phrases, although its mouth never moved, which was quite unnerving.

Outside the Town Hall, a Salvation Army brass band played Christmas carols, while a crowd stood humming along to the music, smiling, wrapped up in their winter coats, hats and gloves. I walked through and hugged my own coat round myself more tightly to keep out the sharp nip in the air.

My first 'point' was at the phone box on Market Place. After thirty minutes on the beat I stood there and waited, in case the station rang through. No one called, so I continued on down Station Road. Towards the end of my shift, one of my jobs was to check the church offertory box, so I walked into the Catholic church opposite the station and stood there for a while, out of the cold, in front of the huge stained-glass window.

The church was perfectly silent, the low winter sun shining through the glass, lighting up a group of angels hovering in the air around Jesus Christ, who pointed disconsolately up in the air. As I was leaving, Father Reilly came shuffling out from the back room.

'Oh, you startled me! But I'm glad I've caught you. I've been meaning to pop by the station. I've something for you and the lads.'

'Hello, Father. Merry Christmas,' I said. 'I just came in to check you hadn't had any trouble with those thieves again.'

'No, thank the Lord. I had a better lock fitted on the thing. Hopefully that'll keep the dogs at bay, as it were. God knows, we could use all the money we can get these days, what with the vaults leaking.'

He disappeared for a moment and I noticed a small nativity scene, in which there appeared to be only two wise men. I supposed one must have got lost.

'Here you go, my girl,' said Father Reilly, handing me a small red package, 'and give these to the boys with my blessings.' He passed me another few parcels.

'Thank you. What a treat.'

'Well, nice to have something to open on Christmas Day. It can't all be Jesus this and Jesus that.'

'Quite,' I said, unsure whether he was joking or not.

'And will we be seeing you here for Mass?'

'I have to work, I'm afraid. But Merry Christmas. And thank you.'

As I left the church with the bundle of packages I had just one more point to make before returning to the office. In the distance, on my way back down towards the railway station, I could see two shapes capering about in the road outside the phone box. Two ladies were standing next to them, waving their arms about in a panic.

I couldn't make out what they were looking at, at first. It looked like two giant rabbits hopping up and down, but, as I got nearer, I realized it was a pair of goats, with small shaggy beards, floppy brown ears and wild orange eyes, standing in the road. They might cause an accident, I thought, and ran over as fast as I could.

'Hoy, what's happening? Are you OK?'

'Oh, thank goodness you're here! We weren't sure what to do. They looked so wild,' said one of the women, who was struggling with her shopping bag, trying to stop one of the goats pecking at it.

'Do they bite, do you know?' asked the other woman, who had backed away so far up the grass verge she was almost on the railway line.

Together we started trying to herd the goats off the road, but our shouts of 'shoo' and 'hey you' failed miserably. They just wouldn't budge. Then they started wheeling around us, thinking we were playing a game, and then around each other.

And there was the rumble of the mid-afternoon bus. It came hurtling down the hill, blasting its horn.

'That's our bus!' shouted the other lady, who had gradually crept down off the verge. 'Will you be all right?' she asked. 'Only we're late as it is.'

'Yes, of course. You go.'

I was just wondering how to get the goats tied up when Francesco, one of the mechanics from the garage by the railway station, saw me struggling. He dropped his cigarette and grabbed a long piece of rope from the workshop.

'You go that side. I'll run them this way,' he shouted over to me. 'We'll meet in the middle and get the rope round them both.'

I ran round the side of one goat and Francesco ran the other way, but no matter how hard we tried, they kept managing to slip through the middle of us. One of the goats got past us and ran into the garage shop, round and round the aisles, knocking things off the shelves, before running back through the door past a customer, who let out a terrified squeal.

'I've got one!' yelled Francesco finally, tying the rope round it and tethering it to the railings in front of the garage. 'You run the other one this way and I'll catch the little blighter.'

I ran up behind the remaining animal with my arms out, and it plunged straight for Francesco, who managed to catch it and hold it steady by the torso. He tethered it with the other goat.

'Team work, eh? What's this anyway? You're taking the goats for a walk, or what?'

'I found them up the road there. They must have escaped from old McGregor's farm. Thank goodness you were here!'

'Hey. Call me Doctor Doolittle. That was a lot of goat for one young lady to handle alone.'

One of the animals started nibbling his shoe.

'Maybe they're hungry?' I suggested. 'Shall we take them up there by the grass and they can eat while I get the farmer?'

As Francesco tied them up on the grass verge they started bleating at the tops of their lungs again, but soon began chomping away. Francesco came with me up the lane to fetch Farmer Joe. The last time I'd seen Francesco I was checking on the aliens in the town, and he'd been just a person on my list. I really knew nothing about why he was living here in England or where he came from. We chatted as we walked.

'My father, he was a doctor. No *fascista*. He was against Mussolini. He lived in Bardi, north Italy. Came to England, found good job here. But when Italy joined the war – I was sixteen – many were taken. It was the middle of the night and they took him. My father was taken, put on a boat, like so many cattles.'

'Where did they take him?'

'The boat was heading for Canada. He met an officer from the British army on the boat. Well, he was lucky. My father had been this officer's doctor in London before the war. So he asked my father to join them at the top table, with all the silver knives and forks and wine flowing. But my father, he said no, I will stay with my brothers. And he stayed in the lower decks with the others. Class, jobs, all that meant nothing. Just all Italians together.'

'So then what happened? Did he end up in Canada?'

'So many bodies.' Francesco looked down sadly. 'Isn't that your Farmer Joe up there? Maybe I finish the story another day?'

Joe, with his wispy grey hair and baggy trousers, was standing in a field, drinking from a flask of tea. Bertie the bullock, who was, by now, more of a fully grown bull, nudged the gate with his nose as we approached and I backed away.

'Afternoon, Joe.'

'Ah, thee again, eh? Come for some more tea? The wife's not here. She's at her sister's.'

'Not this time. I think we've found something that belongs to you. You're not missing two little kid goats, by any chance?'

'I was wondering where they'd got to. Beautiful. Not even a year old yet. Such lovely ears.'

'They're certainly characters. But they could have caused an accident. We've had to tie them up down the lane, I'm afraid. And I'll have to take down your details, report you for allowing stock to stray onto the highway. Again.'

'Will you, indeed?' he said, apparently unmoved, and continued to drink his tea. 'Well, I think you know most of my details already, don't you?'

He did have a point, but I wrote them down in my notebook in any case, along with the time and date.

'If you could make sure you lock them up securely in future, hopefully this will be the last time we meet like this, over escaped livestock . . .' I thought about his wife, remembering all her ailments and the squalid conditions up at the farm. 'How is Mrs McGregor, by the way?'

'She's alive. Which is something, I suppose. We've sold over a hundred turkeys this year already. Nice and fat too. So Christmas is good for something at least. All the lads want is time off and holidays, though, and then there's the wife's sister and her three children to come and we have to feed them and they make such a noise my head hurts.'

'Well. I am sorry to have to report you for this. But you know the law.'

'Aye, lass. I know the law.'

When I got back to the station, there was a hubbub in the parade room. Two of the lads from the station, Ben Carter and Bill Bryant, were in various states of undress, or with their shirts hanging out, at any rate.

'Ooh. Excuse me!' I said as I walked in, and was about to turn and leave.

'You'll be next,' said Ben. 'We're all being measured for our new best uniforms.'

A man with a neatly trimmed beard, small spectacles and an impeccable pinstriped suit came in, holding a large leather tape measure. He bent down and held it against Bill's legs, then measured his chest size and arm length.

'Afternoon. Perhaps you'd prefer to be measured . . .

elsewhere? So the gentlemen won't know your . . . ahem . . . measurements?' he whispered to me.

'Right, yes. Of course. I'll go and wait in the corridor.'

I looked at the peeling paint on the ceiling until the tailor came back.

'All done with the lads. I've done a few women, but we don't see many in the force and few of the fairer sex buy my kind of suit,' said the tailor as he walked down the corridor towards me.

'Yes, there aren't many of us. Only nine in North Riding in total.' I brushed myself down. 'So where do you want me?'

'If you could just take your jacket off that will be fine.'

He ran the tape measure along the length of my arms, and made a note in a small book.

'So . . . what makes a young lass like you want to get mixed up with all this criminal element? Just hold your arms out, stretched like this. All those murderers and thieves! Can't be much fun. With things the way they are these days. All those stories in the papers.'

'I suppose I wanted to get out of Scarborough. Try something different. An adventure, maybe. And it's really not that bad here. Most people are all right.'

'If you say so. Well, good luck, that's what I say. There should be more like you. Women who have a go.'

Once I was all measured up, I went back into the office, and Sergeant Cleese called me over to the desk.

'We're serving a distress warrant this afternoon,' he said matter-of-factly. 'Not a pretty job before Christmas, I grant you. But the law's the law, whatever the time of year.'

I knew what a distress warrant was from training. If

someone hadn't paid a debt, or had taxes owing, then property could be seized and sold to pay it off. We had to go and make it official, identify any goods of value that could be sold and put a notice on them.

As we drove out of the town, I began to recognize the road. It wasn't on my beat in Richmond, but I had been there before, with Sergeant Hardcastle. It was one of the villages to the north of town, where the cottages all had neat little front gardens. We knocked on the door; there was a familiar stone gnome on the garden lawn, holding a wheelbarrow.

Sergeant Cleese knocked loudly and we waited for a while, but no one came. I thought I saw a shape move past the window, but there was no answer. He knocked again and called through the letterbox.

'She's in there all right,' he said to me. 'Mrs Taylor? We know you're at home. Please answer the door. You don't want to make things any worse for you and the girls, do you?'

Still no answer. Then light footsteps on the stairs and the door slowly opened. A small girl with bright blonde hair stood on the threshold, clutching a formerly white teddy bear with only one eye. I remembered her as one of the two young daughters from the incest/bigamy case. The woman, Mrs Taylor, had turned out to have two husbands at the same time, and a daughter from each. We had suspected her husband of indecency with his own daughter, but it had turned out that the second husband had been abusing the older girl, his stepdaughter. They had tracked him down somewhere in Lancashire eventually, but that was the last I had heard.

'Hello,' said Sergeant Cleese, bending down. 'Is your mother at home?'

'She said to tell you she's not in,' said the little girl, glancing briefly over towards the living room door. 'And that she'll be out all day. It's Christmas soon. Do you know what St Nicholas is bringing me?'

'What's that?'

'A bicycle. I saw it!' she grinned. 'He's already brought it. Early. And hid it in Mam's bedroom. But I found it. It's red and has a bell and a basket, and everything. But don't tell I told you!' She looked away, suddenly nervous.

Perhaps realizing that her daughter had engaged us in too much conversation, and that we were not likely to be leaving in a hurry, Mrs Taylor emerged from the living room and walked over, flattening down her apron.

'Oh, officers. I didn't realize you were here. I was quite occupied with . . . some things. What are you doing, Jessica? What silly things you say sometimes. Don't mind the child, she has the wildest thoughts. Don't know where they come from sometimes. What can I help you with? Is it about my husband, because I thought that was all . . .'

'Not this time. I'm sorry, but we're here to serve a distress warrant. Do you know what that is?'

'I do, officer, but . . . if it's about the rent, I told Mr Shuttleworth I'd pay all of it after Christmas. With Clive in prison and the girls . . . I'm getting another job, nights, at the hospital. And Saturdays at the shop. I barely see them as it is.'

'Can we come in, Mrs Taylor? I'm afraid it's not that simple. The money has to come from somewhere.'

As we walked around her house, I noticed there was a strong smell of damp and mould. There wasn't much of any value that I could see either. A lot of thing things that had been in there before, the Indian sculptures and silks, had gone. A small wireless sat on the side in the kitchen, along with a few plates and a hand whisk. In the living room there was a shabby-looking brown sofa and an elephant's foot, which had been turned into a stool.

'From India,' Mrs Taylor said sadly, then quickly added, 'but it's not worth much.'

Upstairs, there were two bedrooms. In the girls' room was a row of ragged teddy bears and, in Mrs Taylor's bedroom, a dressing table with a hairbrush, some make-up and a wooden box.

'What's this?' asked Cleese, looking up at a large grandfather clock with pictures of moons and stars across the face.

'That's my mother's. It's all I have left of her. We sold the mirror and this is all there is.'

Without saying a word, Cleese took out a notice and stuck it on there.

'What's . . . what are you doing?' asked Mrs Taylor, rubbing her hands together in distress.

'What's that?' asked Cleese, indicating a necklace on the sideboard.

'It's fake. Costume jewellery . . .'

'Hmm.' He moved on, looking for any other items of value. 'Rhodes.'

'Yes, Sergeant,' I answered, unsure what was going to happen next.

'Put a notice on that, would you?'

'On what?' I said, looking around, for there was really very little in the room at all. Then I saw what he was pointing at. In the corner, behind the bedstead, complete with bell and basket, was a shiny red child's bicycle.

Christmas was a day like any other at the station, although it was quieter. I was on lates, so I saw my landlady's children open up their presents in the morning, ate Christmas lunch and then worked in the afternoon. Michael got a bright green railway engine to add to his collection, which occupied him for the rest of the day. Fiona was delighted to receive one of those talking dolls, which, after some demonstration, I discovered was also capable of crying real tears like a baby if you filled its head with water.

'Shame you'll miss this afternoon. We were going to play a game,' Janet said as she cleared the plates away.

I had put on my new uniform from the tailor's, crisp and smelling of fresh wool. It was a relief, as my previous kit had been secondhand and never quite fitted properly.

'Well, Christmas is just another day really, isn't it?' I said, trying not to mind. 'But I'm sure you'll all have fun.'

In reality, I missed my family and wondered what they were all doing. I had received a small package from Mam containing some satsumas and nuts, and a lovely green brooch. 'For your next dance' she had written in the card in her tiny handwriting. I had told her in my letters about going up to Catterick and seeing all the handsome officers, though for some reason I had decided not to mention Jim.

'Well, enjoy the rest of your day, all of you,' I said and wished them a happy Christmas again before stepping out into the chilled air.

The station was quite empty as most of the married

PCs were off with their families. Sergeant Shaw was in the office, but he was engrossed in a mound of paperwork so I didn't bother him. I walked around from room to room, then finished some typing.

The Inspector came in for a few hours, whistling loudly, before returning home to his wife and two daughters. Then the Super came in and sat in his office, never once mentioning the fact it was Christmas. I stood briefly as usual, then went into the office and opened up my gift from Father Reilly. Inside was a thick bar of dark chocolate with a scattering of plump hazelnuts. Not so easy to come by, and proper Belgian chocolate too. The lads had been given a carton of cigarettes each, but I preferred the chocolate and savoured every mouthful as it melted on my tongue.

On my evening beat, the town was dark and nearly empty, a slight drizzle in the air. I could hear laughter and the odd strain of a carol drifting from a window, 'Good King Wenceslas' or Nat King Cole crooning something. Children sat in their living rooms playing with toys – or the boxes the toys had arrived in – and the smell of turkey dinners still lingered in the air. Occasionally the sounds of drunken arguments rose and fell, as that extra whisky or glass of port brought festering family feuds to the fore.

I could imagine Mam washing up, humming her favourite Christmas songs, while Dad dozed off in his big chair and my granny sat knitting endless socks.

As I walked past the churchyard, on my way home, I saw a figure in a long white gown shuffling slowly towards the cemetery. I wasn't superstitious, but it was dark and there was no one else about so I steeled my nerves. The figure flashed in and out of view, and then out of sight through the small cemetery gate. I switched on my little torch, directing it here and there, lighting up trees and a statue of a giant angel covered in ivy, its huge wings towering upwards.

As I approached, the figure in white was hunched over a gravestone. I walked over slowly so as not to cause a shock. The figure turned its head, saw me and shrieked, startling some nearby pigeons who were asleep in the trees.

'My ration books! I left them here. Arthur knows. I came to ask him. Can't seem to . . .'

'Mrs Colbert. What are you doing out here?'

She started to panic. 'They put him in the ground, you know. But he was still alive in there.' She started prodding at the mud next to the gravestone. 'He talks to me, you know. Tells me things. I can't for the life of me remember where they are, though. Can you?'

'Let's get you home,' I said, lifting her up gently by the arm.

'But my ration books! Do *you* know where they are, my girl?' She looked up at me pleadingly.

'I'm sure we'll find them just where you left them at home. Everyone will be so worried about you. It's Christmas Day. Don't you remember?'

As we walked back in the dark together, arm in arm, Mrs Colbert chattered the whole way, apparently unaware of where she was, or who I was. Once in a while, she would have the odd moment of lucidity and then a wave of panic would overtake her.

'I can hear his voice still,' she said, looking off into the distance, straining for something. 'But then, when I look, he's not there. Just that pillow. They put him in the ground, you know. He can't get out. Have you seen my ration books? I can't for the life of me remember . . .'

I dropped Mrs Colbert back at her daughter's house again, but by the time I got back to my lodgings the children were asleep and there were just the remnants of Christmas all around the house: bits of paper, an empty port glass, the cake no one could manage.

I wondered what Jim was up to in Germany. How did they celebrate out there, I wondered. Beer and women, he had joked.

That night seemed endless; I tossed and turned, unable to sleep. There was a loud bird singing just outside my window for hours. Its usually beautiful song seemed mechanical, even slightly menacing. I pulled the pillow over my ears and eventually dropped off just as the sun came up. Thank goodness I had Boxing Day off.

7

1952 dawned unceremoniously. We may have been one of the richest countries in the world, but we still clung on to what we saw as the best of wartime values. Those six long years still hung over the nation like an immoveable mist, and most people weren't in a hurry to move on. Clement Attlee's compulsory National Service also meant another generation of young men were being steeped in the rigours of military training and sometimes even front line battle.

'Have you heard this series on the BBC?' called out Janet one early January morning. She was washing up at the sink, and I was at the table eating some toast and jam. 'Been on for a while now. All about farming. Can't see why anyone'd want to listen to that on the wireless, when we get that every day here in real life. Why, you only have to go to the market to hear farmers complaining about this and that.'

Her words faded into a blur as I opened a letter I had just received from Jim. He had been stationed in Germany, but his latest news was that they might be redeployed soon. I hoped he wouldn't have to fight in real life. My memories of the war as a child were of wives and mothers mourning the loss of husbands and sons, and then there was my own experience when the battleship *Repulse* sank, and its crew with it, and all we schoolgirls were shocked to the core.

I walked to work with a heavy heart. Inspector Armstrong called me in to his office. He was sending me to Northallerton HQ for a week, to see what they did there.

'We like all our new recruits to see life at HQ. It's where it all happens. You'll be staying up with Sergeant Freeman and her husband.'

A few days later, I had packed my bag and was leaving the house to catch the train when I saw a new PC, Peter Palmer, across the road. He had joined us after Christmas and was still wet behind the ears.

'Hello, Peter. How's it going? Are you settling in OK?'

'I'm just making a "point",' he said, proud to be using the official police jargon.

He always looked a bit awkward in his uniform, which seemed somehow too big in every direction, even though he was very tall. His front teeth stuck out and he had a slight stammer when he got nervous. Now that Peter had arrived, it meant I wasn't the newest PC at Richmond station.

'So if the Super drives past,' he said, 'do we salute or not?'

'Yes. Salute and make sure he sees you so he can mark in your pocketbook that you were there. But only salute when you first see him.'

'Right, I see. And what about the Inspector?'

'If you're out and about salute the Spec. But not in the station. But you do call him sir.'

Peter started asking another question, but before he finished there was a huge screeching sound on the road behind us and a terrible scream.

'What on earth was that?'

'I've no idea,' said Peter and we ran across the road. Behind a coach, underneath the wheel, a woman lay, white with pain, on the road. The vehicle had driven clean over her leg, and you could see a good deal of blood soaking through her stockings.

By the time we arrived she had stopped screaming and was shaking, letting out the occasional moan.

'Oh my goodness, that's quite a lot of blood,' said Peter, looking quite queasy.

'All right,' I said, 'you go and ring for an ambulance and I'll sort her out.'

I remembered my first-aid training and looked for something I could use as a tourniquet, but couldn't find anything. So I ran back into the house and grabbed a tea towel from the kitchen table and the first coat I could find on the hanger. When I got back, the woman had almost fainted with the pain. Her head was lolling to one side and her face had gone from grey to almost pure white. She was muttering to herself lightly.

'Can you hear me? What's your name?' I asked her.

'No . . . it hurts. My leg . . . the noise.'

I held her head up but she didn't respond again, just nodded her head up and down slightly as her eyes flickered open and shut.

'Can you feel your leg? Can you tell me your name? I'm just going to stop the bleeding.'

'Is she all right, constable?' asked a passer-by. A couple of the curious and concerned had gathered at the side of the road, peering over.

'She'll be fine. Could you just clear away, please? She needs some space.'

They inched back, but continued to hover as I made the tea towel into a tourniquet for her leg. There were further gasps from my audience, but I managed to stop the worst of the blood, although the tea towel was soon soaked a deep crimson. I put the coat over her shoulders to keep in the warmth and kept talking, trying to keep her conscious.

I could hear some of the passengers on the coach complaining that they were now late for various appointments. The driver was stood in shock on the pavement, his head in his hands, as Peter interviewed him. After about five minutes the ambulance arrived, and two young men carried the woman onto a stretcher; as they lifted her up, she let out another almighty scream.

'Oh my God! Is she all right?' asked the driver. 'I don't know how it . . .'

'Can you describe to me exactly what happened, Mr Fletcher?' asked Peter, taking on a sudden air of command.

'She got off my bus. Then I thought she'd walked away. But she must have slipped or something and . . . and I hit the brakes as fast as I could, but it was too late. Then there was a nasty crunch and the whole coach shook. That scream. Oh God. Is she going to die?'

'I don't think so. Try not to panic. She's in the ambulance now,' Peter told him. 'It was her leg. The wheel went over it. But I think we got to it just in time.'

'Peter, I've got to catch a train in thirty minutes. I'm not even on duty today! Will you be OK? Can I leave you to it?' I said, realizing how late it was.

'I think I've got it under control,' he said. The whole

thing had quite shaken young Peter free of his beginner's nerves.

As I looked back at the woman being loaded onto the ambulance, I saw the coat covering her, now all covered in blood. I realized with horror that it was my landlady's special coat. The new red one she'd been bought by her husband as a treat that Christmas, and was planning to wear to a dance that weekend.

The ambulance door slammed shut and whisked the woman away, and my landlady's favourite coat with her.

Compared to Richmond, Northallerton HQ was quite grand and exciting. It was a large red-brick Georgian building in the centre of town, with two floors. As you approached it looked a bit like a stately home, with a grand portico at the front door, and sash windows on either side. There was a blue police light above the door which was lit up at night.

It felt to me, when I entered, that this was where all the drama must happen. I sat in the reception area again as I had all those months earlier when I came for my interview, and Sergeant Freeman came to meet me.

'Welcome to our humble abode. I hope you had a good journey.'

'It's lovely to be here.'

'It certainly gets busy,' she said, as officers in their uniforms charged back and forth carrying files, chatting urgently to one another.

A young lad was being brought in through the front door, struggling a little as he was taken to the cells.

'Shoplifting. Not the first time he's been in either,' she

said, leaning over. 'We get more and more each year, I'm afraid. These young people are getting bolder by the minute. I blame the parents. Anyway, let's have a proper look around, shall we?'

We walked down a long corridor with lots of doors on either side, the sound of voices murmuring from inside the rooms where people were engaged in all kinds of important meetings. At the end of the corridor was the room where I'd first had my interview with the Chief Constable. Sitting outside, three lads and one young woman were waiting nervously for their own cross-examinations. I was relieved I didn't have to go through all that again.

We made our way upstairs and entered a bustling room where a group of men and a few women in civvies were operating radios. They were enormous, box-like things with buttons and wires sticking out all over the place. Nothing like the compact radios we have today. There must have been some logic to it all, but to me it looked completely chaotic.

'Communications,' said Sergeant Freeman with a flourish of her arm. 'The hub of operations. Come and meet young Willis. He'll be showing you the ropes for a couple of days.'

Willis was stooped over with his back to us, taking a message. 'N2LA to N2XN,' he was saying, which meant nothing whatsoever to me but must have been conveying some purposeful communication to whoever was on the other end. When he was finished, he turned round and smiled at us. It took me a while to clock it, but standing before me was Eric Willis, my childhood nemesis, the grubby little boy Mary and I had spent many a day plotting against, and calling names from across the street. And there he was, staring back at me, all grown up, tall and handsome with a neat haircut and police uniform.

'Willis, this is WPC Rhodes. She'll be working with you in here for a couple of days.'

'Hello, Eric,' I said with a half smile, wondering if he would recognize me.

For a while, he just stared back with a rather puzzled look on his face. I could almost see the clockwork whirring in his brain as he tried to place where he had seen me before. After a few moments, a glimmer and then a beam of recognition spread across his face.

'Pam?'

'Yes! How long has it been? What, over ten years?'

'Do you two know each other?' asked Sergeant Freeman, looking confused.

'From old times,' said Eric. 'Pam was a neighbour of mine. When we were children.'

'Well, what a small world! I'm sure you'll have a lot to catch up on. But remember you're on duty, Willis. Not too much chat about old times, eh?'

I couldn't believe that the spotty little boy, who had caused me to have so many vengeful thoughts, had grown into this handsome young man. And to bump into him here, of all places!

'Well, I'll leave you to it anyway,' said Sergeant Freeman. 'Meet me outside at the end of the shift and we'll walk back to my house.'

The communications department, it turned out, was

where all the messages were relayed to and from all the different stations in North Riding, including Richmond. Messages were sent back to Traffic Patrol, and all the officers who were out in their cars as well, letting them know where to go, and they fed back their own information to HQ.

Eric showed me how to use the radio, which was a little scary at first.

'Do I have to speak into this?' I asked.

'Yes. Pick up the receiver, like this.'

I spoke into it and my voice sounded funny, all echoey and loud.

'Shall we call ... which station are you from?' Eric asked me.

'Richmond.'

'Shall we call there and see who answers?'

'OK,' I giggled.

So we rang through and Doris the clerk answered.

'Any news for HQ?' I said, lowering my voice so she didn't recognize me at first.

'No, nothing to report here, over,' replied Doris.

'Doris, it's me, Pam! Rhodes. I'm at HQ!'

'Pam! Ha. I didn't recognize your voice!'

'Anyway, better go, stuff to do here. We're just being naughty. Maybe we'll talk again, though,' I said.

'Over and out,' said Doris.

'So this is what you do in here all day, is it?' I said to Eric.

'Yes. Well, no, not exactly. There's a whole lot going on here. Murders and all sorts. It's where it all happens.'

It was certainly a far cry from our little station, with our one radio and one telephone. But for me Richmond was still home, for the time being at least.

All around the office in police headquarters there were other people taking messages and the room was alive with noise and excitement. As the messages came in and went, Eric showed me the ropes. By the end of the day, my head was whizzing with buzzes and bleeps and codes and who knows what.

'What a day!' I said, as we walked downstairs. 'So what have you been doing since we last met, anyway?'

'I did my National Service. Went to Germany. That was quite an adventure. I think everyone should have to do it, personally. Then I wasn't sure what to do. Village life seemed deadly dull after that. A friend had just joined the police, so I thought why not give that a go. Been here three years now. I've got a little boy, George. And my wife, Carol. Pam Rhodes. Well I never did!' said Eric as he put on his coat.

'Seriously, you were probably the last person I expected to bump into here,' I said.

'I know. Funny how life turns out.'

We stood for a while in the corridor and both thought about times gone past. Neither one of us mentioned what enemies we had been. It seemed that the past was just that now, like a distant dream, and we were both completely different people.

I was staying for the week at Sergeant Freeman's house. She lived with her husband in quite a small police house on the edge of town, with a very neat garden full of rose bushes, and other shrubs which I didn't recognize. Her husband was also in the police; they were quite a contrast to my landlady and her husband.

Sergeant Freeman was a stickler for etiquette. She asked me to lay the table for dinner, so I put out the usual knife, fork and spoon. But when she came in with the meatloaf, her face dropped.

'My dear, you've put out soup spoons for dessert. And what's this? Butter knives?'

'Sorry. I'm not used to so much . . . equipment.'

'A table badly laid is like a mind out of form. Nothing should be out of place, even the simplest of daily rituals. It's a mark of a shoddy outlook on life.'

Her husband looked at me and smiled knowingly as Sergeant Freeman bustled around the table and replaced the erroneous cutlery, before dishing out the meatloaf and greens.

'For what we are about to receive may the Lord make us truly thankful. Amen,' she said, and began tucking in.

'We may work hard in this house but we always eat well, don't we?'

'Yes, dear,' said her husband dutifully.

'Did you notice Charles's roses as you came in? He's got the greenest fingers in North Riding. They're quite the envy of the ladies at the WI. Aren't they, Charles?'

'Indeed.'

'Well, I said to him the other day, you ought to exhibit them, shouldn't you, Charles? It seems such a waste them just sitting there. Do you have any hobbies, Pamela? Interests outside work?'

'I used to perform in plays, in Scarborough. At the open-air theatre. For a while I did think about acting as a career, before I realized I didn't want to spend all my time with actors.'

'Ooh, you made the right choice. I mean, really, I don't see the point of plays and the pictures and such like. We never go, do we? It seems such a frivolous indulgence, when you think there are people out there with nothing. I'd much rather be doing something useful. Actually make a difference. That's why I joined the police.'

'How do you find it? Being a woman sergeant, I mean?'

'Well, it's still a man's world, and there's no doubt about that. I do find myself sometimes in a room, with the others, and they'll be talking about their wives or girl-friends in this way or that, if you know what I mean, and they'll quite forget I'm there.'

'The lads at our station are always very polite when I'm around.'

The Super was ultra strict when it came to matters of decency, and he wouldn't suffer any bad language or innu-endo at the station, at least not in front of the senior officers or girls.

'Well, I'm glad to hear it! But you can rest assured it all comes out when you leave the room,' said Sergeant Free-man. 'Sometimes it feels like I've dropped right into the bar of a public house, the way they talk to one another. They're not as careful as they used to be around me, now that I've reached this far, I suppose.'

She scooped up the last of her food and wiped her mouth with a huge red napkin.

'Well, I may be the first female among all those men, but I won't be the last, I can assure you of that.'

*

The rest of the week at Northallerton was a blur of activity, quite different from what I was used to in sleepy Richmond. It almost felt like I had skipped forward a few years in terms of technology and the pace of life. There was more of everything. More and bigger cars, more officers, more noise and more case files piling up in the offices.

Sergeant Gaunt, the one who had taken my fingerprints for the official police record, showed me again how to take them.

'Now you have a go,' he said, sluggishly passing me the ink-pad.

'Does it matter which one you do first?'

When I tried it on him, the first attempt was just a big blur of ink across the page.

'Oh no. I'd never identify you from that. It's awful,' I said.

'No. I doubt it,' he said, yawning. 'Have another go.'

I rolled each finger carefully in the ink, then placed them straight down on the paper.

'Much better,' he sighed.

Then we went back into the photography room and I tried that too. After I had taken my test picture, there was a young lad, who had been caught shoplifting, due to have his pictures taken. I stood at the back and kept quiet. The young shoplifter sauntered in and stood in front of the board, with his head slightly on one side. He stared sulkily down at the Sergeant's feet.

'Head straight. Look up. We haven't got all day.'

He looked up reluctantly and the camera snapped quickly, for ever catching that moment.

Whatever the crime, however small or large, every face

that came into that room seemed to look equally menacing when photographed, as though everyone was a mass murderer at heart. I think it was something in the lighting.

Despite all the buzz at the station, it was actually Traffic Patrol which turned out to be the most exciting part of the week. We whizzed around in the big black police cars, pulled people over and stopped off for cups of tea at some of the rural stations. I didn't know much about vehicles and things like that, and would often switch off when the lads at the station enthused over the latest models of car, how their engines worked and which would go the fastest, but it was exciting to actually be driving around the country lanes. The cars seemed thrilling to me, even though they were nothing like the vehicles nowadays: the dashboard was a lot simpler, there was no air conditioning or heating or anything like that, not even seatbelts.

'You're from Richmond, are you then?' asked the driver, leaning back as we rattled along the bumpy roads around Northallerton.

'Yes.'

'Strict, isn't he? Your Super? We try to avoid stopping off there if we can. It's not as relaxed as some stations. We like to have a chat, you know. Pass the time of day.'

'I suppose. I don't have anything to compare it to really. We don't muck about much or anything like that, though. At least not when the Super's around. The Inspector's all right, though. And the Sergeants are up and down, but usually OK. Take their roles very seriously, if you know what I mean.'

At intervals, HQ would call into the car radio and ask where we were. Whenever we called back our location on the days I was on the roads, we always seemed to be at a place called Busby Stoop. I never did work out where that was.

The week flew by. On my last day in Northallerton I just had an hour for a quick look round the department store before my train. It took me back to my days at Marshall & Snelgrove. How glad I was I didn't have to work there any more! As I walked to the train, I caught sight of Eric outside the post office. He had the afternoon off, and I hadn't had a chance to say goodbye properly so I was pleased to see him.

'Pam. You're off today, aren't you? This is my wife, Carol. And little George. Our boy.'

A young lad aged about three or four emerged from behind his mother's legs. He bore a striking resemblance to the young Eric, with a wave of thick dark hair and piercing blue eyes. But, unlike the bold and brash young Eric I remembered, he hugged onto his mother's coat shyly.

'He might look like me, but he's got his mother's way. Haven't you, Georgie?'

Eric's wife was very beautiful: a plain natural look, hardly any make-up. She reminded me a bit of a frightened hare, which stops dead still when a car comes along and very gracefully gets flattened to a pulp.

'Eric's told me about you. How funny you bumped into each other,' she said softly. 'I was very impressed when I heard you were a policewoman. I'd never be brave enough to step outside the normal . . . I mean . . . what's expected. Sorry. I don't mean any offence . . .'

'Anyway, we'd better be off,' Eric interrupted. 'Got to get Georgie his tea. The joys of fatherhood, and all that.'

We all shook hands and said we'd stay in touch, but I had a feeling we wouldn't.

As they walked away, little George in the middle being swung in the air, laughing, I had a sudden urge to be part of a family. My own family. Seeing Eric all grown up, and a dad, brought a new emotion flooding in, and it gave me quite a start.

But I hadn't met anyone yet who I wanted to start a family with. After our night outside the castle, it looked unlikely that Jim would be returning to Catterick after his National Service, so it was possible we'd never see each other again. His letters had all but stopped coming and I had the feeling he had met someone out in Germany or wherever he was. Something in his tone was more distant, and made me suspect that our little friendship was over.

How am I ever going to meet anyone in Richmond, I wondered. All the lads were married or engaged and the men at church were either married or twice my age, or else they were bachelors for a reason. For now, I thought, I'll remain Pamela Rhodes, Miss.

Bestiality.

At first I thought I was seeing things. I'd picked up a report about a court case the Spec had left on the desk. I looked again, and no, I had read it right, there in black and white. Well, pencil anyway. Bestiality.

On the handwritten paper in front of me, in the Sergeant's handwriting, was the name of a man, a young lad down at Pringle's Farm, who, it said, had been caught, 'with' a sheep, as it were, one night in the fields off the Darlington Road.

Now I've heard it all, I thought.

'Rhodes, can you nip home and come back in your civvies?' called a loud voice suddenly, and nearly made me jump out of my chair.

'Yes, Sergeant. Any reason?' I asked, still distracted by the strangeness of the case I had just read about.

'Sorry, can't stop,' he replied, rushing past. 'Urgent meeting with the Spec.'

Sergeant Hardcastle never seemed to stay in one place for long these days. He was having to deal with an unusually high number of people coming in and out of the cells. Sometimes they were soldiers from the barracks who had stolen cars to get home, having missed the bus, but a lot were just drunk and incapable cases who we held on to until they'd sobered up.

When I got to my digs to get changed, Janet was baking some loaves of bread.

'You're just in time. Fresh out of the oven,' she said, producing a delicious and perfectly formed tin loaf. 'I managed to get a lovely chicken from McGregor's too. Don did some work for him, casual, like.'

'What a treat! I'm famished. I'll need to eat quick, though. I tell you, there's something in the air these days. We've had so many in this week, I think we're going to need more cells.'

'Yes. I know what you mean. We've always left the front door unlocked, but now I don't know. It's the young ones are the worst. Bored, I don't doubt. Hanging around aimless. Not like in my day when we made our own fun. Now they expect entertainment all the time. Bored wasn't even a word when I were growing up.'

'It's not just that, though. One case I read about today –

I can barely say it. But it was a man and a . . . he was having hanky-panky with a . . .' I leant forward and whispered across the table, 'sheep.'

Janet hardly raised an eyebrow.

'Nothing surprises me these days,' she said, pursing her lips and slicing the bread manically into thick pieces. 'I knew a man who married a horse once. Well, I didn't know him. But someone at the market knew someone who knew him. Not officially, of course, but he fell in love with it. Like it was his wife, if you know what I mean. He even gave it a wedding dress. Can you imagine? It's like everything, though, these days. No stopping it.'

There was a knock at the door.

'Who could that be at this time?'

I heard Janet answer the door. A panicky woman from across the road was talking in urgent tones. When Janet came back, she was white as a ghost.

'It's the King. He's dead.'

When I got back to the station in my civvies, everyone was in shock and Doris had been crying. The King had been very popular. But life at the station had to go on.

A little boy, who didn't look much older than about nine, sat eating a large red apple, kicking his legs up and down against the bench. Sergeant Hardcastle took me to one side and whispered, 'Canteen breaking. Up at Catterick. Broke a window. Caught raiding the kitchen. The little devil.'

'But he looks so young.'

'He says it was some older lads were the ringleaders. Says they ran away and left him to take the fall, the poor blighter.'

'He doesn't look tall enough to reach the window. Let alone climb in.'

'Well, it might be true, what he says. But all the same, the law's the law. Can you take him up to Middlesbrough on the bus? Do you think you'll be able to handle him on your own?'

'I think I'll manage,' I said, and looked over the scruffy young lad, who looked like butter wouldn't melt. He had on a blue cap and shorts, even though it was only February, and a scruffy shirt with holes in it. His hair was slicked back, as though he'd raided his father's Brylcreem.

'What about his parents?' I whispered.

'We had a phone call with the mother briefly but she didn't say where she was. She said to take him to an aunt. But we've got to take him to the station in Middlesbrough first. The Spec got him to talk, bribed him with sweets in the end. The station's expecting you.'

I hadn't had much to do with young children before, except my landlady's children, who were very well behaved. I hoped I'd be able to entertain him. It was a long journey from Richmond to Middlesbrough.

'What's your name?' I asked the lad, as we walked down Newbiggin towards the bus stop.

The boy looked at me for a while, squinting. I got the feeling he was wary of adults, as he kept his guard up all the way into town.

'Cat got your tongue, has it? How about an ice cream, before we leave?'

'Oh yes!' he answered, almost immediately.

Even the most stubborn of children are quick to succumb to the persuasive powers of vanilla and frozen cream.

'Patrick,' he said, after a while, as we walked up the street towards the ice-cream shop. 'My name is.'

'I had a great-great-great-grandfather called Patrick. In Ireland,' I told him. 'Came to England during the potato famine. With my great-great-great-grandmother.'

'That's a lot of greats. What's a potato famine?'

'When the potatoes got a nasty disease, they couldn't grow them and lots of people starved to death. It was bad.'

'My mam said we've got Irish blood. I'm a sixteenth or something.'

'Where is she now? Your mother? We'd really like to find her. Tell her you're all right. She must be worried about you.'

'I don't know. She's gone. Are we nearly there?'

'Yes. Where do you live, then? Is it with your aunt?'

The boy started kicking a stone along the street and looked down, his face tightening up and his eyes narrowing. In the end, I settled for buying a comic to keep him occupied on the journey and gave up trying to find out any more about his mysterious family life.

'The *Beano*'ll do,' he said, as we looked over the shop counter. 'There's a new boy in it, Dennis the Menace. He's got a dog.'

So I bought him the latest instalment of Dennis and Gnasher's escapades. I hadn't seen the character before, although I used to read the *Beano* during the war years. After that he chose a large vanilla cone from the ice-cream counter; I had never seen a child eat something with such gusto. Anyone would have thought he hadn't eaten in weeks.

Once we were on the bus, he settled back with the comic, the remains of the ice-cream smeared across his face, and kept pretty quiet for the rest of the journey. Every now and then he let out a small chuckle as Dennis got himself into ever-deeper trouble.

After I had dropped Patrick off at the station in Middlesbrough, and the officers had taken down his details, I wondered what would happen to him, and where his parents were. I'd gone before now on escort duty up to the children's home in Seaham Harbour. But the truth was, I'd probably never know. Like so much of life in the police, people came and went. Sometimes I knew their most intimate secrets for a fleeting moment, other times I didn't know anything about them at all, just an anonymous crime. But one thing was for sure: more often than not, I never saw them again.

At home that night, the Prime Minister, Winston Churchill, was on the radio, lamenting the loss of the great King George.

'Isn't it just awful?' said Janet, as we sat round and shared the big chicken Don had managed to get hold of. 'So sudden. No one expected it. I mean he was only, what, fifty-five, fifty-six? You know that's not much older than us. And now that little girl, Princess Elizabeth. Well, she's not so little, but I remember when she was. She'll have to be queen and rule the whole country alone, poor thing. Such a burden.'

'Have to be queen? Oh yes, poor thing. She'll have to eat all that expensive food and get driven around in a posh carriage all day,' said Don.

'Oh, you! It's more than that, and you know it. I know your views, anyway, but you can keep them quiet in this house. Your father may have been a communist, but we'll have none of that here.'

'Aye. Well, he was, anyway. And proud, too. He once walked all the way to London to protest about . . . something or other, jobs or something,' Don said to me proudly.

'They said on the wireless that a crowd stood in the rain all night outside Buckingham Palace. Some were crying. The police had to move them back, apparently,' said Janet, ignoring her husband.

'What's a queen for?' asked Fiona, as she warily examined a bit of chicken on her plate that still had a few feathers on it.

'To represent the country. A kind of . . . figurehead.'

'How do they choose, though? Could I be queen?' She sat up, suddenly excited. 'I could wear a crown and live in a castle with a hundred thousand horses and a unicorn.'

'It's inherited. Don't you learn this stuff at school? Anyway unicorns aren't real,' said her brother.

'We learnt about Henry VIII, about how he killed all his wives. Elizabeth, who never had a baby, and the other one. One who burnt some cakes, and William who killed that other king, with an arrow in his eye. Is that what our king did? The dead one?'

'Fiona! Don't say such things. Eat up your greens and enough of all this. I, for one, am very sorry. He was a good king all through the war. And now he's gone.'

There was a line of tears in Janet's eyes as she cleared away the plates, and for that moment, as the whole country mourned, it felt like the end of an era; as if we were all on the threshold of something, though no one was quite sure exactly what.

*

I had been the only WPC at the station for nearly six months now. Apart from Doris, the clerk, I was the only woman, and I hardly saw Doris, because she worked office hours and I was on duty lots of evenings. Occasionally, though, we did meet up in Philpot's Tea Rooms if we got the chance, for ice cream or a cuppa.

Doris was quite glamorous-looking outside work, and always seemed well turned out in gloves and a hat, with curled dark hair, which she normally tied back at work. She spent a lot of time talking about her boyfriends. She had a succession of them but they all seemed to be called Henry.

'Henry's got a car!' she said excitedly one Saturday, as we tucked into a large piece of Mrs Philpot's finest carrot cake between us. 'You can take the roof off and everything. Oh, it's beautiful, Pam, you should see it. I think it's really essential a man drives these days. Don't you?'

'I hadn't given it much thought. I suppose it's quite useful. But expensive. And a bit scary, don't you think? They go so fast.'

'My last Henry, with the limp – not dark-haired Henry, the other one – he didn't drive. After a while I got so bored with walking everywhere, and buses. Waiting around for hours. Now we can just hop in and go where we like. It's freedom, that's what it is.'

She sat back and closed her eyes, smiling, as if deep in the memory of a particularly unforgettable country drive, then she sat back up suddenly.

'Ooh, by the way, have you heard?'

'What?'

'Well, I could be wrong, but I heard the Spec on the

phone to HQ about it the other day. I could be wrong, but I think we're to be joined by another woman.'

'Really? Gosh. I wonder what she'll be like.'

'Well. I don't like to pry, you know me. But I did happen to catch sight, quite by accident, of a document on the Super's desk. I was just dusting. Anyway, it said she'd be arriving in the next week or two.'

'So soon!'

'I'm surprised they haven't mentioned it to you.'

'So am I.'

When the Inspector called me into his office the following Monday, I had to feign surprise at the news of a new female PC.

'You know how much we value you, and your contribution at Richmond,' he said, putting his hat on the desk beside him and settling into his chair. 'But I'm aware it's a lot for one person. There may also be another opportunity for you coming up.'

'Oh?'

'But we'll discuss that later.'

'Right. I suppose it will be good to have someone to cover the other shifts. What with things getting so busy.'

'Exactly what I said. Now that we're used to having a woman around, we might as well make the most of them. She starts on Monday. I trust you'll make her welcome. Jeanette Farthing. That's her name. Like the coin.'

'Thank you, sir.'

All week, I wondered what Jeanette would be like. Although we had Doris, I had got used to being the only WPC at the station. It wasn't so much that I would resent another woman, more that it would take a slight shift of identity. I wouldn't be unique any more.

Jeanette arrived at the station the following Monday. She was quite a bit taller than me, a couple of inches at least, with dark glossy hair which looked long, somehow, despite being well above shoulder length. Her uniform was immaculate, and everything about her seemed to ooze confidence.

'Morning. You must be Pam. I've heard so much about you from Dorry,' she held out her hand. Doris was leaning over the desk, facing her and smiling.

'Welcome to Richmond,' I said. 'You seem to have settled in already.'

'Yes. I'm like that. I always just fit in, wherever I am. I don't know how.'

'Jeanette was telling me about her last job,' Doris said. 'She worked in a slaughterhouse for a whole year! Can you imagine? Such guts.'

They both laughed uproariously.

'No, actually I worked in an office,' Jeanette said after they'd stopped laughing. 'Nowhere near as interesting – but a lot less blood. Most of the time.'

More laughter.

As it turned out, I hardly ever saw Jeanette. Whenever I did cross shifts with her she seemed to spend a lot of time talking to Doris. And it wasn't long before I was sent on my own little journey. I would soon put Richmond, and everyone in it, behind me altogether, for a while at least.

'There's someone in reception. Says she'll only talk to you,' said Sergeant Shaw as I put down my handbag on the desk. I was on the afternoon shift, and had just said hello to Doris, who was in the corner, typing.

'Who is it?'

'An elderly lady. Something about marmalade. She said she wants the police lady.'

I walked out to the front and there was Mrs Colbert, sitting on the bench, hunched over her walking stick. She looked as though she had been crying; her nose was all red and her cheeks were flushed.

'Look, Gladys, here's the lady police officer. She'll take you home and we can sort this out.'

Sergeant Shaw took me aside. 'Swears blind she had some marmalade or something, and now she can't find it. Says she's looked everywhere. Thinks they might have had an intruder. In the night. You better go with her and check.'

'Come along, Mrs Colbert,' I said, helping her up.

'Will you catch them?' she said and wiped her nose.

'I hope so. Let's go and see anyway. I'm sure it's probably nothing.'

We walked past the workhouse, where people with no homes or jobs were taken. I wondered who was in there now and how you'd end up in a place like that. As we shuffled up the street, I looked down and noticed that Mrs Colbert was wearing her slippers again. They used to be pink, but now they were all blackened at the edges, from walking about outside, no doubt. The last time I had seen her she had been in the cemetery on Christmas Day, looking for her dead husband. Before that, she was wandering up the street and her daughter had been out of her mind with worry. Perhaps they can't cope, I thought. The daughter worked full-time as a nurse and couldn't keep an eye on her mother through the day.

'So tell me what happened, exactly? With the marmalade or the noise or whatever?'

'Well. I woke up in the morning, as usual, and went downstairs. I fed Billy, but I had thought to myself that I'd heard a noise. Scraping. I was making my breakfast. Searched everywhere for the marmalade. Everywhere.'

Her voice rose and was getting quicker as she spoke. She had on a lot of powder puff and blue eye shadow, and spoke through nervously pinched lips.

'Cupboards, drawers, even in the cellar. Salt, pepper, butter, Spam, all there. But no marmalade. I seem to forget everything these days so I even looked in the garden. Just in case. Since my husband went, things just don't seem to be as they were. Things . . . move, of their own accord.'

She looked warily into the middle distance as though she had got quite used to being haunted by one thing or another.

When we got to her daughter's house, we both began looking through the cupboards again. The kitchen was filled with washing up – her daughter had obviously been too busy to tidy up before she had to be at work again.

'Did you have it at breakfast yesterday?' I asked as I rooted through the sink and then tried to remove a sticky substance which had made its way into my sleeve.

'No, I don't think so. No. I had porridge yesterday. I think. Or was that the day before? Oh, I don't know any more.'

After a while she began to look sheepish and looked away, then up at me with small eyes.

'Well, I may have had it yesterday. Perhaps I finished it. I don't know. Oh, Lord.'

She sat down on a rickety chair at the kitchen table and started to cry again, her head in her hands.

'Don't worry,' I said. 'We all make mistakes. Did you eat it then?'

'I think so.' She looked over at the sink.

I rummaged around in the pile of washing up and there it was, the empty marmalade jar.

'Is this it?'

'Yes. But I thought I . . . I don't know what I thought any more.'

'Well, that's a relief to find it anyway, isn't it?' I tried to sound chirpy.

'Oh, please, don't be cross. I'm so stupid. To have brought you all the way down here.'

'I'm not cross. Don't be silly.'

I was doing my best to comfort the woman, but feared that her state of confusion had gone beyond anything I could help with.

'Well, at least you know you haven't had any intruders anyway, don't you?'

For one brief moment of clarity she seemed to agree, but it was all too short-lived.

'You're right,' she said. 'I do. I know that much. Don't I?'

When I got back to the station, the Inspector wanted to see me in his office. I racked my brains as to whether I had done anything wrong. There was that little boy who had fallen over on the road when I was on the school crossing patrol. But nothing seemed to have come of that. Or might I have filed something in the wrong place, or made a mistake with my typing?

'Sit down,' said the Inspector. I couldn't read his expression.

The walls of his office were lined with legal books, and on the desk was a photo of his wife and their two daughters, twins in matching dresses and hair ties.

'I've got some exciting news for you,' he said, leaning back and fiddling with his pen. I relaxed; at least it wasn't a telling off, then.

'Have you ever been to Redcar? On the coast up north.'

'No, I haven't, sir.'

'Well, they're looking for a WPC during the coming busy period, and now that we've got Jeanette, we can spare you. So HQ has asked for you to be transferred for the summer, to help with the tourist season.'

'Oh, right. Well. That should be different.'

'It should be a change. Anyway, you'll be leaving next week. That gives you the rest of the week to find some digs. Shouldn't be too hard, but ask if you need any help. Be pleasant to take in the sea air at any rate, I'm sure. Wish I was going too, to be honest with you.'

I had just less than a week to sort out some new digs; and I had to let my landlady, Janet, know I'd be leaving. She was quietly relieved, I think, if truth be told. Her children were getting older now, and the house seemed to be getting smaller and messier by the day.

I telephoned Mam from a pay phone and told her my news.

'She's moving to Redcar,' she called out to my dad, who was listening to a new comedy on the radio. '*The Goon*

Show. I can't get him off of it,' she said to me. 'He laughs for hours.'

'Isn't that where Annie and Colin moved to?' he called back, and then I heard him laugh loudly at a man with a funny voice.

'Ooh, yes, you must get in touch with them. They're bound to know somewhere you can stay.'

So she gave me the details of their friends, and Annie immediately offered to put me up for the summer. They had no children, so plenty of room, she said. Well, I thought, at least that's sorted.

On my last day at Richmond, I sat in the station office and finished off my final report. I was about leave when Sergeant Shaw came over and produced a small brown package tied up with string.

'For the journey. We thought you could use it.'

I opened it up and it was a large bar of chocolate.

'We all chipped in,' said Peter.

'That's kind!' I said. 'Delicious. Thank you.'

'You might even meet a nice man out there,' said Doris. 'You never know, all that sea air and those sunsets. Bit of romance.'

'More to the point, look out for those donkeys,' Ben warned. 'They can give you a right good kick in the shins if you stand behind them.'

'Thanks for that. Thank you all. I'll see you in a few months then.'

8

As I stepped off the bus, the air in Redcar smelled different from Richmond; it reminded me of home. There was that familiar sound of gulls squawking overhead, and the open, fresh feel of a salty sea breeze that had accompanied so much of my teenage life. The roads were already filling up with holidaymakers in their cars, and several families trooped off the bus with me, carrying bags and big sun hats.

It wasn't actually sunny, and in fact there was a sharp easterly breeze. But it didn't stop people leaping about in the sea, building sandcastles and playing cricket on the beach. Dads sat reading the newspaper with handkerchiefs on their heads, while their children dug huge holes and buried each other in the sand. Girls showed off the latest in swimwear, splashing about in the sea laughing, climbing on each other's shoulders or dunking each other under the water.

I tried to find the police station from the instructions I had written down myself on a piece of paper, but I struggled to read them. In the end, I had to ask someone, and by the time I found it I was exhausted from my travels.

Redcar was a much bigger station than Richmond; it was a rather imposing and grand red-brick building which went back for quite a long way. I waited around in the main entrance until a sergeant came over and called me in.

'Rhodes?' he asked, without smiling. 'You're later than I was expecting.'

'Yes, sorry, I got a bit lost.'

'Well. You need to be punctual here. Sit down. I'm Sergeant Ditchburn. The duty sergeant. We've got seven other PCs, and now two WPCs. And Inspector Sharpe – you won't see much of him, but he's in charge from on high, as it were.'

As we sat down, Sergeant Ditchburn began picking his nails. He had a sharp pointy nose, and had scraped his remaining hair across his bald patch. He had the air of someone who is always just a little bit put out by life. Behind him, in the office, there were two female clerks noisily typing, but neither of them said hello or even looked up.

'You won't need to do any office duties here. That's all taken care of. Everything here has its place, though heaven knows it's a struggle to keep them all in check sometimes. I suppose you want to know what you'll be doing then? Why we've brought you here?'

'That would be nice. Yes.'

'Patrolling the seafront mainly. Moving on cars, giving directions, that kind of thing. We don't have any females stationed here usually. But they're bringing in two this summer. So we'll be positively overrun.'

As he didn't smile, I wasn't sure whether it was a very dry joke or a serious comment, so I kept quiet and sat with my hands in my lap waiting for his next move.

'You and another girl. A Miss Treadwell. Maureen Treadwell.'

I sat up. The name sounded familiar. Where had I heard it before? Then I remembered: it must be Maureen from

Scarborough! Jane had introduced us and I'd given her some advice about the questions which came up in the exam and that kind of thing. But I hadn't heard from her since. Well I never! Maureen Treadwell had got into the police too, then.

'What's wrong with you, girl? You look like you've had a horrible vision.'

'Sorry. No. I was just thinking. I know Maureen. Miss Treadwell. From home.'

'Hmm. Anyway. Report for duty tomorrow and I'll get PC Featherstone to show you your beats. Any questions?'

My head was full to the brim with questions, but I didn't dare ask Sergeant Ditchburn any of them.

When I arrived at my new digs, I was nearly in tears. I was so tired and Sergeant Ditchburn hadn't seemed at all friendly. I was relieved when Annie answered the door with a beaming smile.

'Come in, come in. You look shattered.'

She was plump, not very tall and always seemed to be wearing her apron. Her short grey hair was covered with a scarf, and she had permanently rosy cheeks as though she had just emerged from a boiler room.

'You're just in time for tea. Come and sit down.'

I was so exhausted I could have fallen down and slept right there and then. But my hunger got the better of me. As we sat down at the table, to my relief there was none of the fuss over cutlery I'd had with Sergeant Freeman, just a single knife and fork and a nice chicken pie.

Colin was at the table already, with a napkin tucked into his shirt, drinking a bottle of stout.

He had on an oversized green cardigan and slippers, and was small and skinny compared to his wife. Despite their size difference, they had the look of a couple who have been together for so long that they've started to resemble one another in mannerisms and facial expressions.

'I'd better watch what I say with the law in the house. Have you arrested anyone then?' asked Colin, gulping down his pie.

'Not really, no,' I said.

'Oh, leave the poor girl alone,' said Annie. 'He's always winding people up. Ignore him.'

'How do you know my mam and dad?' I asked.

'Your father and I worked for Mr Saville, this millionaire in Bradford. Made his money in textiles. I was his driver for ten years. Your father was his PA. He lost the lot, though, the millionaire, in the depression.'

'The whole fortune,' said Annie. 'Can you believe? He just wouldn't lay people off. Nice, I suppose, but in the end everyone lost their jobs so . . .'

'Anyway, yes, so he had to lay a lot of us workers off. Your father, being the kind of bloke he is, he set up his own business, as you know.'

'I understand he's quite successful now, isn't he? Your father?' asked Annie.

'Yes. I think so. Well, we've got a telephone anyway!'

They laughed when I said this, but I wasn't sure why.

'Good man. So, anyway, we decided to move out of town. I found a job at the steel works. Made foreman eventually. And here we are.'

'Wouldn't live anywhere else now. I need to be by the

sea,' Annie said. 'How's your mother, by the way? I've been meaning to write to her.'

'Good, I think. The tourist business is doing really well in Scarborough and she takes care of a lot of the financial side and everything now.'

After the pie, Annie brought out a large bowl of rhubarb and custard and we all tucked in.

'Redcar was a Victorian seaside resort, you know. Queen Victoria came here and everything, probably,' said Colin, after we had finished eating.

'No, she didn't. You're thinking of Hull,' Annie told him.

'Why's there a street named after her, then?'

'I don't know. Probably the Jubilee, or something. Anyway, love, I have to ask: what's it like being a policewoman? Do you get much . . . trouble or anything, from the lads, ever? Or tricky criminals to deal with and things like that?'

'Oh no, they're all very polite mostly and I've never had any real trouble yet.'

'Do you know what you'll be doing here then?' she asked, and began clearing away the plates.

'A bit of patrolling, I think. I'll soon find out, though, I suppose.'

I felt very comfortable with Annie and Colin, and I got the feeling they were actually pleased to have some new company.

That night, in their little guest bedroom, I slept like a bear in hibernation and didn't remember a single dream. The alarm clock was ringing for some time in my ear the next morning before I could bring myself to completely wake up.

*

When I got back to Redcar police station, the atmosphere seemed a little more welcoming. One of the PCs took me round the station, pointing out all the different rooms. John, he said his name was. He was a little bit younger than me and was full of energy, like an overgrown rabbit.

'This is where we file all the reports, and that's the radio room. The cells are down there, and that's the Chief Inspector's office. He's not around much. At least we don't have much to do with him. He's all right, though.'

'How long have you been here?'

'Three years. For my sins. I started as a police cadet and then worked my way in. I do like it, though. We haven't got any WPCs here normally so it's a bit of a novelty your being here. A nice one, mind.'

'What about your digs?' I asked him. 'Are they all right?'

'I live above the station with three of the other lads, Steve, Malcolm and Tony. Nice lads. It's our own little bachelor pad.'

'Wow. No wonder the building's so big.'

'It's a bit like being at boarding school sometimes. Silly pranks. You wouldn't want to be there when some of us get back from town some nights, either. The things they talk about. But we mostly get along all right and play by the rules. Honest. You have to be with Ditchburn around, any rate. Anyway, let's go into town and I'll show you what goes on around here.'

As we strolled through Redcar, we walked past the pier and the ballroom and John pointed out the main places to make a point. He showed me the big hall where they held summer shows every year and the amusements on the beach.

We seemed to spend most of the day either giving directions to lost holidaymakers or moving on cars which had parked along the road and blocked the route. But although the duties seemed to be a bit limited, compared to what I'd been doing at Richmond, it was nice to take in the sea air and be somewhere different.

The following day I was on the beat on my own, and I walked up and down the promenade for hours, directing people towards various amusements. I passed John coming the other way at one point and it was nice to see a familiar face, as I didn't really know anyone in Redcar apart from Annie and Colin.

Down on the beach, I said hello to the donkey man, who was helping a group up onto the animals. He was quite a dapper-looking chap, in a scruffy kind of way, with a tweed jacket, scarf round his neck and a moustache.

'Morning. Nice day for it,' he said.

'Everything OK?' I asked, thinking I ought to say something that sounded a bit official.

'Aye. All fine and dandy here. You'll not find much crime along this way. Apart from the crime of having fun that is!' He laughed loudly at his own joke.

I stopped for a while to take it all in, and marvelled at the way he handled all those donkeys and riders at once. He had created a clever rigging of ropes which tethered them all together as he pulled them up and down.

There were four donkeys in all: a tiny little dusty-coloured one, on which a small boy sat pulling at the animal's ears, and a slightly larger brown one, on which another little girl was screaming with fear and didn't seem to be enjoying it at all. There were also two larger black donkeys; a couple of older girls in swimsuits climbed aboard them and giggled. The donkey man winked as he hoisted them over, and they all trooped off along the beach, their parents watching, feeling a mixture of relief at the chance to have a break and slight fear for their children's safety.

I made a point at a phone box just beyond the promenade, and, somewhat to my amazement, the phone actually rang. I picked it up a little nervously.

'Hello?'

'Rhodes?'

'Yes, Sergeant.'

'Good, you're there. I need you to go up to Stanley Grove, there's been a complaint about a dangerous dog. Some woman up there. Her baby, she said. Attacked. Do you think you can handle that?'

'Yes. Of course, Sergeant. Right away.'

So I left the seafront behind me and made my way into town with a brisk walk. I eventually found the house, after asking a few people directions. It was along a steep terrace of houses with different coloured doors, and a very flustered-looking woman answered, with three young children at her feet.

'Oh, good. You're here. Oh, I can't tell you, constable. It was terrifying. They came running over and nearly knocked my Timmy clean over. They were three or four times the size of him. At least! Teeth everywhere. He could have been killed.'

The woman's voice was rising in panic.

'Just take a few minutes to calm down, Mrs . . . ?'

'Trent, Anna Trent. I . . . only will you be able to catch them? Because I'm afraid that if you don't something awful's going to happen. It wasn't like this before the war. You just didn't see them like you do now. But these days . . . And I don't blame the dogs. They can't help it. It's the owners.'

She was losing her breath and I thought she might hyperventilate at any moment.

'If I could come in for a few minutes? Then I can take a statement, and we can try our best to find the animals.'

As we sat down on a small sofa, the children all piled in and climbed on with us.

'Sorry, do you mind, officer, only they're all still a little shaken, aren't you, babies?'

'Mammy, why is that policeman a lady?' asked the little boy, who was chewing the head off a toy soldier and squashing right up against my shoulder.

'Timmy, put that thing down. You'll swallow it. She's not a policeman, she's a policewoman. And don't be rude. Sorry about him,' she said to me. 'They just say whatever comes into their heads, don't they?'

I took out my notebook and pencil, and waited for the children to settle down.

'Can you tell me what happened then, Mrs Trent? With the dogs?'

'Well, I was coming out of the post office. I have to admit I was quite distracted, what with the three of them, and then I was looking at my shopping list, and it was windy and, oh, everything seemed to be going wrong. You know how it is. Anyway, before I know it, there are these two enormous dogs, like wolves they were, foaming at the mouth, and running right towards us.'

'Like the Hounds of the Espadrille,' said Timmy, who had chewed the soldier in two and was now curled up at his mother's feet, the headless infantryman lying at his side.

'Baskervilles. Yes, it was like that. Something out of a horror film. They just kept running faster and faster, and I couldn't even see an owner anywhere. The children were screaming, and I stood in front of them trying to ward those dogs away. But they just kept coming.'

'Can you describe these animals? What colour were they exactly?'

'I would say . . . they were dark brown. Brindle, is that what they call it? Brown with flecks of other colours in it. One had a white patch on its nose. One had a long tail, I think. It's so hard to remember details, though. You know what it's like. In the heat of the moment.'

'And then what happened?'

'Well, the animals lunged forward, and one ran right at Timmy and knocked him over. Then it put its paws on his shoulder and started licking his face. I thought he'd rip his head off. I really did. I thought, it's only a matter of time before he has the poor child for lunch.'

'Was he injured? Timmy?'

'Not exactly. Shaken up, mind. Oh, well, yes, actually he did get a nasty bump on the head, didn't you, love?'

'Yes. It was the size of a pickled egg, you said, Mam. Exactly right here,' Timmy said proudly, parting his hair to reveal the bruise.

'Anyway, I wasn't going to hang around and wait for any more ravaging, so I picked him up and tried to pull the others behind me, and the shopping. And we ran all the way home, didn't we? Not even stopping to talk to Mr Pringle. And then I rang you lot from the pay phone. And I haven't stopped shaking since. And that was a few hours ago now.'

'Well, you're lucky you didn't get bitten. And you say you have no idea who owns these dogs?'

'None whatsoever. And if I hadn't seen them in flesh and blood I would have sworn some supernatural force was behind it, they were that big. I wouldn't be surprised if they belong to the devil himself.'

'Right. Thank you, Mrs Trent. You've been . . . informative. But for now, all I can do is be on the lookout. Do let us know if you get any more information that might help us.'

On the way back to the station I saw several dogs and wondered if they could be the offending creatures. But they all seemed to be trotting along quite innocently.

As I walked back along the promenade, the beach itself was, by now, absolutely packed out with people. You could hardly see the sand, as the crowds sat among a colourful array of windbreaks, or used upturned fishing boats as hideaways or makeshift climbing frames.

Suddenly, as if out of nowhere, a man in a loose jacket and open shirt, with a pipe in his mouth, stopped beside me and looked me in the eye.

'There's somebody at it back there. By the pier,' he said after a while, and tossed his head back nonchalantly in that direction.

'At what?'

He laughed and continued along the front, then stopped and called back, 'You'll soon find out.'

I scoured the beach for whatever it was someone was at, but couldn't see anything out of sorts. Now I can admit to knowing exactly what he meant, of course, but at the time I honestly had absolutely no idea.

I was looking forward to seeing Maureen Treadwell, the other WPC, who I'd met at home in Scarborough, but I didn't bump into her for a few days as we never worked the same shift, and I began to wonder whether she was actually in Redcar at all.

Eventually we met up. She was coming off her shift, on her way out of the door, and I was whizzing by on a bicycle my landlady had lent me, trying desperately to stop my skirt from flying up in the wind and keep my hat on. I very nearly toppled off when I saw Maureen.

'Pam!'

'Hello, Maureen. They told me you were here,' I said, managing to stop the bike and hop off just before hitting the wall of the station.

'Not the easiest mode of transport in a skirt and hat,' she said and we laughed.

'How've you been?' I asked. 'Where are you staying?'

'I'm with two lovely ladies, Pam and June. They had an ad in for a lodger. They're not sisters but sometimes I find it hard to tell them apart. Both have got the same curly hair and they even finish each other's sentences. They also make the most delicious greengage jam on the planet.'

'Sounds wonderful. I can't stop for long. I've got to get in for my shift, and you know what old Ditchburn's like. Such a stickler for punctuality.'

'Isn't he, though? Well, how about a dance, when you

have an evening off, down at the Pier Ballroom? They've got a Mexican night! Can you believe? We should go maybe. We could wear hats!'

The rest of my day was much like the previous, mostly strolling up and down the seafront. I kept an eye out for dogs that matched the description Mrs Trent had given me. There were no telephone calls in on my points, so after a few hours it was back to the station and then home. As I was leaving, climbing onto my bike, Sergeant Ditchburn called after me.

'Miss Rhodes, before you leave. I almost forgot. Can you come in wearing plain clothes tomorrow? Something . . . nice, if you know what I mean. We've got a special job for you.'

Sounds ominous, I thought. 'Of course. What's it all –'
But before I could finish he interrupted me.

'You'll find out the details when you get here. Tony'll be with you so there should be no . . . danger, we hope.'

Danger? What on earth could this job be?

Annie did most of the cooking at my digs, but every now and then Colin would be seized by the desire to cook his signature dish, shepherd's pie.

'It's the only thing I can cook,' he said. 'Other than that I don't cook, I just heat. Milk, eggs, baked beans. That's about it. But I do love making a good old shepherd's pie. The way my mother used to. Her father was a drover. They were seriously poor people. But she always managed it. No matter what.'

'He doesn't like my shepherd's pie,' said Annie, without looking up from the newspaper.

'It's not that I don't like it, as such. I just . . . prefer mine. You don't cut the carrots up properly. And not enough onion. And the gravy. It's all about the gravy. Has to be thick.'

'Whatever you say, dear. I have to sit in here while he's clattering about out there for hours. I tell you, it plays havoc with my nerves. Then he uses every single utensil he can find, and never washes a thing. He'll be the death of me one day.'

I couldn't remember ever having seen my dad in the kitchen, except making the odd cup of tea. He just about knew where the kettle was and that was about it.

'Anyway, there's some left if you want to heat it up.'

I had come in late from my shift, and even though it was nearly bedtime, I eagerly agreed. I never did quite get used to having meals around shift work. It was always either too late or too early for proper food, but you have to eat, don't you? I wolfed the shepherd's pie down. I had to admit it was very tasty.

'So what did you get up to today, love?' Annie asked as we sat round the wireless.

'Walked along the seafront mainly. Past the man with the donkeys. The pier.'

'Not much to it now, is there?' said Colin. 'I remember when it was hundreds of feet long. That was before the war, of course.'

'Really?'

'Yes. Used to stick right out to sea – miles of it, there was.'

'It's only, well, can't be more than fifty feet now, isn't that right?' said Annie.

'Forty-five. The Jerries wanted to land there at one

point during the war, you know. They had it all planned. Then it got damaged beyond repair, terrible business. And that's all that's left, what you see now.'

'How sad,' I said.

'Built in the 1800s originally. The pride of the north.'

'He's got this thing about piers,' said Annie, standing up to go to bed. 'Obsessed.'

The following day, I stood outside the station in my plain clothes, wondering what activity Sergeant Ditchburn had planned for me. I was particularly wondering what he had meant by asking me to wear my 'nice' clothes. I'd chosen a smart blouse and skirt that I usually wore to church, and a light coat, and hoped that would suffice.

'Ah. Here you are. Very good. Tony'll look after you. Don't worry, but we've had reports of this fella flashing, would you believe, in broad daylight, at women in the park. Not a very nice situation, I can tell you. Some of them were quite distressed.'

'My goodness. How horrible. What am I to do then?'

'You're to act as what we call in the business a "decoy". It's nothing to worry about. Just walk up and down a bit, look your best. And we'll see if we can lure the devil from his lair, so to speak.'

When someone says there's nothing to worry about, I always think there must be something very much to worry about.

'Right. What do I do if I . . . see him?'

'Tony here'll be right behind you all the way. Any action from that department, and he'll come in and take control of the situation. You're just there to . . . attract him in, as it were. Like a spider catching a fly.'

The Sergeant, whose demeanour had been entirely serious throughout, had his back to Tony, who was smirking into his hand. By the end of the Sergeant's speech, Tony couldn't help himself, laughing out loud at the bit about the fly.

'What's so funny, Stokes?' said the Sergeant, turning round sharply. 'Women are at risk here. It's a serious business. I put you on it because I thought I could trust you, but I can just as easily take you off the job, you know.'

'Sorry, Sergeant.'

'Right. Good. All in order. Rhodes, just make yourself look like you're having an ordinary stroll. Don't draw attention to yourself. I'm relying on you two to deliver on this one.'

'Yes, Sergeant.'

'It's all right for you,' I said to Tony as we walked away. 'I've never even seen a man's . . . with nothing on.'

'He won't be wearing nothing. I'm sure he'll have a coat. They always do. Anyway, there's a first time for everything.'

I felt around in my coat pocket to make sure I had my whistle. That would be my only form of defence. I stretched my mind back to Sergeant Wooding's ju-jitsu classes. Would any of that come in useful, I wondered. I think there was one move where you could break a man's fingers if he attacked you, but I wasn't sure I fancied that. Then I supposed you could always kick him where it hurts, if it came to it.

'Why do men do things like that. Flashing?' I asked after a while.

'Can't say the urge has ever struck me, I must say. Maybe they're not quite right in the head. Frustrated? Who knows? You get all sorts, these days.'

'Tell me about it,' I said, thinking back to the bestiality case I had read about in Richmond.

When we reached the entrance to the park, we agreed to split up and take different paths.

'You go that way, into the park, and walk down the main drag. I'll come in the side gate and keep a good way behind you.'

'You won't lose sight of me, will you? Promise?'

'You're all right. I've got your back,' he said, and tapped his nose.

Something about Tony gave me the impression he wasn't taking this mission entirely seriously. But I had no choice now. I was the decoy and that was that.

'Keep your eye out for anything . . . suspicious,' I said.

I could feel my hands shaking as I walked away. I felt like a young gazelle being thrown into the lion's den, wide-eyed and petrified. But really, what do I have to fear, I thought? Just a silly old man with nothing better to do than show his bits to a few girls. What harm could he do?

And yet, in those days, flashing was quite shocking. Young women just weren't exposed to that kind of thing; there was no internet revealing everything to everyone, or anything like that. It could really be quite distressing for some people; the fear was it could end up leading to rape or something worse.

I steeled my nerves, strode into the park, and wondered

how you 'make' yourself look like a normal person having a stroll. It all felt very silly and awkward, particularly as I didn't want to walk too fast or I would get to the other side of the park too soon and have to turn back. I stopped for a while and pretended to admire some roses. I sniffed a few, which made me sneeze, then watched a couple of bees as they darted in and out of the petals.

From the corner of my eye, I could see Tony sitting on a bench, pretending to read a newspaper, and I felt reassured that at least he was still there.

An elderly lady came past with two tiny terrier dogs and waited as they sniffed round a lamppost. She smiled at me as I passed.

'Lovely day, isn't it? Summer's well and truly here now.'

'Beautiful,' I said.

'These two practically dragged me out for a walk this afternoon. Wouldn't stop scratching at the door until I brought them here.'

'They're very nice. How old?'

'Just a year. They're twins! Anyway, they keep an old lady happy. If it wasn't for them I'd probably never go out since my Albert died, God bless his soul.'

As she walked off I hoped she wouldn't get the full 'flasher' experience before I could catch up with him. I thought it might finish her off.

I walked a bit further into a slightly wooded area, and the air went suddenly damp and cold. I looked up ahead and caught sight of a strange-looking figure. As the shape grew closer I made out the form of a hunched-over man who was coming right towards me. He looked a little scruffy, perhaps a tramp, with a shabby long coat and greasy hair.

He wasn't that old, only about forty-five, but his stoop and the lines round his eyes made him seem older.

He sniffed and wiped his nose across his sleeve, then stopped for a while just in front of a large oak tree and looked around the park.

I felt for my whistle in my pocket and braced myself. I was almost tempted to cover my eyes, like you would watching a horror film, but I managed to resist, and continued on past, keeping a wary eye on him.

The man bent over, and took several minutes fumbling for his bootlaces.

'Don't want to trip up,' he said. His deep, gravelly voice made me jump. 'That wouldn't do at all.'

'Of course not. Safety first,' I replied, and stopped walking. I was keeping my distance, though.

He stood up and held onto his back for a moment.

'Not as young as I once was,' he said and took a small bottle out of his pocket. 'Doctor's orders.'

I looked up the path and saw Tony watching covertly from behind a tree. Tony looked more like the flasher from that vantage point, I thought.

The man sat down on a bench and leant back with his arm on the rest. He took a large slug from the bottle and looked down at a one-and-a-half-legged pigeon dragging its way across the ground. He reached into his pocket, took out a piece of bread and when it came over to him he started stroking the bird's little head. I could hear him talking with a gentle growl as he fed the injured creature.

'We're the same you and me, aren't we, sir? Lone soldiers.'

I found it hard to believe this odd but kindly character could be the flasher and I left him to it.

After another hour and a half I had exhausted every possible form of leisurely strolling I could muster, and still had nothing of any interest to report. There was no sign of the flasher anywhere, so I met up with Tony back at the entrance and we walked to the station, with a mixture of anticlimax that our mission had failed and relief that I hadn't seen the flasher in action.

'The Sergeant'll be disappointed we didn't come up with the goods. Though can't say I'm sorry we didn't get a ringside view at that particular sideshow,' I said.

'Nothing much we could do anyway,' said Tony, smiling. 'Must be his day off. Although you know what that means, of course. He'll most likely be back at it tomorrow.'

The hours went by quite slowly on the beat in Redcar. Not a lot happened during the day, and when Friday night eventually arrived we were relieved to be going out. Maureen and I, and a few of the lads, were meeting at the Pier Ballroom for a dance.

Tony had got hold of a load of Mexican hats from somewhere, which he produced as we all arrived. A Mexican band had come all the way from a tour in London to play in Redcar. This was in the days before package holidays to foreign locations were the norm, and the whole thing felt very exotic indeed.

'How ridiculous we all look,' I laughed as we walked into the hall.

'That hat actually suits you,' Maureen said. 'Perhaps you should go and live in Mexico.'

The band were all wearing big ponchos and playing a very new kind of music, to our ears at least, with an unusually jumpy beat, accompanied by panpipes and guitars.

'Is that Spanish they're singing in?'

'Yes. I think so. Or is it Portuguese?' asked John.

'No, that's Brazil you're thinking of. That's in South America. Mexico is Central America.'

'I always get my Americas muddled up. I don't know why there are so many Americas.'

The lads all stood in a row in their hats. Steve was good-looking, with dark hair and a freckly nose. He asked me to dance. And then, next to him, there was Malcolm. I hardly noticed him that night, but it wouldn't be long before I did.

Steve was quite a good dancer and an easy talker, and we got on quite well as we shuffled around the floor to the strange Mexican beats.

'There was this bloke at home who went to Mexico once. Said you could buy a house out there for about three quid. Seriously.'

'What would you do with it, though? I mean, isn't it dangerous?' I asked.

'He bought a donkey too. Or was it a mule? What's the difference?'

'Not sure.'

'Anyway. It's not like in the films any more. Cowboy films, and all that. But they do have gunfights. Out in the open sometimes, he said.'

'I've never been abroad, ever. I'd love to one day. My dad goes to Spain and Portugal and things now, with the church. Organizes it himself. They went to Rome in Italy this year. It was so hot you could fry an egg, apparently.'

'We took the boat to Calais once, just for the fun of it,' said Steve as he swung me round. 'My dad made me go and buy him a packet of cigarettes. I was only about nine! I'll never forget. *Un paquet de Gauloises, s'il vous plaît.* I could hardly see over the counter.'

After the dance, Maureen came over with Malcolm and Tony, laughing.

'Look what we found,' she said, holding up her glass. 'Blue drinks! The mind boggles. Must be a Mexican thing.'

'Have you tried them yet?' I asked warily.

'I don't dare. Tony, you try it.'

'Ooh, it's bitter,' he said and scrunched up his face.

'Don't they drink maggots in Mexico or something?' asked Steve.

'Ooh, it makes me shiver to think,' said Maureen. 'Tequila, isn't it?'

'How disgusting. I'm glad we don't do that here! I'll settle for port and lemon any day.'

At the end of the night we all said goodbye, then Steve walked me back to my digs before returning to his room above the station. He was much more lighthearted than Jim had been, and it was a nice relaxing walk back, both of us freely talking and laughing.

'How about the pictures then? Next week?' he said as I put the key in the door.

'Sounds great.'

It was a date.

Some of us were excited the next week as we had been detailed to the Redcar races. That meant getting out of town for a few days, to the racecourse.

'What's it like?' I asked Tony as we walked over. He would be joining me on the shift.

'A lot of horses.'

'Well. I guessed that much.'

'Actually, to tell you the truth, I didn't do the races last year. But it's usually fun when I've been not on duty.'

As we got closer to the racetrack, there were lots of people milling about. Men in cloth caps, some taking bets, scribbling with chalk on long boards and passing around bits of paper. Others held up their binoculars, inspecting the horses, and the women were quite smartly dressed in their best hats and dresses, tottering along in the mud.

As we got nearer, I thought we were about to enter the ground itself, but instead Tony steered me towards a small white van on the edge.

'This is us, I think,' he said, looking around.

'Hoy!' yelled a voice. 'We're over here.'

It was a lad I had met once at HQ. They called in police from all over the area, but I was the only woman.

'I've seen you before.'

'Yes. You were there when I had my photo taken at HQ, I think. With Sergeant Gaunt?'

'That's it. I'm Kevin.'

'Pam.'

'You mash the tea here and serve here, in these mugs. And the sink's here for washing up.'

As I surveyed the scene, I realized to my disappointment that, stuck in this van, we could only just about see the racecourse through a gap in the trees. My job, along with the other PCs, was to make the tea for the officers out in the grounds. We could hear the loudspeaker calling each race, and every now and then the roar of the crowd would swell up, rising and falling as the horses sped around the track.

'Two teas, please,' said a voice through the hatch. I turned round and filled up a mug from the big urn, and watched as the policeman ran back to where he was supervising the crowds in the thick of the action.

'That rain'll cause havoc with the track,' said Kevin as a light drizzle began to fall. It wasn't long before it became heavy rain.

'My father's into racing,' Kevin said. 'I once saw a horse slip so badly its legs nearly split in two.' He demonstrated a mock fall in the tea van, which nearly sent the urn flying. 'Another time a woman – this was before my time – ran right into the tracks. Protesting she was, for some cause, women's rights or something. The vote. You know. Had her head knocked right off. Are you a betting man?' he asked Tony.

'Only the Grand National. I wouldn't want to get hooked. Haven't got the money for it.'

'My mother swears she knows which horse to put her money on. Waits until the horses are all lined up at the starting line. Then she watches carefully, to see which one does his . . . business. And which business is the biggest. And she puts all her money on that horse, quick as she can, before the race starts. Says they'll be lighter and faster. More often than not she's right, you know. She has a real knack for it.'

Just then, the crowd let out an almighty roar, which was followed by an eerie silence. A few policemen began running from different directions, like ants in the distance, and we strained our necks to see what was going on. Gradually we began to hear what had happened from a variety of sources.

'Rider fell at the last jump,' said a young PC who was just walking over to get some tea. 'Lost his grip on the reins, and the animal just reared up. Slipped in the mud. Then the jockey had a heart attack right there on the track.'

'I heard the rider had a stroke,' said another. 'Then fell off. The horse just kept running and won the race on its own. Although it doesn't count, of course.'

We heard a few more variations on the story, including one in which the jockey actually managed to get back on the horse and went on to win the race. But we never did find out what had really happened.

A while later, as we were packing up the tea things, we saw the jockey himself being stretchered off into an ambulance. He looked pale, possibly even unconscious. A little way behind him, a skittish-looking horse, neighing and snorting frantically, was being led away into its box by two stable lads. I wondered whether that would be the end of its track career.

And that, I'm afraid to report, was my one and only glimpse of the action at the Redcar races.

9

The air was shimmering in the heat above the road, and there were streams of people packing out the beach each day as summer hotted up. Some dipped in the sea to cool off from the heat, others just lay stretched out like smoked kippers on the beach, too hot even to speak to one another.

I walked past the donkey man, who smiled out from under a broad-brimmed straw hat. He was red in the face and sweating as he led the animals along the seafront. A little girl was intently trying to maintain her grip on a fast melting ice cream as she clung onto the reins of the smallest donkey, an undertaking which was proving increasingly difficult with every step. The little boy next to her was kicking his animal, trying to get it to go faster, but it just stared straight ahead and plodded on in the heat. As I made my way up and down the promenade, day after day, in my uniform, sometimes I could really identify with those poor beasts.

As I arrived at the pier, one of the lads from the station was approaching from the other direction. We both stopped as we reached the entrance.

'Hello,' I said, 'we've overlapped.'

I hadn't spoken much to Malcolm over these past few weeks. Just the odd greeting here and there. He seemed to be the quiet one, a little offhand the few times we had spoken, so I had it in my head that he was a bit grumpy.

'Afternoon,' he said, putting his hand on the wall of one of the onion-domed brick buildings which marked the way onto the pier, and wiping his forehead. 'Sweltering, isn't it?'

'I know. I just want to put my swimming costume on and dive right into the sea, right now.'

We both stared out across the beach for a while at the hundreds of holidaymakers.

'Look how red that bloke is. Like a big lobster.'

'Where do they all come from, anyway? A month or so ago, this beach was almost empty and now you can't move. Who are they all? That's what I want to know,' said Malcolm.

We stood for a while on the pier, near the ballroom. A pair of elderly ladies arrived next to us. They looked out to sea, sharing a packet of chips.

'Do you think seagulls talk to each other?' asked one of the ladies. 'I mean, what do you think they're saying?'

'If they do it's all probably very mundane, telling each other to go away and things like that most of the time, I would have thought. You know, marking their territories. They're not called seagulls, actually. They're just called gulls. That's a common gull. My Frank's quite the bird-watcher, you know.'

'Really? I thought they were called seagulls. I could have sworn.'

Just then, a huge bird with a big, yellow beak glided down and made a dive right for their chip packet.

'Cheeky! Get away! Did you see that?' she called over to us. 'You should arrest that blessed gull, whatever its name is.'

The gull swooped round, circling above, and seemed to laugh, *squawk squawk*, as it flew away into the distance.

'Hey, do you fancy a dance here one evening?' Malcolm asked, out of the blue.

Well, that was the last thing I'd been expecting. I didn't even think he liked me.

'Um. Well, I'm not really free,' I said quickly, trying desperately to think of an excuse.

'What about the variety show?' he said, almost desperately, as though he couldn't bear to lose. 'It's fun. I suppose. Some comedian, a fat woman who sings, apparently. And some dancers, and . . .'

I looked up at Malcolm as he spoke. I hadn't noticed how clear and blue his eyes were before. And now, with the sun shining on his hair and his lovely complexion, he really did look quite handsome.

'One day I'm going to leave a bottle here with a message in it and see who gets it.' He stared away and out to sea. 'I wonder how far it would go, anyway. It might just end up down in Scarborough or something. Or would it go all the way across and end up somewhere exotic, like Denmark?'

'Yes.'

'What? Scarborough or Denmark?'

'Yes. I'd love to go to the variety show with you,' I said.

'Oh, that. OK. I'll pick you up next Friday then, shall I? Around seven.'

I couldn't figure Malcolm out. One minute he seemed keen as mustard and now he didn't seem to care at all.

As we walked back towards the promenade, everything seemed like it was in glaring, cartoon Technicolor. The sky had never been so blue, the sea never such a rich mix of greens and frothing whites, and the sand was so yellow it seemed to spread like butter out into the sea.

'See you then,' I said, continuing on my beat. He hardly looked back as we went our separate ways.

'So, anyway, there's been another incident and I need you to go and check it out.'

Sergeant Ditchburn's voice had been murmuring on in the background for quite some time but I hadn't been able to concentrate on what he was saying.

'Sorry, Sergeant? What incident?'

'With the dogs. Aren't you listening?'

Everyone was getting hot in the station, and we were all finding it hard to do anything. This was long before the days of air conditioning, and as the day went on the room just got hotter and hotter, like a huge brick oven.

'Sorry. I was distracted.'

'We're all hot. It doesn't mean you have to shirk your duties. Anyway, as I was saying, there's been another report of dangerous dogs. Where these animals are coming from I don't know. Must be something in the water. Up by the park. I need you to go there now and check it out.'

The last time I had been near the park I was in my civvies, acting as a decoy for the flasher. I hoped I wouldn't see him there this time. The Sergeant had given me the location, and as I approached, a gaggle of women were gathered with their children, in deep and earnest discussion.

'Well, I think if we see those animals again we should take matters into our own hands. I know where we can get some arsenic.'

'Jean, really! That's a bit extreme.'

'Well, who else is going to do it? Tell me that?'

'But the poor animals! They would suffer so . . .'

'I agree with Jean. We have to deal with this ourselves now or who knows what might happen?' said another.

As I walked up to them from behind, Jean, the tall woman in thick glasses, swung round.

'Oh, constable! You made me jump. Thank goodness. We've all been beside ourselves.' She broke away from the group and approached me confidingly. 'We were taking the little ones through the park, that is myself, Elsie and her sister Joan. And these two huge animals came running over. One of them went straight for Ruby.'

'Nearly bit her legs right off. Tell her that,' called Joan, trying to get in on the action. 'Would have had them too, if it wasn't for that kind man over there.'

'Ruby? Is that your daughter, madam?' I asked, suddenly very concerned. 'Does she need to see a doctor?'

'My little Ruby. Here,' she said, and produced a shivering creature from behind her legs. It was a little dog, with a white head and a brown body. There was a small scratch on one leg, but otherwise I think it was just in shock. 'He had to prise one of them off the poor creature. The other one – he was the ringleader, I'm sure – he just stood and barked, orders probably. So loud it was, we all had to cover our ears, and the girls were crying. Oh, it was mayhem.'

Over on a bench, a man was sitting quietly. He looked familiar, and then I realized he was the man I had seen feeding that pigeon last time I had been in the park. His hair was even more dishevelled and his clothes were ripped. He had a small grey knapsack underneath the bench, and I wondered for a moment whether he was actually living in the park. Perhaps those were all his worldly belongings. If he was, I might have to move him on. But he seemed so kind and harmless, I didn't think that would be right somehow.

I looked back at the woman who was waiting for my response.

'So can you tell me what happened exactly?' I asked her, taking out my notebook and pencil.

'Well, as I say, these two creatures came out of nowhere, barking their heads off. No owner in sight anywhere. Feral, I wouldn't wonder. Living up in the woods, probably. Like wolves. One was a brown thing. Large, almost like a small horse. The other one was white with black spots. But it all happened so fast. And my poor Ruby bore the brunt of it, poor love. She's only just plucked up the courage to come out at all. She's a bit of a house-dog, really. Then that gentleman over there, he came over and pulled the dogs off. God only knows how he did it, but he did.'

I was about to go and ask the man some questions, and thank him for helping, but when I looked back again, he was gone. Not a trace of the grey knapsack, nothing. It was as though he'd never been there.

After I had gathered all the descriptions, I had a picture of some very strange dogs. According to reports they were brown, but also grey. Tall, fat and skinny, with big ears and small ears; one was as big as a horse, with teeth as sharp as razors, while the other was small and sly and looked more like a long stoat.

How many dangerous dogs are there in this town, I wondered as I walked back. I had yet to see any of them.

*

As I was leaving the station that afternoon, Steve ran out after me.

'What time shall I pick you up later? I've forgotten what we said.'

'What? Oh . . . um . . . seven?'

'Righto. See you then. You hadn't forgotten, had you?'

'Of course not! No. Can't wait.'

All this business with the dogs, and the heat, not to mention Malcolm inviting me to the variety show later in the week, and I had completely forgotten my arrangement with Steve to go to the pictures.

I wasn't sure if it was wrong to be going out with two of the lads in the same week. But we were all just friends, weren't we? And anyway, I wanted to see the film.

I spent the rest of the afternoon lying on the beach, and dipping in and out of the sea. It was nice to be able to enjoy the sun and not be on duty for once. I saw Maureen walk past on the promenade on her beat, and called over to her.

'I'm envious,' she shouted. 'I wish I was out there in my swimming costume too, not up here in this boiling old uniform.'

'Much happening?' I asked.

'Not really. Moved a few cars on. They didn't like it, but what can you do? Hey, do you think we're allowed to eat ice cream on duty? I could kill for one right now.'

'I doubt it. You know what old Ditchburn's like.'

'You're probably right! See you.'

I watched Maureen walk off up the promenade, and felt quite proud to see a fellow policewoman out there on the beat.

The sand was so hot it was burning the soles of my feet, so I had one last dip in the sea to cool off.

Even when it was this boiling, it still took my breath away, going into the icy water. I tried to run in all at once, in a big enormous splash, instead of walking in tentatively, which always seemed like slow torture. A pair of girls around me were half screaming, half giggling, holding their arms up in the air as they trotted in up to their waists and stopped.

'It's too cold!' said one. Then the other one dived in and came out again, choking and laughing.

'Come on, May. It's easy.' She lay back and started kicking the water with her feet.

'Get in, you wimp,' said one of a group of lads. May screamed even more, before taking the final dive in.

I lay on my back and floated for a while, listening to their screams of laughter and looking up at the gulls whirling above against the clear blue. A group of younger lads came splashing by, shouting and chasing a big blow-up ball. I lost my balance and went underwater for a moment, spluttering on seawater, salty in the back of my throat. But I didn't care. It was bliss. Eventually I stood up and shook out my hair. Where had the time gone, though? I suddenly realized I only had an hour before Steve was turning up.

When I got back to my digs, my hair had caked dry with salt and my skin felt fresh and warm. I loved that feeling of having been in the sea on one of the few really hot days of the year. As I walked through the door, I imagined I had been stranded on a desert island for years, and was just returning home to my family, who might not even recognize me, I was that sunbaked and wild.

'Had a lovely swim, did you?' said Annie. 'I try to go every morning. No matter what the weather. One morning it was so cold – ooh, must have been January. And when I came out my feet had turned completely green.'

'That's what keeps her so young,' said Colin, leaning out from his chair.

'What, green feet?'

'I only go in when it's really hot,' I said. 'I just wish I could spend more time doing that, and less time working!'

I ate my dinner quickly, barely stopping to breathe, and just had time to run upstairs, brush my hair and get changed. I wasn't sure how smart to be to go to the pictures with Steve, so I went for fairly casual and didn't even wear any jewellery. When he knocked on the door, I felt a slight nervous tingle.

'You look nice. Glowing or something,' he said.

'Thanks. That's what the sun does for you.'

I said goodbye to Annie and Colin and we walked off towards town.

'What have you been up to this afternoon, then?' I asked.

'I had to take my old lady out. My mother. She's not well. Cancer.'

'Oh. I'm sorry.'

'Yeah, well. She's all right. She just keeps going really. But she's not that capable any more. So I take her to the shops. Get her things, food and so on. But let's not talk about that tonight.' He bounded off up the road like a greyhound after a hare. 'Let's enjoy ourselves. Hey, can you do this?' He swung round a lamppost, all the way, on one arm.

'No. You're crazy. Lucky I'm not on duty. I'd arrest you for that.'

'I don't know. Sometimes I just feel like I've got so much energy I could run right the way round the world in a matter of seconds. It's like I'm about to burst. Maybe I should try to climb St Paul's Cathedral, or Everest or something.'

While he had been speaking, Steve had hoisted himself halfway up the lamppost. He hung there for a moment, jumped down again with a springy bounce and leapt up like a giant rabbit.

'You need tying down, you do.'

'That's what Mam always says. She never could control me. I was always out jumping off roofs and all sorts. That's why they made me join the police. Said it would drum some sense into me. Never did, though.'

'Well, you'll have to sit still at the pictures. I want to see this film.'

'Scout's honour.' He saluted with three fingers.

The film was about a boxer, played by John Wayne, who goes to his home town in Ireland after accidentally killing a man in the boxing ring. It was in colour, which was a real treat. Steve didn't fidget that much either. But more than that, I enjoyed just spending time with him. His energy was infectious and I came away smiling but slightly exhausted, as though I had spent the night with a very excitable puppy, who I would now be relieved to shut away in the kitchen for the night.

'See you back at the grindstone, then,' he said, as we neared my house.

'See you then, then.'

And with that, he ran off down the street, whistling loudly.

I woke up in the middle of the night as a huge crack of thunder rattled around the whole house. A few seconds later the room was illuminated: for a moment I caught sight of the mantelpiece, Annie's selection of porcelain shepherdesses, the old chair with my dressing gown slung over it and the Victorian cupboard, so large and foreboding, who could tell what was inside it. This was swiftly followed by another enormous *boom*, which shook my bones. Outside, some neighbourhood dogs started barking. Then the rain came, showing no mercy, as if a giant gardener in the heavens had just tipped the contents of his slosh bucket right on top of us. I was on the beat in just a couple of hours and I wasn't looking forward to it.

I couldn't get back to sleep after that, so I tried to read a book. I gave up on that and then just looked out into the dark at the rain splashing against the windowpane. In the garden next door, a skinny brown dog was chained up to a railing, howling at the top of its lungs.

When I got up at five a.m., the rain hadn't abated, although the temperature had finally dropped, which was something of a relief. As I crept down the stairs, I could hear Colin snoring like a felled animal. For a moment he stopped breathing altogether. I waited on the stairs to make sure he was still alive and then he let out an almighty spluttering growl.

I ate some toast, then grabbed my raincoat and stepped outside. I hadn't seen Redcar in the pouring rain yet. We'd had a few showers, but this was something else. Dawn had broken already, but huge dark clouds swept across over-head and kept out most of the daylight. Bert, the milkman, was running from house to house with his bottles, trying to shield his head from the rain.

'Morning, constable. You should have stayed in bed,' he said as he ran back to his van to fetch Annie and Colin's bottles.

'I wish I could have,' I told him, putting on my hat and looking up at the dismal sky.

Bert had not long moved from using a cart that his dad had used before him, pulled by his old horse, Jemima, to a new electric milk float.

'It might keep me dry, but it's not the same. No person-ality, if you know what I mean. Now all Jemima does is sit in the field, poor thing. I see her looking sadly at me as I leave. Why can't I come? she says with her eyes. Mary says I should get rid of her but I never could. They make glue out of them, you know. Not on my watch.'

I said goodbye to Bert, then walked as quickly as I could all the way to the station, splashing through puddles as they formed along the roads. When I got in, Sergeant Ditchburn sent me right out onto the promenade again.

'The rain won't keep people away. I still need you out there, manning the place,' he said.

For a few hours I was literally the only person there, along with a collection of gulls scavenging on yesterday's picnics. After a while, a couple of old men turned up with two young lads and started fishing. They sieved the sands for cockles and worms, baited up their lines and waded out into the sea.

By about eleven o'clock the sun was blazing down and

a trickle of eager holidaymakers, undeterred, made their way onto the beach, spread out their towels and produced their obligatory buckets, spades and hampers.

Then, as if by some stroke of curious magic, the clouds parted and silver streaks of sun shone out again, drying everything up in an instant. As people began to fill up the beach again, cars arrived in their dozens, great growling things, and started parking all over the place; on verges, and up on pavements. I rapped on the window of one vehicle which was parked too close to a corner.

'Excuse me, could you move your vehicle from this dangerous . . .'

As I was asking him, rather sternly, to move on, the window wound down and there inside, with a big smile on his face, was Father Reilly, all the way from my church in Richmond.

'Now, you wouldn't make a man of the cloth move, would you?'

'Oh, I had no idea it was you or I would have been more . . . polite.' I flushed a bright scarlet and wished the pavement would swallow me up right there and then.

'You're only doing your job. I don't expect the special treatment. I'm up here visiting my sister. She's had a loss. You know. And I couldn't find a place to park. The husband. Awful business.'

'I'm sorry. How is everyone back home?'

'Oh, you know. The same. We plod on, doing God's good work. Anyway. I best be off, eh?' and he gave me a little wink, before starting his engine. 'We'll be seeing you again soon, I hope,' he called.

'Oh yes, not long now. Take care now, Father.'

After that I was too nervous to move anyone else on, in case I got any more shocks, so I walked on to my next point and waited to see if any calls came through.

As I stood in the phone box, I thought how nice it had been to see someone from Richmond. I realized now that I missed them all, and the little town; I had quite put it all out of my mind these past few months. It had been nice being by the sea, and Annie and Colin were wonderful. But I didn't have as many duties here and it was beginning to get a bit repetitive. I even found myself missing Sergeant Hardcastle, who in my memory seemed like a gentle giant compared to old Ditchburn.

I had just a few weeks before the season would be over. Before that, I had the small matter of my outing with Malcolm to the variety show on the pier. For some reason my stomach was in knots that afternoon, and I began to wish I was meeting Steve instead. He was so easygoing, and I never felt nervous at all with him. But, for some reason, Malcolm scared me a bit. I never knew what he was going to be like. Sometimes he was up and jolly, and then the next he was steeped in a kind of intangible, silent anger. As though the world was a bad place and there was no escaping its dark forces.

I was walking through the corridor at the police station when Malcolm walked past, as if he was in a hurry.

'So, see you tonight then,' I said, smiling.

'What? Oh yes. See you then,' he said distractedly, and kept walking. I began to wonder if I was making a terrible mistake.

After dinner that evening, I confided in Annie as she washed up and I dried the dishes.

'Some men are like that,' she said. 'One minute they're up, the next down. It's the war. It comes down through the generations, father to son and so on. The Great War, I mean. My brother was the same.'

'But it's funny because I'm quite drawn to him. Not like thunderbolt stuff, but he's kind of enigmatic. Like a mystery I want to solve. Do you know what I mean?'

'Well, I can't say Colin was ever exactly enigmatic. But he made me smile. And that was good enough for me.'

There was a sharp knock at the door.

'Well. It's too late now anyway, love. He's here,' said Annie. 'You look lovely. I'm sure you'll have a grand time.'

As I opened the door, my stomach had tied itself into a thousand knots.

'Hello.' Malcolm smiled, a beaming broad smile.

My stomach relaxed a little. At least he's in a good mood, I thought.

'Are you up for some fun tonight then?' he asked quietly, almost shyly.

'I am if you are.'

The variety show was a strange affair. First there was a very small Welsh comedian in a black wig, John Bach, he called himself, who told a string of jokes in quick succession, so fast I could hardly hear a word he said. Then a few dancers came on, with feathery headdresses, and then a woman with a huge hat and a small ukelele sang some songs about how useless her husband was. All the women in the audience laughed uproariously at this.

Every time I looked over at Malcolm, he had a kind of taut expression on his face. As if he was finding it hard to stay sitting there for that long. He only laughed once, very loudly, at a joke about a man falling down some stairs.

When we walked back along the seafront, the sun was just setting, the most glorious sunset I had ever seen, or ever seen since, in fact. I'll never forget it. There were so many colours, it was as if an artist had decided it would be his last ever work, and he had to use up every last bit of paint in this final explosive statement.

'Nice, isn't it?' said Malcolm, staring intently ahead.

'Very.'

'Almost beyond words.'

And it was nice, if that's enough of a word for it. But somehow Malcolm didn't seem happy, even set against that glorious scene.

After a while we walked back towards my digs. We said very little most of the way. As I was about to say goodbye, and was getting my key out of my pocket, Malcolm opened his mouth. For a moment nothing came out, then a small voice.

'Do you . . . ? I mean . . . Can I visit you? When you go back to Richmond? I'd like to. If you would.'

I waited for a moment. This felt like a kind of turning point. One where, if you make the wrong decision, you might regret it for ever.

'Yes. I would,' I smiled, but I was making it up. Life, I mean. Making up life on the spot, there and then. I suppose there are no answers, I thought, no right and wrong. It's all one big improvisation. We do what we do. And then that's that. Curtain down.

*

By the final week at Redcar, I couldn't wait to get back to Richmond. For starters, I was finding it hard to be around Steve now. I liked him a lot. In fact, I'd never felt so relaxed and happy than when I was around him. But somehow that wasn't quite enough. I felt bad, but in the end I hardly spoke to him again, and then, one day in the corridor I blanked him completely. He looked back sadly, but I was relieved the next day, because I saw him leaning on a wall, talking to Maureen. Steve was never down for long.

'Thank you for all your efforts, Rhodes,' said Sergeant Ditchburn, nodding his head. 'It's been a pleasure.'

Well, that was a surprise too, as I never thought Ditchburn liked me that much. Maureen was just going on shift as I was leaving; it was her last day too, and we wouldn't see each other again.

'Thanks again for all you did. When I was starting out. I honestly don't think I'd be where I am if it wasn't for your help,' she said.

'I'm sure you would have done just fine without me,' I told her.

Malcolm walked me back to my digs.

'So I'll come to Richmond then. We've got some friends with a farmhouse nearby. I can stay there.'

'Fine. Great. Lovely,' I said. When I went inside, my heart was beating so fast I thought it might give up with the effort.

'We'll be sad to lose you, love,' said Annie, as I stood in the hall with my bag all packed and ready to leave. 'It's not often we have a young face around here.'

Before I left, I had one question I had been meaning to ask all summer. I finally plucked up the courage.

'Was there a reason you never had any children yourself? I just wondered,' I asked cautiously, not wanting to offend.

After a while Annie looked up.

'We did try, but . . . well, we did have one. Little Norman. But he only lived a few hours. I held him for a while, like a little monkey he was. All furry. But there was nothing they could do. He never even opened his eyes. Colin was inconsolable. Just wouldn't accept it. I've never seen him like that. I thought, I can't do this again. The loss. And we never mentioned it again.'

'I'm so sorry. I had no idea.'

'I said to myself, there's no room for dwelling in this life. And we'll meet Norman in the next. We get along just fine, the two of us, as we are.'

She inhaled and brushed down her apron, then went into the kitchen for a moment and came back with a small package.

'Anyway. You take care. I made you these, for the journey. Some of my best apple cake, and some sardine sandwiches. Should keep you going. Don't eat it all in the first five minutes, though.'

'Thank you so much. I can't thank you enough for being so kind.'

'Oh, you're off,' said Colin, coming in. He had been out in the garden sweeping. He packed his pipe tight with tobacco, then put it in his mouth, and shook my hand. 'Do visit again, won't you? If nothing else, it's nice to have someone to keep the wife busy.'

'Cheeky!' said Annie.

'Thank you both for everything,' I said. Then Annie

gave me a bear-like, all-encompassing hug, before pushing me through the door.

'Now, you'll miss the bus if you hang around any longer. Off you go, lass.'

I thought I saw a little tear in the corner of her eye, and then the door shut. As I walked off down the street I looked back to see if they were waving through the window, but they had gone.

Once I was on the bus I felt all excited, as though I was going back and starting a new life in Richmond again. The station had arranged for me to live in new digs, with a new family, so it would be exciting finding out who that would be. And Malcolm would be visiting me in a few weeks. I felt like I had grown up suddenly, and the world seemed like a newly clear place, full of possibilities.

Outside the bus, the countryside whizzed by. I changed buses twice before the lanes and farmsteads gradually began to look familiar again. We passed by Pemberton's farm, and then Joe McGregor's; I could just make him out, with his pigs, sloshing buckets around. That means we're nearly home, I thought.

I had eaten the sandwiches already, but saved the cake until I couldn't wait any longer. Annie had a secret ingredient, she said, which made it irresistible. Finally, I opened it up and savoured every mouthful with its rich, appley flavour, finishing it just as the bus came to a stop outside Richmond town hall. I was back.

10

'Did I miss much?' I walked into the office and plonked my suitcase down on the floor.

'Rhodes,' said Sergeant Shaw. 'How nice to see you. Well. Can't say that much has happened really. Oh, we did have a leaky pipe in one of the cells one night. That was quite an adventure. We had to move out the prisoners for a whole night, and keep them all in one cell, while it was fixed. Otherwise, much the same as usual.'

The other WPC, Jeanette, came in with Sergeant Hardcastle. They were in deep discussion about something.

'Ah, good. You're back,' Hardcastle said. 'Timely. Jeanette here has just given me some news.'

She held up her hand, and there on her finger was a large, shiny engagement ring. Blimey, I thought. That didn't take long.

'So she'll be loving us and leaving us in a few months.'

'Congratulations,' I said as she showed me the jewel.

'Yes. It all happened so fast. But I know he's the one. He got down on one knee and everything.'

'Oh, by the way, I have the address of your new digs here somewhere,' said Sergeant Shaw, digging around among the papers on his desk. 'A Mrs Pritchard. On Beechfield Road. You might as well go up there now.' He handed me the piece of paper. 'But don't get too settled.

First thing tomorrow, I've got a job for you up at Durham Jail. So be bright and early and ready for action.'

I arrived at my digs with a feeling of trepidation. Over the past year I had felt like a nomad, moving from house to house. Hopefully this would be the last move, for a while at least.

My new landlady, Caroline, was older than Janet. She was in her early forties, and I think a little better off. She lived with her husband, Terence, in one of the new houses at the top of town. It was a lot bigger than Janet's house, a semi-detached, and they had a big garden at the back full of flowers. There were even a few cars on their street. Where Janet had always seemed a little flustered, Caroline was the epitome of calm. When she first opened the door, the whole house smelled of scent.

'You must be Pamela? I must say, we are so honoured to be helping out the police. When they rang I thought, how lovely, to have a policewoman in the house. She must have lots of stories. Come in, come in and let's take your things up.'

'You've got a lovely house,' I said as we walked up the carpeted stairs.

'This is Lily's room.' She pointed. 'And this is Katy's.'

'How old are they?'

'Twelve and fourteen. It's gone so quickly, I can't tell you. And we won't go in here,' she said, shutting the door to her and her husband's bedroom. 'I haven't tidied up properly or anything. And this is yours.'

My room was very clean and sparse, with no ornaments, just a lovely vase of freshly picked blue flowers on the desk, a carriage clock and neat white bed linen. On the wall were a few little watercolours of flowers and country scenes.

'I like to dabble,' said Caroline, looking at the paintings.

'Oh, you did these? They're beautiful. That one's the castle, isn't it?'

'It's so lovely to paint. All that stone, and the wildlife there. And the river too. I go up there when I get time. Which isn't very often. But it's a bit easier now that the girls are getting older. My father-in-law makes the frames. Ooh, the girls will be home from school soon. They'll be so excited to meet you. Get yourself settled and then you must come down for a cup of tea.'

I sat on yet another new bed, and looked out of the window at the street below. Children were coming home from school and playing games on the street, laughing and chattering to each other. Some were skipping or playing hopscotch, others were kicking a football. It felt like a nice friendly neighbourhood.

When I got downstairs, two young girls were sitting at the table in their school uniforms. Their mother busied about, bringing out some hot buttered teacakes and putting a big red teapot in the middle of the table.

'Katy, Lily, this is Pamela. She'll be staying with us for a while.'

'Hello. Pleased to meet you,' said the younger girl to me, and then turned back to her mother. 'Mrs Hirst gave half the class the slipper today.'

'Oh dear. What for?'

'It was a horrible dirty old slipper too. Because someone let in a cat. And then no one would admit to it. It just sat there and licked its paws. And a window was open, so someone must have opened it.'

'I'm sure that woman enjoys hurting children.'

'When I was in her class, she used to give us the ruler every day, whatever we did,' said Katy, trying to better her sister's story.

'You never told me that.'

'Well, she did.'

As Katy spoke she examined her teacake, picking out the raisins one by one, before placing them carefully at the side of the plate.

'I thought you liked those. I put them in especially.'

'I've gone off them. I can't help it. They remind me of dead insects.'

'What can you do?' Caroline said to me, sighing and clearing away the plates. 'It can never be too soon, getting these two off my hands, I can tell you. I've a good mind to marry you both off to the butcher's sons tomorrow.'

'Mam!' they said simultaneously, clearly appalled by the notion.

'Well. You'd never want for sausages.'

When I got to the station in the morning, we had inspection with Sergeant Cleese. I had forgotten how rigorous they were at Richmond. No room for anything out of place. There had been none of that in Redcar, where I had hardly seen any of the officers in charge.

'You might have been away, Rhodes, on the seafront, but we run a tight ship here. Those shoes aren't nearly shiny enough,' Cleese said as he strolled up and down the line.

The men had to present their 'appointments': truncheon in one hand, handcuffs in the other. I didn't have to show anything.

'Right. Cosgrove and Rhodes, I've got a job for you. They're bringing in a woman, needs driving up to Durham Jail from court this morning. You think you can manage that between you?'

'Yes, Sergeant.'

The woman was brought out of the cell and put in the station car, to be taken to the jail.

'Do you know what she did? To be going to Durham?' I asked before we got in the car.

'Murdered her husband, maybe? Mrs Slater's her name. I don't know her. She's not from Richmond.'

'Blimey.'

'Actually I think it was theft. But you never know . . .'

The woman was wearing a brown cardigan and skirt, with her hair in a neat bun. She wore small spectacles and didn't look at all like my expected vision of a female prisoner. She didn't look up as Bill guided her into the back seat, and we stood outside for a moment.

'You wouldn't think it to look at her, would you?' I said. 'Murder or theft or whatever . . . She looks so ordinary, like you might see her on the bus or anywhere.'

'I suppose. But then what do murderers and thieves look like? She does look like that woman who works in the library, though. Wouldn't say boo to a ghost, that one. She won't last five minutes up at Durham,' said Bill as we got into the car.

Every now and then I looked at the unlikely criminal in the back seat next to me, but she didn't speak the whole way. It looked as though the court case, and the whole affair, had drained the life right out of her, and this was just a shadow-woman.

When we got to Durham Jail we walked through the imposing main gates.

'We'll take her from here,' said a female prison officer and took her off down the corridor towards the cells.

Bill handed over the paperwork, as though we were making a goods delivery. I watched as the officer took her through a giant steel door, which slammed immediately shut behind them.

'Fancy a mug of tea, up at Scotch Corner?' said Bill as we got back into the car.

We would often stop at the transport café on the side of the road for a cuppa after making trips like this.

'Traffic's terrible today,' he said as we climbed towards Ferryhill, on the way up to the café.

Suddenly, behind us, there was a loud bang and a horrible crunching of metal on metal.

'Flippin' heck! What was that?' he said, and stopped the car, narrowly missing the one in front. He pulled off to the side and we swerved to a halt in the verge.

'It's an accident,' he said, opening the door, almost falling out onto the road.

'Bad one?'

'Not sure yet.'

I scrambled out of the car too, and surveyed the scene behind us. The fronts of two vehicles had been mangled; one had both the headlights completely smashed, and the other was buckled up, with the bumper coming off.

'Must have crashed head on,' shouted Bill as he ran over.

Traffic was starting to build up on the road in both directions but we had to get to the passengers before we could deal with that.

'Can you sort out these, while I go and try to get hold of Durham?'

'Sure,' I answered, and felt for my notebook and pencil, tape measure and first-aid pack.

I yanked open one of the car doors. Inside was an elderly man and two women dressed all in black. They were both sitting staring straight ahead, in shock. The man in the front seat had a small cut on his cheek where he had been flung forward and hit the dashboard; his hat was in his lap and he had a pipe in his hand. In the back, the two women sat with their hats all askew, looking stunned.

'We've just been to a funeral,' said one of the women with a quavering voice.

'Are any of you hurt?' I asked, but they didn't answer. I suddenly saw a great shadow behind me, and the looming figure of a man spoke in a very gruff voice.

'Can I help, officer? I saw everything from up in my cab.'

I looked up and saw his vehicle, a huge lorry parked up behind us. 'British Road Services' it said along the side.

'Thanks. You're a godsend. Well, let's get these lot out, and check the next car.'

We helped the three funeral-goers out of the car and sat them on the grass verge, huddled together in their mourning finery.

In the next car, a young couple were getting anxious. They had come off slightly worse. The woman had hit her head on the dashboard quite badly and there was a bruise forming already. The man had a cut on his hand where he had caught it in the steering wheel.

'I don't know where they came from,' said the man. 'One minute we were driving along and then they were on our side of the road, heading straight for us. There was nothing I could do.'

'Let's get everyone out first, and we can take it from there,' I said.

I looked back at the traffic building up along the road. Cars wound their way down the hill, some beeping their horns, and people were getting out, straining to see what had happened.

'You were all lucky, if you can call it that,' said the lorry driver. 'I saw it all. Could have been much worse if you'd been going any faster. You get a lot of accidents up here. Bit of a black spot. Something should be done about it really.'

Out of nowhere, a woman in a blue coat appeared with mugs of tea. I couldn't work out where she had come from, as there were no houses that I could see, but the hot drink was very welcome.

I dug out the first-aid kit from my pocket and dealt with the injuries as best I could. I wrapped up the older man's arm in a small bandage. It had started bleeding a little where he had caught it on the door.

'I don't know what happened, officer. I honestly don't.' He was still shaking from the shock as I pinned the bandage on. 'Did I do something wrong? I'm a very good driver usually. But I'm just not all here today. We've been at my sister's funeral, you see. On our way to her house now. Everyone will be wondering.'

'I'm sorry about your sister. Don't worry. My colleague's in contact with Durham, and I'm sure they'll get you where you need to go.'

'Hello, there! My wife feels sick. She doesn't look at all well,' said the driver of the other car. 'She's pregnant. I'm worried it might be the baby.'

'Don't worry. We'll get her to a hospital as soon as the others arrive.' I tried to sound as calm as possible.

Once everyone was settled, and drinking the tea that the woman in the blue coat kept supplying from her mystery source, I thought I'd better get on to clearing the traffic. It had built up quite a way in both directions by that time.

'Will you be OK here for a minute, while I sort this traffic out?' I asked the lorry driver.

'No problem. I'll keep them all talking,' he said, and started to make them smile with a few jokes.

I managed to direct the cars using the hand signals I had learnt at Bruche and practised every market day in Richmond. I tried to keep my arms out as straight as possible, as we'd been taught, and I was surprised at how easily it all came to me in the heat of the moment. After about ten minutes, I had cleared away most of the backlog, directing the cars one way and then the other, building up a system to get them round the obstacles. When Bill finally arrived back, behind his car were two Durham police cars.

'Thanks, constable. We'll take over now,' said one of the officers who got out. 'You seem to have handled it all very well anyway. Anything we should know about?'

He had an official and brisk air about him, as though he did this kind of thing as easily as brushing his teeth.

'I patched up a few cuts and bruises, but the lady over there probably needs to get to a hospital. She's expecting. A bit shaken up. Cut on her head.'

'I saw the whole thing, officer. That's my lorry back there,' said the British Road Services lorry driver, edging his way forward eagerly.

'Very good. If you could stay that would be great,' he said to the lorry driver, then turned to me and Bill. 'Right. We'll start taking measurements and notes then. You've been very helpful. Lucky you were here. But we can take over. You should get back to your station.'

Bill and I got back into the car as the Durham officers began surveying the scene. We drove back in surprised silence most of the way home, leaving the wreckage behind us. I was thinking about the people in the cars, wondering who they all were, and how fate had brought them all together like that, at the side of the road. This car fad, I thought, was proving dangerous.

On the road behind the police station in Richmond was a racing stables. That's something you don't see much in town centres any more. One morning, as I walked up Goal Bank past the stables, I stopped to look at the race-horses for a moment. They stamped their feet and snorted, their glossy coats shining in the sun.

'Lovely, aren't they?' Sergeant Hardcastle came up behind me on his way into the station.

'Yes. So big. Do you think they're happy in there?'

'Well. Perhaps they'd prefer to be wild on the moors. Who knows? But they look well kept enough. And they don't have to look far for food and a bed.'

'I suppose so.'

One of the horses snorted again, as though in answer, though I wasn't sure what his answer actually was.

'Oh, by the way, I'm glad I saw you. We've had a call from Startforth station. About a young girl who's a funny shape – unusually big, you know, for her age. Only thirteen years old. They've asked us to go and take a look.'

'Oh? What's the problem then?'

'Between you and me, we think she might be pregnant, but we can't speculate. I need you to come with me to see the family.'

We took the car that afternoon and drove out to Bowes, which was just about in our area. We were driving through a winding country lane when we heard a clanking and ringing of bells from just ahead of us. A large red fire engine came round the corner.

'Someone's left toast under the grill or something!' said Hardcastle, as he swerved to make way. The engine just about squeezed past, and the fireman gave us a wave from his cabin as he sped on.

'So what happened with this girl then?' I asked.

'We're not sure yet. That's what we've to find out from Mrs Dixon, that's the mother. Not sure what she knows.'

We passed the village sign and drove into Bowes, past a small church and a little post office on the corner.

'Here it is. The one with the yellow door, they said.'

It was a quiet village that looked straight out of the seventeenth century. Picturesque cottages with thatched roofs, hardly a car in sight. It looked as though no one was actually living here and it was just a model village or the picture on a biscuit tin. But as we walked up the Dixons' path and to the yellow front door, I did see a couple of curtains twitching in neighbouring front rooms, as the locals kept a beady eye on us. When she opened the door, the woman looked genuinely surprised to see the police on her doorstep.

'Has something happened?'

'That's what we're here to find out, Mrs Dixon,' said the Sergeant.

'Oh? Well, in you come, then. Sorry, I would have tidied if I'd known. Or made cake.'

'Not at all. We're just here to do our business. No need for any fuss.'

'Well, let me get you a cup of tea at least.'

She came back a few minutes later with a large tray covered in tea and biscuits. As she sat back down, I could see she was on edge, fiddling with a chain round her neck.

'It's a matter of some sensitivity, Mrs Dixon,' the Sergeant began. 'We wanted to talk to you and your daughter about some rumours. Have you heard any rumours? About your daughter?'

'What about my daughter?'

'Why she's . . . larger than usual?'

I was beginning to wonder how many ways the Sergeant would come up with of broaching the difficult subject.

'What!' She nearly spat out her tea. Then she laughed a little. 'Larger than usual? It's puppy fat. Is that really a police matter? With all due respect, Sergeant.'

'Perhaps.'

Mrs Dixon collected herself and began sipping her tea

again. The door creaked slightly as a young girl in a pretty blue dress walked into the room. She was small for her age, but with a chubby face and a small pot-belly visible through the dress.

'Here she is. Bella, love, come and sit here, would you?'

'Hello, Bella,' I said.

She looked back at us slightly stunned, then a little sulky, then at her mother for an explanation.

'We just want to ask the girl some questions, Mrs Dixon, if you'll permit that?'

'What? I really don't understand what this is all about. Why do you want to talk to my daughter? You can see she's just a child.'

'That's exactly the reason we need to talk to her. I think it might be best if you and I leave the room, just for a moment, while PC Rhodes here has a chat with your daughter.'

'Well, I'll put the kettle on again then, I suppose, if you like, but . . .' Mrs Dixon got up reluctantly, and left Bella with me in the living room.

We sat there in silence for a while. I wasn't sure what to ask.

'Can you tell me who your friends are, at school? Do you have many friends?'

'My best friend is Lucy Trotter. And Charlotte. I used to be friends with Maureen Barts but she . . . we don't get on any more,' she said.

'Any friends who are boys?' I asked brightly.

She reddened. 'Why? I mean . . . I suppose. What's . . . ? There's Tom Griffin, and Roger — I don't know his surname. He's older.'

'And did you do anything with any of these boys?'

'No!' she said quickly.

Silence.

Then she said, 'Well ... we did try it out once. The birds and the bees thing, that we learnt in class.'

She seemed to be relaxing a little now that Sergeant Hardcastle was out of the room.

'Really. What did that involve?'

'Nothing. Just that. We tried it out. What we learnt in Mrs Jones's class.'

I had never faced a situation like this, with a child, talking about such a subject. I wondered who was more embarrassed: her or me. I put my hat to one side and took out my statement sheet. She just stared back at me with enormous blue eyes, and fiddled with an ornament in the shape of a horse that was sitting on the table.

'So you have a few friends who are boys, then?'

'Yes. We all do,' she said, her elbows on the table. She looked a little bored now.

'Tell me more about when you tried it out. The birds and the bees. What exactly did you try?'

'We tried it out,' she said again.

'What?'

'*It*. You know. What they told us. In the shed.'

'Go on.'

'Mrs Jones. She showed us pictures of how to do it. So some of us, we tried it out.' Then she looked a bit cross at having to sit here and talk about all this, and clammed up again.

'Can you tell me what you tried out, exactly?'

She paused for a while, and looked up, then back at me.

'It wasn't for long. Just to see. You know. What it was like. It was horrible, anyway. It hurt when the boys, when Roger and . . .'

'Who was there while you tried it out? Just you and . . . Roger, is it?'

'Oh no. There were a few of us. Me and Charlotte and three boys. Roger, he's fourteen. The others were in my class. It was during the dinner hour, in the shed. I didn't think anything bad would happen.'

'Did anyone make you do it, Bella?'

'No. We all decided. It was funny . . . at first. Then . . . not very nice. Then later I was sick. I thought I was just ill. I thought I was just getting fat. Puppy fat, Mam said. You'll have to tell, won't you then, if I'm going to have a real live baby?'

'Well, let's wait and see, shall we? What the doctors say.'

After I had finished talking to the girl, I read her statement back to her.

'Anything you want to add or change?' I asked.

She sighed and looked at me.

'No. That's all.'

I opened the door and ushered her mother and the Sergeant back in.

'We've had a little talk, and I'm sure she'll tell you what happened at the school. Won't you, Bella?'

Mrs Dixon sat back, bewildered, as her daughter told her what had happened in the school shed. She'd really had no idea why we were questioning her daughter.

'And so I think I might be having a baby, Mam,' said Bella finally.

Her mother was so shocked she couldn't speak, and

looked as though she wanted to burst into tears and hug the girl all at the same time. We told Mrs Dixon it was up to her what they did next, and she said she'd take her to the doctors first thing in the morning, to confirm things either way.

It would be up to her whether to press charges in court, but most likely the lad who was fourteen would be held responsible as the others were younger. Bella would have to have the baby, as abortion was against the law, but of course they'd never know for sure who the father was.

We left the Dixons' house and got in the car. 'A little knowledge can be a dangerous thing, eh, Rhodes?' said Sergeant Hardcastle.

I noticed the curtains twitching again as the police car pulled away from the sleepy village of Bowes.

It was all change at Richmond. Jeanette was leaving, off to get married to her new soldier boyfriend. I hadn't seen much of her, really, and would hardly notice she was gone. We also had a new addition to the station, a police cadet called Charles. He was a tall seventeen-year-old lad, fresh-faced and keen as mustard. He would help out in the office, and was learning what he could from Sergeant Shaw, with a view to joining the police himself when he was old enough.

'Shaw's got something for you. He asked me to give it to you,' said Charles as I walked into the office one day.

'Oh, hello. Running the station now, are you?'

'No.' He looked a little hurt. 'Just trying to help.'

'Don't worry. I'm joking. What is it then?'

'Oh . . . umm . . .' He fumbled about on the desk for a while. 'I had it here. Oh yes, an address. You're to go and tell a lady her father died. Sounds grim. Last night, in his sleep.'

'Oh, that's sad.'

'The lady's address was in the occurrence book. She hasn't got a phone. So you have to go round there personally, Sergeant Shaw says.'

I took the address from Charles and headed out. This was a new one for me. I'd never delivered a message like this before. I rehearsed it in my head all the way there. How should I start?

'I'm so sorry to say . . .' That was such a cliché. I didn't want to sound too sad, right from the off, that would worry her. How about, 'I have some news for you. You might want to sit down'? No, too foreboding. Oh, I'm sure I'll think of something, I told myself.

Eventually I found the place, number 37, up a narrow alley near the marketplace. I knocked and a woman peeped cautiously round the door, her hair in curlers.

'Mrs Jackson?' I asked, looking down at the name scribbled on the piece of paper.

'Yes. That's me,' she said, opening the door wider.

'I have some news for you. Can I come in?'

'Of course. I don't get many visitors. That's why I'm always a bit, you know, careful.' She smiled. 'Is everything OK?'

I had tried not to put too much gravity in my voice, so I could get her seated and comfortable before letting her know the tragic news, but now she had put me on the spot.

'Yes. Well, no, I mean. Let's sit down, shall we?'

We walked through a dingy hallway, which looked like nothing had changed there in at least fifty years. The skirting was thick with dust, and there was dark wallpaper with sooty roses on it all along the hall. There was a rich musty odour pervading the place, it smelled to me like a combination of sweetcorn and stale cabbage.

'Let's sit at the table. Can I get you anything? Tea?'

'No, don't trouble yourself. Really.'

'I insist.'

She clattered out into the kitchen and I sat at the table

in the small living room, opposite an enormous grand-father clock. When it got to twelve it started to chime loudly, and made me jump almost out of my seat.

'Sorry about that!' she called through the hatch in the wall. 'I'm used to it now. It is a bit loud, though, in't it?'

Finally, she came back with a tray covered in doilies, with cups, a milk jug and sugar pot and all manner of biscuits, which looked as though they may have been sit-ting in the kitchen for quite some time. She set the offerings down in front of me and sat down.

'Help yourself. God knows I can never eat it all myself. I buy it and then I don't get many visitors so . . . anyway, how can I help? I haven't been robbing banks in my sleep again, I hope. Only joking.'

'No. Not at all.' I laughed, then recomposed myself, remembering the seriousness of the situation. 'Nothing like that. I'm afraid I have some bad news. I'm afraid . . .'

'Oh?'

'Your father,' I began, taking on the hushed reverential tone I felt most befitted the situation.

'My father?'

'Yes. He died. Suddenly. I'm so sorry.'

I pulled out a hankie from my pocket in readiness for an outburst of grief. But none came. I was just met with a very confused look from Mrs Jackson.

'What, and they've only just sent you now to tell me? Well I never.'

'I'm so sorry. We only found out ourselves this morn-ing. I came as soon as I could. I'm really terribly sorry for your loss.'

I was surprised that she didn't seem that upset, or even

274

shocked. She paused for a moment and poured out some more tea. This ceremonial event took some time, as she held it at a great height over the strainer and watched it flowing into the cup.

'You get the best flavour this way,' she said seriously. 'No one ever believes me, but you do.'

When this was done, I thought she might show some grief, but instead she spent another few moments selecting a biscuit, picking one up and examining it, before replacing it and moving onto another. She even sniffed one. Perhaps she's in denial, or shock, I thought. It must be hard to face such tragedy.

Finally she made her selection, then dunked the biscuit right to the bottom of her tea cup and shook it about a bit.

'I mean, after all. He died five years ago.'

'Pardon?'

'Yes. I'll never forget it. October 22nd, 1947. Bill found him. Oh, it was awful. His face was all twisted up, poor love. He'd fallen, you know. From his stepladder. I always did tell him not to try to fix things himself, at his age, but would he listen? And then he lay there for hours, still clutching the screwdriver in his hand, like a little claw. All for a lightbulb. He'd had a heart attack, hadn't he? Right there on the floor. It was awful. We buried him up at St Margaret's. Over a hundred people, you know. So he had a good send-off, anyway.'

She looked up with a few tears in her eyes at the memory of it.

'Why, you police are a bit slow on the uptake, aren't you? Only coming round to break the news to me now, five years after the fact.'

'But you are Mrs Jackson, though, aren't you? Number 37 Tanner Street? I have it here in writing, that he was found at his home last night. A stroke, they suspect. Died in his sleep.'

'Oh, dear, dear. Oh no, this is awful. This is 37a. 37's next door. Bob, that's my husband's brother, he lives there with his wife, Dora. She's Mrs Jackson too. Poor Dora. So old Jack's passed now, has he? She'll be devastated, poor love. She was always was his little girl.'

'Oh my goodness! I'm so sorry.' I stood up and went to put my hat on, knocking my tea cup over in the process.

'Don't worry. I'll clean that up. You sit down. Finish your biscuit. Then you can go and break the news to poor Dora. You've had a bit of practice now, haven't you?'

I sat back, dazed, ate the biscuit as quickly as I possibly and politely could, before heading next door to repeat the whole scene again. Only this time, I made sure I had the right Mrs Jackson.

It was a week of letters. First we had received a letter from Durham, to thank us for helping with the road accident. Then there was another one that my landlady stood waving at me when I came in after an evening shift.

'It looks like a man's writing. All small and twisty, if you know what I mean,' said Caroline, with a sly smile, as we sat down. 'Anyone nice?' she asked eagerly.

'Oh. You know. Anyway, how was your day?'

'Oh, fine. The girls are in the school play, so they're rehearsing tonight. Katy is to play Juliet. We're so excited. And little Lily, she's playing Mercutio. Can you imagine?

There aren't enough boys to fill all the parts. She's quite a good little actress, actually. How about you? Arrested anyone today?'

'Not really, no. Spent most of the evening going round the pubs checking for underage drinkers. Saw my first bar fight, at the Bishop's Blaize, which was odd. At least I nearly did, but Sarge did his best to get me out of the bar before the fists started flying. I think he was trying to save me from the worst of it. One of them got quite a bloody nose, though, I did see on the way out. They took him up to the station.'

'Oh, you don't get too much of that round here. But when you do it's usually those boys from up at the barracks. They just get bored, I suppose. Anyway, here's your letter.'

I looked at the envelope, and, even though I'd never seen it before, I just knew it was Malcolm's handwriting. It had been written very carefully, in tiny characters, and he had drawn faint pencil lines underneath each line of the address. Sure enough, the postmark was Redcar.

'I'll go upstairs now then. I'm shattered.'

'Righto. Good night then.'

When I got into my room, I sat on the bed and pulled out the letter.

Dear Pam,

I said I'd write and so here it is. I feel like we parted quickly when you left. Life in Redcar is much the same, but without you in it.

I thought you might be interested to know that Sarge finally caught one of those dangerous dogs the other day. Turns out it had bitten clean through a small boy's finger. They had to put the brute down in the end. The dog, not the boy.

I have a few days' leave in two weeks' time and have planned to visit you in Richmond. I can stay at a family friend's farm nearby. Let me know that this is suitable.

Yours sincerely,
Malcolm

The letter was such an odd mix of formality, banality, forwardness and hesitation, I didn't know what to think. It was hardly a love letter, but at least he'd kept his promise.

Dear Malcolm,

Thank you for your letter, which I was pleased to find. Thank goodness they finally caught one of those dogs. I spent so many days chasing them, without success, I was beginning to wonder if they existed at all. Though it's always sad when one has to be put down. It was probably raised badly by the owner and . . .

I stopped writing for a moment. How we had ended up focusing our entire correspondence on dangerous dogs, I didn't know. Oh well, it's too late now, I thought, and concluded the letter hastily.

Anyway, further to your suggestion, yes. That's my weekend off. We can meet in town on Friday evening and see a picture. If you like.

Yours,
Pam

I sealed the envelope and addressed it to Redcar police station. For a moment I did wonder about Jim, and where he was. Still in Germany? Back home by now? Married, even? He hadn't written for nearly a year now, and I had almost forgotten what he looked like. Then Malcolm's face came back into my mind, with his funny, serious, blue eyes. I wondered what went on behind them, and made up my mind to forget all about Jim.

When the girls got home from their school play rehearsal they were full of beans and leaping about the house. I went downstairs to fetch some water and say good night to them all. They were midway through demonstrating their dramatic enterprises when Caroline's husband came home too, from his billiards night.

'We have to have a sword fight!' said Lily, brandishing an imaginary sword at her father as he came through the door.

'Well, I hope you do better than that, or he'll have your head off. Hello, love,' he said, kissing Caroline on the cheek.

'I have to die. Or at least pretend to die. And then really die,' said Katy. 'And Lily's not taking it at all seriously. She keeps corpsing. That's when you laugh uncontrollably, Mr Walker says.'

'I do not!' said the younger girl, as she leapt up onto the stairs and then down again in a giant star-jump.

'You think it's just a big game. But you're embarrassing me. I want to do it properly. Mam, tell her.'

'I'm sure you'll both be wonderful. Now off to bed. You're late!'

'Mr Walker made us stay until we had completely rehearsed the whole of the first act word perfect!' said Lily. 'He said I was the best Mercutio he's ever seen! But Katy kept forgetting her lines.'

'I did not. You were putting me off. She kept pulling faces. She thinks she's the clown of the class.'

'I am.'

'Mr Walker says . . .'

'Mr Walker says . . .' mimicked her sister.

'I can help you both with your lines,' I said, remembering back to the days I had been in theatre in Scarborough, and hoping to diffuse the situation. I thought it would be a nice way to get to know the girls a bit anyway.

'Thanks!' they both said in unison.

Caroline looked at her husband, relieved that the sibling bickering had stopped, for a while at least.

'Well, I'm expecting great things then!'

As I got into the routine of police work, my time at Richmond began to fly by and, before I knew it, another Christmas was gone. Joe McGregor's early lambs had been born and were scattered all across the hillside.

'How's Mrs McGregor?' I asked Joe one morning on my beat, as I walked up the lane to the phone box on the way out of town.

'Haven't you heard?' he said, leaning against the gate. 'She were taken in. Last night. A high fever. I'm only here keeping an eye on the lambs, then I'm straight back to her bedside.'

'Oh, Joe. I'm so sorry.'

'Well. We never let things like this pull us down. We're

fighters, me and the missus. Well . . . she . . . At least I hope she is.'

A small lamb came trotting over and nuzzled up against his leg. He reached down and stroked its straggly back and it trotted off again.

'That one was born just a few hours ago. You wouldn't believe it, would you? How quickly they stand up and run about. I just hope he doesn't freeze out here.'

That afternoon, after my shift, I went home and changed into my civvies, then popped into Mrs Philpot's for a cup of tea.

'Just the way you like it,' she said as she came out of the kitchen with the nice hot brew. 'I even saved you some sugar. When this rationing will end, I don't know. But you must try my Beetroot Surprise. It's something I used a lot during the first war,' she said, and cut off a thick slice of a deep reddish-orange cake from the front of the counter.

'What's in it? Such a lovely colour.'

'Carrots and beetroots – they give it a natural sweetness, some spices . . . and a secret ingredient which will go with me to the grave.' She tapped her nose. 'I learnt it from my old grandmother. We always had this big book in the kitchen. Leatherbound. So old the pages kept falling out and smothered in who knows how many generations of cake mix. But I'd never use anything else.'

I had to admit, it was the most delicious cake I had ever tasted.

After the war, bread, potatoes and even petrol were still rationed, but by the fifties it was mainly sugar and meat that were hard to come by. Mrs Philpot certainly had no trouble baking cakes, though, whatever the rations.

As I scraped the remaining crumbs from my plate, someone behind me put a hand on my shoulder and made me jump.

'Miss Rhodes.'

'Francesco!' Last time I had seen him, we were tethering up Joe McGregor's goats. 'How are you?'

'Not bad. Not good. I'm leaving the garage – and Richmond. Got a new job up in Leeds. More money. One pot of tea please, Mrs Philpot.'

'Why don't you join me?' I said.

So Francesco pulled up a chair, still wearing his mechanics uniform, all stained with oil and grease, his dark hair flopping over his eyes.

'Where did you learn about cars?' I asked after a while.

'My father. Always playing with this and that. Old engines. Even though he never did it for a living. I suppose I just picked it up that way.'

I was a bit concerned as I looked around that people might talk. It wasn't usual to sit with young men in cafés, alone, unless you were courting. So I drank my tea quickly, and was about to leave when Francesco spoke up.

'Wait. Before I leave, don't you want to hear the rest of the story?'

'Story?'

'The boat. That took my father and his people.'

'Oh! Yes, of course.' I clutched on to my tea cup, anxious to get away before someone saw us.

'So you remember what I said? They, the police that is, came in the night, and took the men on the boat, all my father's friends: my godfather, waiters, hairdressers, all

Italians who had made a life here in Britain. Because Italy was the enemy now. You know what happened?'

'No.'

'Bombed and the boat sank to the bottom of the ocean. Hundreds and hundreds of people lost.'

'My goodness. I'm so sorry.'

'Rumour was they shot at the lifeboats so people couldn't escape. But who knows the truth.'

'And your father?'

'Washed up on the coast of Ireland in a lifeboat. Taken in by a family there until he could find his way back home to us. He hardly spoke about it after that, only telling me that the sound ringing in his ears every night, until the day he died, was the sound of men crying "Mama" as they drowned.'

'Would you like more cake?' called Mrs Philpot from the kitchen.

'No, thank you. I must get going,' I told her. 'Bye, Francesco. Thank you for your story.' I pressed his hand. 'And good luck.'

'Goodbye, Miss Rhodes.'

I wanted to hear more, but I didn't want the consequences, the whispering and gossip, that would surely come if I stayed chatting to Francesco all afternoon. So I stood up, collected my gloves and turned round to leave. And there, standing behind me with a grim look on his face, was Malcolm.

As planned, I had met up with Malcolm after my summer in Redcar. We had been to the pictures quite a few times now; when he visited he had stayed in a farm up the road. He had got into coming regularly now, but I wasn't expecting him this week.

'Hello, Pam.'

'Heavens! You made me jump right out of my skin.'

'Who's this?'

'Oh, this is Francesco. He's . . . I mean, I had to go round and check him. Aliens. Sorry, I mean, that's what, you know, Sarge said. He's from Italy,' I blabbered.

Francesco held out his hand. 'Delighted to meet you. You are a friend of Miss Rhodes?'

'You could say that.'

'Of course. Francesco, this is Malcolm . . . he visits me. He's a policeman too, in Redcar. By the sea.'

'Don't let me interrupt your little . . . whatever it is,' said Malcolm, turning to leave.

'No. Not at all. I was just going. Wasn't I, Francesco?'

'Yes. I mean no. I'm leaving. It's my fault, I imposed myself on the young lady. I'm leaving town tomorrow.'

'Italian, eh?' said Malcolm, raising an eyebrow.

There was a bit of an awkward pause.

Then Francesco said, 'Anyway, I must go and pack my things up, and say goodbye to the lads at the garage. Goodbye, Miss Rhodes. Goodbye . . . Malcolm.'

I sat back down, and Mrs Philpot came over. 'More tea then?'

'Yes, please!'

We sat at the table for a while. Malcolm was fiddling with one of the plants in front of us, and began pulling the leaves off absentmindedly.

'Stop it. You're destroying the poor thing.'

'Sorry. Italian, was he?'

'Who? Oh, Francesco. Yes. I told you. I know him through work. He helped me tether some goats. It's a long story. Don't worry.'

'Goats! What do you get up to out here?'

'It's just work.'

One thing I had learnt about Malcolm, since we had been meeting up, was that he had a jealous streak. He did his best to hide it, but I could see it bubbling up like a poison if I spoke to the lads from the station when he was with me. Even the Inspector, sometimes.

'How long are you staying?'

'A few days. I wanted to see you.'

'I'm on earlies tomorrow, but we can meet in the evening, if you like?'

'Sure.'

For the next few days I was working, but on Monday I had the day off, so we went for a walk around the castle. It was a relief to be outside together. There was a chill in the air as we approached the looming building, though, and I realized that the last time I'd walked up here with a man it had been that night with Jim, when we hadn't kissed, and he'd gone off to Germany so soon afterwards.

'I've been thinking,' said Malcolm suddenly as we stood at the foot of the castle. 'You know. Life. Death. What it's all for?'

'What's what all for?'

'It. I mean, look at this castle. All those people who used to live here. Who built it, even. Slaves, who knows?

All the money and the slaughters that went on, every meal, every breath. I just wonder what it's all for, that's all. When it comes to this. A big ruined castle. Nothing more.'

'Oh. And what did you decide?' I said, confused.

'I haven't yet.'

'I think it's quite a nice castle.'

I took his arm as we walked back down into town. Then, out of the blue, and for the first time, he kissed me on the cheek. It wasn't a long kiss. It wasn't even particularly passionate. But it was definitely real and warm and close, and my first. When we parted I looked into his eyes.

'See you then,' I said, suddenly giddy and shy all over again.

'See you.'

'So you'll be going to York, to the assizes.'

As the Inspector came in to the office one morning and announced that I'd be going away again, for a week, I was in a dream.

'Are you listening?'

'Yes, sir. Sorry, sir. York. Assizes.'

'You might find it easier to travel from your parents' home in Scarborough each morning. They do have a house there, don't they? It's quite a trip from here. Nice chance for you to get back for a bit too.'

'Yes, sir.'

I hadn't seen my parents for months, as it became harder to fit in Malcolm's visits and trips home along with all my shift work. I was looking forward to catching up with them all. I packed up my police things and said good-bye to Caroline and the girls. I'd miss the performance of the latest school play, which was a shame, as Lily was playing a lead part. But I gave them all a big hug and wished the girls luck, then set off back home.

As I arrived into Scarborough station, the first of the summer visitors were arriving, full of holiday cheer as they walked down to the beach with their buckets and spades and windbreaks. I walked past Marshall & Snelgrove, where I'd worked all that time back, and past the ice-cream shop where I had last seen Jane. It felt funny coming back, as though I was a stranger in a very familiar place. Everything was etched into my memory from growing up: the shape of the cliffs rising up on either side, even silly things like a post box with a big graze on one side, where a lorry had hit it one night, and the missing R on the theatre sign, which had never been replaced, so it read THEAT E.

Although I was familiar with the smallest details of the town, all the faces were somehow strange, as though they had been swapped while I was gone. There were new shopkeepers, and new children leaping about on the beach as I once had with my friends. Every now and then I would see a face I recognized, slightly older and wearier, but more often than not it was all new and strange.

'She's here!' I heard Mam shout upstairs excitedly as I knocked on the door. Then there was a pattering of feet, and it opened. 'You're taller somehow,' she said, and held my shoulders to get a good look at me. 'Are you eating enough? You look thin.'

'Yes. My landlady, Caroline, she's a good cook actually. Always manages to get a nice piece of meat somehow.'

'Well. I've got a surprise for you!'

'Oh, Mam. I'm tired. Can it wait? I just want to flop and unpack.' I started to walk up the stairs.

'I'm afraid not.'

She signalled me to go into the living room and as I walked in, there sat Granny Steele, who we had lived near to as young children growing up, before we moved to Scarborough, but who I hardly ever saw now.

'Granny!' As I gave her a hug she smelled of powder puff and jasmine, and looked exactly the same as I remembered her all those years ago. She had lived in an ancient cottage in the village, which she always used to say had been in the family for years. When we stayed with her, we would go to bed by candlelight and watch the shadows flickering on the ancient stones, imagining who used to live there.

'Happy birthday for next week,' I said, remembering.

I had never been able to work out how old my granny was. It was something of a state secret, and I made it a challenge for myself to try to find out. She said she was born in the 1800s and could remember Queen Victoria. One day, at her house, I saw a picture of her and asked how old she was. Without thinking, she said she was twenty at the time of the photograph. Then I asked when the picture was taken, thinking that might be a way to find out, but she cottoned on too quickly and said she couldn't remember. But when I turned the picture over there was a date on it: 1898. Which would have made her about seventy-five now. She looked well for it, too. She was quite short and stout, but this kept her skin looking young, and she had a big shock of naturally curly hair, formerly dark brown but now quite grey, and wore horn-rimmed glasses.

'You look so well. Younger even,' I said.

'I feel it too. It's the dogs. Keep me active.'

She always had two little terriers, and she always called them Bit and Bob. There had now been at least three generations of Bit and Bob, so it seemed like they were kind of immortal.

'Coming here is the only rest I get. I've left them with the neighbours this week. Too much to bring them on the train. So what news have you got? I hear there's a man on the scene.'

'Oh. I don't know. Yes. I suppose.'

That evening Mam and Dad told me what they'd been up to. They had bought another house in Scarborough, and business was going from strength to strength. After pudding, summer fruits and a big pile of fresh cream, which was a treat for Granny's birthday, she produced a piece of paper from her handbag.

'So I wanted to show you all this. It's our history. Where we're all from, if you like.'

The paper had a large family tree on it, in scrawly writing, and there was a typed letter.

'From America,' she said proudly. 'This man in Philadelphia, turns out he's our relative, cousin or something. He dug about into the family history, and you'll never guess.'

'What?'

'We're related to Bonnie Prince Charlie!'

We all gasped.

'Really?'

'Well, almost.' She laughed. 'Actually one of his troops. You know the cottage?'

'Your cottage?'

'Yes. Well, this man found out that our ancestor, Joseph Bayley, he was abandoned as a newborn baby at the side of a well. His mother was with Bonnie Prince Charlie when they came through the area in 1745, on retreat from a battle.'

'What would they want with Hanging Heaton?' asked Dad, looking up from his newspaper.

'I think it was just a stop, for the night, you know, a campsite sort of thing.'

'And?' I was getting interested now. It seemed exciting to be part of history in this way.

'Well, one of the soldiers, his wife was with child and she'd accompanied them. And she had the baby right there in the camp. In those days they brought their wives and girlfriends along. But she didn't want to take the child back to Scotland, in case it died on the way or something.'

'Did she abandon it then? By the well?'

'Well. She did it for the child, I like to think. Anyway. She left the boy by the side of a well. No bigger than a kitten, poor lamb. Joseph, that was his name. He ended up in the poorhouse, then got work for a local farmer, and eventually got his own piece of land and a built a little cottage. My cottage.'

'Heavens. I didn't realize it was so old,' I said, trying to imagine how it would have been then.

'Anyway, they became weavers, and millers, and farmers and such like, and Joseph Bayley, he was my great-great-great-grandfather, I think. Eventually he built up a nice little smallholding.'

'And what about his mother?' I asked.

'She came back, nineteen years later, from Scotland. Knocked on the door, right out of the blue, and tried to persuade him to go back with her. But he refused. Said his home was there now. But she gave him his name, Bayley that was. So next time you come round, you'll have something to think about, eh?'

But I didn't have long to dwell on my ancestors. The next day I was in court, and back to some very living stories.

I had never been to York before, so this was a first. It was a lot bigger than Scarborough, and surrounded by a real Roman wall. York Assizes, the main courthouse, was a very grand and beautiful building, like a huge Roman villa, and it was worth the trip just to see that. I walked up the stone steps and into the courthouse, where a court official came and met me.

'Miss Rhodes?'

'Yes.'

'First time in the big smoke?'

'It is. It's so grand,' I said, looking up and around at the huge building.

'You wait 'til you see inside,' he said and we walked down the corridor together.

The walls were made of elaborately carved sandstone, and there were arches and decorations like a huge Gothic cathedral.

'Do you know what we'll be doing?' I asked.

'The courtroom is in there.' He pointed through a doorway. 'You'll stand behind the defendant and call in the witnesses. Have you done that before?'

The room looked so imposing. There was a great desk and an elaborate chair at the front, where the judge would sit, and separate areas for the jury, the defendants and the witnesses. Even the air felt formal in there and it sent a shiver down my spine. I sat down to wait in the chair the official pointed out.

After a few minutes, loud voices could be heard coming along the corridor, then the judge came sweeping through into the courtroom in his gown, officials scurrying along behind him. He walked right past us into another room, where he sat looking over his glasses, taking notes from the case, before a clerk shut the door. He looked a bit scary to me.

Eventually the official led us into the court room, and then the jury came in nervously one by one, and were shown up into their seats. There were two women, one quite young and another in her fifties; the rest were men of varying ages, one in an army uniform. Once we were all seated, the judge came in, and the whole court stood up until he sat down in his seat. He took ages arranging his gown and shuffling papers before opening proceedings.

Eventually, they began to call the witnesses up. There were two defendants, a man and a woman who had been caught in a compromising position in a car parked along a road north of the city. It was an indecency case. Two police officers were called up to testify that they'd happened upon a man and a woman in a car ('having it off', as someone had said to me before we went in).

The first policeman came up to the stand. He was tall and thin and spoke so quietly hardly anyone could hear what he said.

'So, PC . . . Holder. Tell the jury what you saw that evening.'

'Well, I was on my beat, about to make a point up Greylag Road, when I saw a shape. It was dark and I got quite nervous, as I know the road well and it's usually very quiet.'

His voice trailed off.

'What?' asked the judge. 'Can't hear a word he's saying,' he said to one of the court officials.

'IT'S USUALLY VERY QUIET,' said the policeman loudly, and the members of the jury jumped in their seats. 'Anyway, so I approached and it was a car, a Morris Minor, green. And . . . well, I saw a woman in there first, then I realized she was with a man and, well, her buttocks were bare. So I knocked on the window. And they got dressed, hurriedly, like, and that was when we took them in.'

'Thank you, constable.'

Next they called up his colleague, PC Finch, who had a similar story.

'And so when I got to the car, I saw the young lady in question, and her buttocks were bare,' he said, and I thought it was very odd how they had both used the same expression.

Next they called up the woman, who was claiming that she hadn't consented to be in the car at all in that situation, and that in fact the man had tried to rape her. The young woman, about twenty-two years old, was led up. She was smartly dressed in a sensible suit with gloves.

'You claim, Miss Shields, that you were forced into this . . . position . . . by the other defendant.'

'We had been walking out for about a month,' she started. 'We packed a picnic and everything. Then he changed his mind, Martin did. Said it was about to rain, so we should pull up the car and have the picnic there instead. Right in the car. Well, I was a bit dubious. You know, I hardly knew him really. I mean we'd danced together and that, but it was early days.'

The more she spoke, the less she allowed herself to breathe, and the story came out like a torrent, getting faster and faster.

'Anyway, after we'd eaten the sandwiches, he brought out a hip flask, one he had in the car, he said, and it was full of brandy. Well, I'm not much of a drinker, but he, you know, persuaded me it would be all right. We played a game, and before I knew it we'd drunk it all. I was feeling quite sick and dizzy, you know, and I got up to go and leave the car for some fresh air. But before I could go he . . .'

She hesitated at this moment, and pulled out a gigantic hankie from her pocket and blew her nose loudly.

'He pulled up my skirt and . . .' At that point she exploded into tears.

The barrister for the prosecution didn't relent.

'So you allowed yourself to be taken into a car by a near complete stranger . . . Can I ask, then, what you expected to happen, Miss Shields?'

'I tried to stop him.'

'Really, Miss Shields. A complete stranger, and you were surprised? I put it to you that you planned the whole thing. And you had no shame about it whatsoever; that you led this man, this complete stranger, on.'

'No!' she shouted. 'It wasn't like that. Anyway, I didn't

say he was a complete stranger. I mean, we've been to the pictures twice. I trusted him, I suppose. I thought we'd be having a nice picnic, that's all. We brought Scotch eggs!'

'Really?' said the barrister knowingly. 'No more questions, Your Honour.'

After that the young man was called up. He was only about nineteen, and had the short crop hairstyle of someone on their National Service. He stated his name and swore his oath, before being cross-examined by his barrister.

'Can you tell me what happened that evening?'

'Betty . . . Miss Shields . . . said she wanted to go for a picnic. So we packed it up and she insisted I took the car, in case it rained. I wanted to walk but she was very . . . persuasive.'

'Go on.'

'She made me park up, on a verge by the old farm. I thought we might get into trouble, you know, so close to the road, but she grabbed out at the steering wheel. I thought we might crash. She insisted we stop there. She said she knew it was a good place.'

'What happened then? Tell the jury.'

'Well. She pulled out this flask. Like what you use for shooting and things. One of her dad's, she said. She said it was full of brandy and we should drink it. I didn't think it was such a good idea. What with me driving and all. But she forced it to my mouth and said she'd give me a treat if I drank it. So . . . well, you know what it's like, and I . . . well, I gave in, didn't I?'

'Did she force you to drink the brandy?'

'In a manner of speaking, yes.'

'What happened next?'

'Well, it all happened so fast, but before I knew it she had ripped off her . . . skirts . . . and was climbing on top of me. That was when the officers knocked on the door. I tried to push her off, but she's a strong lass, you know.'

'And at any stage did you force or try to engage Miss Shields in any kind of sexual activity?'

'Never.'

'That will be all.'

After all this, my head was a confusion: they both sounded so convincing. Next they were cross-examined by the woman's barrister, and they gave the same stories, equally convincingly, except her barrister made the man sound more like he was in the wrong. How the jury would ever decide, I had no idea.

In the end, in a master stroke, the young man's barrister produced the hip flask in evidence, and managed to convince everyone that it couldn't have been his, because it was inscribed with the initials P. S., which was supposedly the young woman's father, who was called Peter Shields. But then her barrister counterclaimed that the young man had bought it from a secondhand shop, and those initials could be anyone's . . .

At the end the judge summed up and looked sternly at the jury, reminding them that their decision could affect someone's life, and that they could only find the defendants guilty of sexual indecency if they were sure beyond all reasonable doubt.

He then excused them to make their decision. Another young PC and I walked behind them along a passageway and into a small room where they would discuss the case.

They weren't allowed to talk about it outside the room, so we had to stand guard together outside, making sure no one came out or went in. As we waited we could hear their voices rising and falling inside the jury room.

'Looks like we might be here a while,' said my companion, who'd introduced himself to me as Jeff. He was leaning on the wall, looking at his fingernails.

'Yes, looks that way.'

'Hey! Do you like dancing?' he said suddenly.

'I do, yes. Why?'

'How about it?' he said and held out his arms as if to start a foxtrot or something.

'Are you sure?' I said, looking around warily. 'Mightn't the judge or someone come along?'

'Nah. They're all upstairs having lunch. The jury might be a while. So, how about it anyway?'

'OK, why not!'

So Jeff led the way and up and down the corridor as we danced; first a military two-step, then a bit of a tango and we even tried a waltz, but ran out of space. We'd almost collapsed into a heap of laughter when a voice called down the hallway.

'Ahem. We've reached our decision. When you're quite ready.'

It was the foreman of the jury, a large man with a huge Edwardian-style moustache, standing in the doorway of the jury room. I went bright red, having been caught out dancing, but Jeff didn't seem to care at all. He just walked casually over to the clerk to the court and informed him that the jury were ready to return.

When we were all seated, and had gone through the

procedure of standing and sitting on the judge's arrival, he looked up from his notes.

'Well. Has the jury reached a decision?'

'Yes, Your Honour. The jury finds the defendants not guilty,' said the foreman grandly, his moustache twitching. And that was that.

Neither party showed much emotion at the result. The girl just looked down, then left the courtroom with her barrister. The man didn't smile either, though, and I got the feeling it had been a horrible experience for both of them.

I never quite got used to the contrast between work and home life. I would come back to my landlady's house after a day interviewing a young girl who'd been assaulted, or back home to my parents' after listening to a court case about possible rape, and then have to come in all smiles, as if everything was normal.

When I got home that evening, sure enough, Granny, Mam and Dad were all sitting round the wireless listening to the Light Programme. Dad was laughing, an enormous great chortle which welled up from deep down in his belly, as a bumbling policeman tried to solve the mystery of a missing diamond.

'I don't get it,' said Granny. 'I just don't understand this new comedy . . . if you can call it that,' she sighed, and got back on with her knitting.

'Oh, Pamela, have you heard this on the wireless?' Mam asked. '*PC 49*. It's hilarious. Your father and I are hooked. You can tell us all whether it's true.'

'No. Not really. I mean, no, I haven't heard it.'

'How was your day?' asked Granny as I kicked my shoes off.

'Fine,' I said, deciding not to mention the courtroom and the description of the woman's bare buttocks. 'I danced in the corridor with one of the PCs. Jeff. That was funny. While we waited outside the jury room. I'm pretty tired, though.'

'We never could stop you from dancing,' said Dad. 'Remember how you used to tell me you were off to the cinema, and then you'd trot out of the house and collect your shoes from the bushes and go dancing at that ball-room anyway. Don't think I didn't know what you were up to!'

'Did you know about that, really?' I asked, amazed by my dad's powers of deduction.

'Can't fool a Rhodes.'

'Oh, leave her alone,' said Mam. 'I couldn't be more proud of you, of what you've done. Did she tell you she's saved over a hundred pounds already?' she said to my granny.

'Do you get what the lads get, do you? As far as wages go?' asked Granny.

'Nearly. We get five pounds and ten shillings a week. They get about six, I think, plus a boot allowance for repairs. So not too bad. One day maybe we'll get the same, though. Who knows?'

'How you've saved that much, I'll never know. Anyway what are you going to do with it all?' asked Granny, looking over her glasses.

'Who knows!'

And in truth I hadn't really thought about what I was

saving for. My mind flickered back to Malcolm. We'd been walking out now for some months, but the word marriage hadn't yet come up. A hundred pounds wouldn't half come in useful if it did, though.

As I made my way up to bed, the sounds of PC 49 sleuthing for diamonds and questioning a lady in a mink coat and crocodile shoes drifted up the stairs, followed by another of Dad's great guffaws.

On the way back to Richmond, thinking about my time at the assizes put me in mind of other court cases. I thought about the local magistrates court in Richmond, at the town hall, and my weekly duties there if there were any cases with women involved. There was also the court in Leyburn, which involved a lovely drive through the countryside. After a case there we'd go to the Sergeant's house for a midday meal cooked by his wife. This was always a treat, and a chance to catch up on what the village bobbies had been up to. On one occasion there, I remember hearing that one of the lads had applied for a police house for him and his new wife, but there were none left so they had been given two rooms to start their married life. I'd been told I would be going on a refresher course at Bruche, and wondered if any of the old gang would be there too.

Every court case was different. One of my first was for a milk van that had crashed with an insecure load. I had taken the driver's details and told him he would be reported. When he was in court there was a solicitor present and I had to appear and answer some questions, which was a bit nerve-racking. Where had the bottles landed, on the road or pavement? What was the road like? 'Wet,' I answered. Was the road straight? 'It had a camber to one side,' and so on.

Other cases were held at the juvenile court, which was more relaxed than an adult court, but often more shocking. One case which sticks in my mind, even now, was an indecency case, in which two little girls were asked if they could see the man who had allegedly abused them in the room. They both said no in the court, but when I spoke to them later on they said he had been there, but they hadn't dared say anything. There was nothing I could do about it, though.

I also remember taking a statement from a little girl in another indecency case. She said a man in khaki had asked her if she wanted an ice cream, and when she closed her eyes and opened her mouth, he had presented her with something quite different. All these cases could be quite shocking; I never understood how someone could do that to a child.

When I get back to Richmond, I thought to myself after the drama of the courts, it'll be back to doing reports with my usual two-finger typing. 'Sir, I beg to report,' they would all begin. But I'd be glad to be back.

12

'The girls have really missed you, though they'd never admit it,' said Caroline as I sat down, back in my Richmond digs, and told her about my time away in York. Lily had blown the audience away with her performance in the school play, apparently.

'I've got this letter for you too,' she said, knowingly. 'Isn't that Malcolm's writing?'

It was. For some reason, I hesitated before opening it. I went into my bedroom and shut the door, before pulling out a thin piece of blue paper. His letters were never fulsome.

Dear Pam,

I hope all is well at the assizes and that you're not getting into any mischief. I've spent the past week at the races, making tea. It's just like you said, only worse, and it's done nothing but rain these past weeks. I did have a laugh with the other lad in the van, but I never want to see a tea-leaf again, I can tell you.

I have another piece of news too. I've been posted to Catterick. Just up the road from Richmond. Must be fate. So we can see a lot more of each other.

Let me know you're happy and keep safe.

Yours,
Malcolm

I folded the letter back up and lay on the bed. Malcolm was getting closer, and there seemed to be no turning back now. I was excited, though. Wasn't I?

A few weeks later, Malcolm was settled into his new job, and I had quite a start when I came into the station at Richmond and there he was, in his uniform, sitting in the parade room.

'Hello!' I said.

'Surprise.'

'What are you doing here?'

'Oh, that's a nice greeting. Thought you'd be pleased.'

'I am but, I wasn't expecting . . .'

'Well, actually, I'm here on a job. With you.'

Before he could explain, Inspector Armstrong came over.

'Miss Rhodes. I believe you know Stevenson,' he said, cleaning his reading glasses with his tie. 'He's off to pick up a young woman in Rotherham. A Miss Baxter. Been stealing up at Catterick. Milk bottles or something. Anyway, Rotherham have picked her up, but we need to question her. Bill's out with the car so you'll have to take the train.'

'Stealing milk bottles. How odd.'

'It happens quite a lot actually, the lads say. They nick them from outside people's houses in the mornings.'

'To do what? Drink them?'

'I suppose so. I don't think she was selling them on for export. Some people like stealing stuff, anyway,' the Inspector said. 'For no particular reason.'

So we took the train, having to change a couple of times, and eventually ended up in Rotherham, at the police station there, where a duty sergeant showed us in. Another PC came in with a young girl in tow, who couldn't have been more than about nineteen or twenty. She was a boyish imp of a creature, with a short crop, sharp nose and scruffy mackintosh.

'Lucy Baxter. Caught up in Catterick, but her family brought her back here, so you'll be wanting her back up your way for all the paperwork, and so on.'

'Thanks, Sergeant. We'll take care of it.'

'Philip'll drive you back to the train station if you like.'

We all trooped outside and a young PC showed us into a huge Black Maria, a large van for transporting prisoners. I'd never seen one before in North Riding, so this was a real treat, a giant black shining hulk of a thing with huge doors and enormous wing mirrors. I climbed in the back with Lucy, who sat hunched up in the corner the whole way and didn't say a word.

As we got out and walked towards the trains, Philip whispered a warning in my ear.

'Watch out for this one. She might look innocent, but she's a wild one, I can tell you. Just keep an eye on her, is all I'm saying.'

'Thanks. I will.'

'Good luck.'

When we got on the train, Lucy, Malcolm and I sat together in a carriage next to a woman with a baby who wouldn't stop crying. No matter what she did, it just kept screaming and had gone completely red in the face. None of us could talk much, what with the din, though occasionally I'd see something out of the window and remark, ooh, look at the cows, or that lovely cottage, but we mostly kept quiet the whole way. I even tried to make some small talk with Lucy, but got little response.

When we got to York we had twenty minutes between trains, and the girl spoke for the first time.

'I need to use the toilet,' she said quietly.

'Can't you wait until we're on the train?'

'No. I need it now.'

'Right, you take her then,' said Malcolm. 'I'll wait here and keep an eye out.'

So we walked to the public toilets on the platform, and when we got there I realized I was in need too. So she went into one cubicle, and I went into another. I kept an eye on her coat under the partition, safe in the knowledge that Malcolm was outside too.

When I came out, though, I looked into her cubicle and the coat was on the floor but there was no sign of the girl. Panic set in. I couldn't believe it. I'd been charged with this duty and I'd let her get away. How could I have been so stupid?

'Malcolm, Malcolm!' I hissed. He was standing by a hoarding outside the entrance to the toilets. 'Did you see her?'

'What?'

'Lucy. I think she's gone.'

'What? No! I've been here all the time. But, well, I did go for a quick walk on the platform. But I would have seen her. You idiot! How could you have let her go? In broad daylight?'

'But I had to go. Anyway, you were supposed to be keeping an eye out too!'

'Oh, Pam! The Sergeant's going to kill us. You and me both.'

'I'm sorry,' I said, feeling a little hurt by his response.

'Right. You go that way, I'll walk up the platform. Meet back here. And you'd better find her or this has been more than just a wasted journey. It could cost us our jobs.'

As we separated I rushed up the platform, sweat streaming down my forehead as the panic rose up in my stomach like a thousand barbed-wire butterflies. At one point, I thought I saw the back of her head in the crowd, and called out.

'Lucy! Lucy, stop.'

But when she turned round it wasn't her at all. It was a young lad. He gave me a funny look so I turned away and continued on.

I scanned every person I could see: an old couple sitting on a bench, a couple of soldiers in uniform, smoking and laughing, and a woman and her two children, all standing innocently on the platform. But no sign of the little milk thief. The announcer on the platform began to call our train, and then I could see it puffing its way into the station with a great screech of coal and iron. There was nothing to do but run back to the spot where I'd left Malcolm and work out a plan of action.

'We'll have to tell someone. A guard or something,' I said as I arrived back, completely out of breath.

But then, just as I looked back, Lucy came wandering out of the toilets nonchalantly.

'Left my coat,' she said, looking at us both. And her impish eyes lit up ever so slightly. 'I could have got away from you, you know. But I didn't,' she said, turning sort of glum.

'Thank goodness you didn't. Where have you been anyway?'

'Over there.' And she pointed to a cubbyhole in the wall, just big enough to fit a small girl in. 'Just watching you lot panic. That's all.'

I looked at Malcolm with a feeling of relief. I didn't care if we'd been duped. At least she hadn't escaped.

'So why didn't you, then? Run away?' asked Malcolm, as we took our seats on the train.

'What would I do?' she said quietly. 'For food? Steal bread and milk? No thanks. I've had it with that.'

For the rest of the journey I didn't take my gaze off that girl for a moment, until she was safely inside Richmond police station and under the Sergeant's watchful eye. But something about her made me believe she was telling the truth, and that maybe this brush with the law meant that her milk-thieving days were over.

With Malcolm now based in Catterick we saw more of each other and, although nothing 'happened' in that sense, he would come over to see me at my landlady's occasionally. We'd read books together, or sit and chat, but since our first kiss I'd been adamant that nothing more would happen without a ring on my finger. I had seen enough of pregnancy out of wedlock in my job to know the repercussions. In those days it meant being ostracized from your community, maybe even your family too, such was the stigma. So, for the time being, we stuck to holding hands and the occasional kiss.

One evening towards the end of March, Sergeant Hardcastle came out of the office looking very serious.

'Ah, good. Rhodes. You're on tonight.'

'Yes, beat three. Up Theakston Lane.'

I expected him to leave at that point, as he usually did, but for some reason he lingered for a while, and rubbed his chin.

'Before you go . . . there's been an All Stations, you see. The Met,' he said, straightening up and broadening his shoulders. 'They're looking for a fella, Christie. He's wanted for questioning. Looks like he could be anywhere in the country. Biggest manhunt in history, they're calling it. Got the whole lot out looking for him. Some pretty grisly murders, looks like it might be, but there'll be more news tomorrow, no doubt.'

'Gosh. What did he do?'

'Women. Scores of them at his house in London, I was told. Off the record, HQ says it looks like they've turned up several bodies already. Urgent they catch him before the full moon, they said. Not sure why. Perhaps he's a werewolf.'

'My goodness. Where is he, then? Have they got any idea?'

'That's the thing. He moved out of his house not long ago. New tenants found the bodies. As I say, looks like it's pretty nasty. Anyway, they reckon he could be anywhere. But hear this, he has connections with Yorkshire, they're saying. So when you're out there tonight, keep an eye open, won't you? He's targeting women.'

'Will do,' I said, less than pleased to be out at night with this on the possible cards.

As I traced the line of my beat along the map, I realized I had only ever done it in the daytime. It was a route that went largely on the outskirts of town, where there was little light and not many houses either, mostly woodland and farmland and a few dirt tracks.

I picked up my torch and my whistle and headed out through Market Place, past a few pubs and the Market Cross, where a couple of squaddies stood smoking cigarettes and chatting. I bade them good evening as I walked past, made my way down Station Road and across the River Swale, which was rushing down in torrents after a heavy rainfall. It was eerily empty as I crossed the bridge, only the sounds of the water swishing by and the odd dog barking in the distance. As I walked up the lane, I saw the bright beam of the evening bus and an army lorry disappearing off up the hill towards the garrison. Then there was complete quiet as I made my way further out of town.

Although I'd walked up here before during the day, by night it was a different matter. Things I thought I knew as familiar – the post box on the corner, the fence post at the top of the hill – all took on shifting shapes and gave deceiving flickers as I approached them. One minute they looked like a man in a greatcoat, the next a giant creature, poised to pounce. At one point I thought I felt something brush against my cheek, but before I could look back to see what it was, I felt compelled to run as far as a big tree, where I leant against the trunk, panting to get my breath back.

I had to get to the only phone box on this beat, which was on The Green, a mile or so away. First, though, I had to make my way past the outlying farms. In the eerie silence, the buildings took on a sinister air at this time of night, the chimneys of the old farmhouses crooked against the moonlight.

The further I walked the darker it got, and eventually I had to flash my torch from one side of the road to the other, just to ensure I didn't trip in a pothole or get tangled up in any overhanging trees. The more I walked, cold air filling my nostrils, the more I could hear. At first it had seemed like silence, but as I left the town behind I began to hear not human sounds and traffic, but things which only ever come out at night. I heard scrapings in the bushes, curious animal shufflings from across the fields and a sudden, loud snort which made me jump and pick up my pace.

The darkness was pressing in deeper and deeper as I walked on, into a particularly thick section of woodland, the road overhung by trees. Suddenly I heard an almighty scream from in among the trees. It sounded like a woman. I stopped dead still in the road and flashed my light around, picking up the odd darting insect, the track below, a wayward moth attracted by the light. But I could see nothing else. As the screaming persisted, it sounded muted and unearthly, but seemed to be getting louder. I held onto my whistle, flashed my torch around again and walked on.

Horrible images jumped into my mind. A woman lying on the floor, her face blue as the last breaths of life were expelled. Or a Jack the Ripper scenario, in which a woman had been neatly and skilfully dissected. I opened and shut my eyes a few times to expel the horrible images.

A few pigeons flapped and flustered round my head, and suddenly the screaming stopped. It was completely silent again. I held my breath as I put one foot in front of the other. But before I could relax, the screaming started up again, this time getting louder and louder and more desperate.

Could it be that Christie had made his way here after

all? But why would he choose Richmond, of all places? It seemed so unlikely. But it was possible, wasn't it? Sergeant had said the whole country was on alert. My shoulders stiffened as I clutched on tighter to my whistle and torch.

The screaming was by now so loud I felt like I could reach out and touch it. And yet I couldn't find its source; no matter how far I walked it never seemed to arrive. I was almost across The Green when I flashed my torch over to where the sound appeared to be coming from, fully expecting to see the man himself, mid strangulation, his poor victim on the floor at his feet.

Instead, my torch lit upon two eyes at ground level, then a bushy shape; another face with some pointy ears in hot pursuit. I stopped and they stopped and we all looked at one another, me and two enormous foxes out on a night's prowl, their eyes flashing before they disappeared into the bushes.

I had never felt such relief in all my life as the realization dawned that a fox screeching sounds like a woman being strangled. As I waited in the phone box I leant back, panting with relief, before stepping back out and on towards Goal Bank and the station.

Before I arrived back I did have one more start, though. There was a shape on the pavement. A body still juddering in the throes of death? Oh my God. I almost couldn't bear to look. But as I flashed my torch over on full beam, there, looking up at me, was a giant badger, white stripe down its long nose, big black legs and white pointy ears. He had a look on his face as if to say, what are you doing out here at this time, human? This is badger territory.

I looked at him for a while, and he at me, but neither of

us moved. My dad used to tell me they could give you a nasty nip, but this one came nowhere near me. Eventually I turned one way and he the other, as if in mutual agreement to allow one another to pass undisturbed; before I knew it, his large speckled back disappeared along the lane.

I very nearly ran back to the station after that, and once I hit the pavements along Goal Bank, and on to the stables and the station, I was a jangling mess of nerves.

'You look like you've seen Napoleon's ghost,' said Peter, who was just going out on his beat on the other side of town, all geared up in a warm winter tunic and cape.

'Almost,' I said, as I stretched out my arms over the open fire.

As I sat there and watched the flickering flames, it felt like I had encountered all the beasts of the wild on that journey. But, thank goodness, the one beast I didn't encounter was John Christie.

All week at the station everyone was talking about the manhunt. After ten days they found Christie on a bridge in London. They had found bodies in the garden at his address, and under the floorboards, in kitchen cupboards even. One was his wife, but there were also prostitutes too, it looked like. I came in one morning and overheard two of the lads on Motor Patrol who had called in. They were in the office having a cuppa from a flask, the newspapers spread out on the table in front of them.

'See that?' said Peter, pointing at a grainy picture of a man on the front page, in a raincoat and glasses. 'Mad as a March hare. Gassed during the war. Didn't speak for three years. Led him to a life of sexual perversion, so they say.'

'Yeah, but plenty of people were gassed during the war, and they don't all go strangling women and hiding their bodies in alcoves,' said Tony, as he took a big gulp of tea.

'Says here he's admitted it all, though. Unbelievable!' said Jack, flicking through another newspaper. 'Look here. Had sex with the bodies once they were dead. Eurgh! They found bits of women's ... hair ... in his shed in pots. That is disgusting.'

I didn't think they'd noticed me so I sat down quietly and went through some reports on the desk left by the Inspector. They carried on talking.

'Remember that bloke, Evans, hanged a couple of years ago for killing his wife and baby?'

'Vaguely.'

'Wasn't all there, apparently. Well, looks like the wife and kid might have been killed by this Christie fella too. Same house and everything. See, that's what's wrong with the death penalty, right there in black and white. An innocent man hanged probably. And for what?'

'Yeah, but do you want Christie still alive, after this? A life of luxury in prison, paid for by Joe Public?'

'They should lock him up, granted, but once the country itself becomes a murderer, can we really take the moral high ground?'

'Well, I say there are just some people not fit to live in this world. If he'd killed my daughter, I'd hang him myself and that's for sure. I'd enjoy it too. I couldn't give two hoots for no moral high ground.'

They sat for a while pointing out other new and gruesome aspects of the case that the newspapers were revelling in reporting.

'Hey, hey,' said Jack after a while, sitting up in his chair. 'Ring-ring.'

'What?'

He went as if to pick up the telephone on the desk in front of him. 'Christie here.'

'Yes?' Tony answered, going along with it.

'Come on over, and I'll dig up a girl for you!' Jack sat back on his chair and laughed uproariously.

'You're sick,' said Tony, struggling to suppress his own smile, more at the audacity of the man than the joke itself.

'Well, if you don't laugh you'll cry, right?' Jack said, and downed the rest of his tea.

After that, the whole country awaited Christie's trial with bated breath, and everyone knew that if he was found guilty, whatever anyone's views on the matter, it would be death for him at the gallows.

Off duty, walking home to my digs, a hearse suddenly appeared, coming slowly toward me down the road. It was followed by a procession of vehicles and mourners, with lots of flowers everywhere.

As the hearse carrying the coffin drew level, I stood to attention at the side of the road, and saluted. I wondered if it was anyone I'd met.

As I resumed walking, I thought to myself that we can never know what is round the corner. Life is full of surprises.

13

While the country geared up for the trial of the decade, the nation was also readying itself for the party of the century as Elizabeth II, who became Queen on her father's death, got ready for the coronation at Westminster Abbey. All the papers were full of anticipation: what would she wear, who would be there? But what was most exciting for everyone was that we'd all be able to watch it, live as it happened, on the television. It would be the first time most of us would have seen the Royal Family in the flesh, apart from pictures in the papers.

'For the first time ever, we'll all be able to see it. Actually see it, in our own houses. That's what's so marvellous,' said Caroline one morning over breakfast. 'Mrs Fisher across the road has promised we can all go round and watch it on her television set. He still won't get one, Terence. Says it's too expensive, and a malign influence on the nation, beaming images in. Could be used for devious purposes by the government, he thinks. But I'm rather excited about the whole thing.'

'How does it work exactly, television?' asked Lily, as she neatly sliced the top of her egg off, and sprinkled a pinch of salt over it, like she was enacting a sacred ceremony.

'Heavens. I don't know!' said Caroline. 'Ask your father when he gets back.'

'How do they get them into the TV set in the first place,

the people, and then into every single person's house at the same time? That's what I want to know.' Lily was not giving up easily.

'Do you know?' said Caroline, looking over at me.

'Can't say I do. I've never even seen a television set. My mam says she's getting one for the coronation too, but it's all new to me.'

'Isn't it something to do with light waves?' said Katy, who was the scientist of the household, and could often be found examining insect specimens on the kitchen table. She had even built a small wireless set once, with the help of her grandfather; they managed to pick up Radio Luxembourg for a few minutes, and something in French. 'I read something says they beam the pictures over as electrons through the air,' she went on. 'Like radio but with light, and that makes what we see on the set.'

'Well, that's more than I know. All I can say is, I'm looking forward to seeing that little princess become a queen. I think she'll more than fill her father's boots, and that's a tall order in itself. And seeing the dress she wears, of course. I bet she'll look beautiful. Like a swan.'

But before we could watch the ceremony, and before the party could start, I still had work to do. This time up at Gallowgate Camp, an army barracks nearby. Back at the station, the Sarge had given me a message to deliver; I didn't read it, but it seemed quite urgent.

As I stepped out on the grass at Gallowgate, the camp seemed windswept and desolate, just a few tanks driving up and down, some army lorries in the distance and Nissen huts behind. There didn't seem to be many people around, but eventually I found the main office and was shown to a seat by a young lad in uniform, who offered me tea you could stand a spoon up in, it was that strong. Nice for warming your hands around the mug, though. When the Corporal came along and took the note briskly, I was quite relieved to be able get out of the camp, which had such an eerie air.

As I walked back down the hill to the bus stop, I saw the bus that would take me all the way home to my digs already waiting. I had to hurry to make sure I made it. I hopped on board the big double-decker just as the driver was about to leave, and the conductor saw me in my uniform and gave me a big smile.

'Afternoon, constable,' he nodded. But instead of continuing on his way and taking fares, he hung on for a moment and stroked his chin, unsure whether to speak.

'Is everything OK?' I asked.

'Yes. I mean . . . well, maybe not.' He lowered his voice to a whisper and clutched my arm. 'It's just that. Well, it don't add up,' he said, his nose pressed up right against my face and breathing all over me, pointing further up the bus.

When I looked over, there was a young lad in soldier's uniform sitting on his own and looking out of the window.

'He just doesn't look right to me. Something in my bones. And I'm usually right about these things.'

Finally he relaxed his grip on my arm and went on up the bus, collecting fares and whistling a warbling tune at the top of his lungs.

As I approached the young soldier he saw me coming, averted his eyes and looked back out of the window.

'Excuse me. Have you got your passbook?' I asked. He

didn't look much older than about eighteen; he was very gaunt in the face, and quite ill-looking.

'Pardon?' he asked, pretending not to have heard.

'I said, have you got your papers?'

'Oh. Umm . . .'

'What's the matter?' I asked, as he looked as though he was about to burst into tears. 'Are you AWOL or something?' I said, half joking. But the look on his face told me I was right.

He hesitated before answering. 'Suppose I am.'

He looked down sadly, as though he'd given up.

'Where have you been?'

'Living in the woods. Three days. Under a tree. I made a shelter, like what they taught us. Survival and things.'

'In the woods! What have you been eating?'

'Not a lot. I caught a rabbit but then I couldn't bring myself to kill it in the end. I never wanted to be in the army. I was trying to get home. I think this bus goes the right way. Think it does, anyway.'

He looked faint, and as though he might pass out at any moment. I felt sorry for him, but I had to take him in to the station because that was procedure. I didn't have any handcuffs or anything, as we WPCs didn't carry them, but when the bus stopped at Victoria Road roundabout we got off, and I asked him to come with me. He didn't look like he was going to put up much of a fight.

'You sure you'll be all right with him?' asked a man at the front of the bus.

'I think I'll manage.'

The young lad didn't look like he was capable of walking far on his own, let alone running away.

When we got to the station, the Sergeant rang the Red Caps, the military police, who came to take him away. And although I knew I was doing my job, I did feel a little sad for him as they carried him off into the van, and back to the garrison he'd been so desperate to leave.

Over the following few weeks, the whole town was talking of little other than the coronation. Summer was in the air, and a party feeling with it. Even the most ardent anti-monarchist couldn't help but succumb a little to the special occasion.

I'd never seen a television set before, and for me this was going to be the real treat. I eagerly awaited the rota, to find out whether I would have the morning off to watch the ceremony. Eventually I found out I would be starting at two p.m., so I could watch it.

On the big day, Caroline, Lily, Katy and I all trooped over the road to Mrs Fisher's. Mr Fisher was a headteacher at the local school, and they always seemed to have all the new technologies before anyone else in the neighbour-hood. TV sets were still few and far between at this point, although a lot of people had splashed out on one just for this day.

'Where shall I put this lot?' asked Caroline, as we all trooped through the front door and into the living room. 'Oh, how lovely. Sandwiches, and what's this?'

'My special apricot cake,' Mrs Fisher told her. 'I stayed up late last night and made two.'

'Well, we've certainly got enough food in here to feed an army.'

There weren't enough seats in the room for everyone

so the children, Carol and Bobby Fisher, and Lily and Katy, all sprawled out on the floor together. When we walked in, Carol was working intently with glue and brown paper, pasting in pictures of the Queen that had been in the papers all week.

'I'm making a scrapbook,' she announced proudly as we stepped over her. 'I cut up this ribbon to make the flag. Look!'

'Beautiful, darling, but can you move it for now, so our guests can all sit down? Sorry, she's a little enthusiastic. She wants to be a queen herself, I think.'

'Oh, my Lily's the same!' said Caroline as we all sat down.

'No I'm not,' said Lily, who was a little sulky that we had to spend the morning cooped up inside when she could just as well be outside playing.

'We got given mugs at school. With a picture of the Queen on. Did you?' asked Katy.

'Oh yes, we got them too!' answered Carol delightedly.

I offered to sit on a small stool, while the others squeezed onto the sofa and chairs; it felt like quite a crowd in there.

'Let's get the beast started then,' said Mr Fisher, wearing his slippers, and carrying a pot of tea.

The television set was a large wooden box, with a tiny screen in the middle.

'You know you have to wind it up, don't you children?' said Mr Fisher, winking at me and Caroline.

'Really?' said Lily, suddenly interested. 'Can I do it?'

'I thought it was a thing on the front,' said Katy, going over to peer at it. 'Yes. Here!'

'Well. Yes, all right. You got me there,' he said, his joke foiled.

We all sat back and stared at the screen, and waited.

'What happens now?' whispered Lily excitedly to me, a little nervous.

'I'm not sure. Watch and you'll see.'

There was a hushed silence, broken only by Mrs Fisher slowly munching on a sandwich.

'You just wait,' Mr Fisher said.

So we waited.

After a while, a small light began to appear in the centre of the screen, and then finally an image, in grainy black and white. We all gasped.

'Ooh, look. It's so clear!' said Caroline.

'Who's that funny man?' one of the children asked.

'The newsreader. At the BBC.'

'He's so posh.'

The coronation hadn't started yet, and instead there was a news report of two men, Edmund Hillary and the Sherpa Tenzing Norgay, who had climbed Mount Everest as part of a British team.

'Where's Mount Everest?' asked Lily. 'Is it in France?'

'No, it's in Tibet, silly,' said her sister. 'It's the tallest mountain in the world, isn't it, Mam?'

'Gosh, I don't know. Yes, I think so.'

'Why did they want to climb it if it's so high? Did they get as high as the clouds?'

'Probably.'

'What's it like in the clouds? Are they like ice cream or . . . what are they made of anyway?'

'Water,' said Katy.

'Water!'

'Well, steam or, you know, vapour.'

'Be quiet, girls. It's starting,' said Caroline, settling in her seat with a big plate of sausage rolls and sandwiches.

On the screen were images of people all across London, in the streets and along the Mall near Buckingham Palace. They were waving flags and were dressed up for the occasion. It was incredible to think it was happening right at that moment, while we were all tucked inside this small living room, hundreds of miles away.

'It's amazing, how they do it,' I said, as the camera panned inside the interior of Westminster Abbey and the commentators spoke in hushed tones, awaiting the arrival of the Queen into what they grandly called the 'Coronation Theatre'.

'Where's this now then?' asked Mrs Fisher, her mouth full of pastry.

'He just said. That's Westminster Abbey. Don't you remember, we went there once when we were down in London,' Mr Fisher said. 'You had an ice cream and we saw those horses.'

'Oh yes. I see it now. It looks smaller somehow. Even the throne – is that the throne? It looks so small.'

As the camera panned back outside the abbey and across London, we saw shots of schoolchildren and ordinary people, women in headscarves and men in caps, swarming up the streets in their hundreds, dressed up in Union Jacks; even some dressed as television sets, so momentous an occasion was it.

After a while, the bit we'd all been waiting for arrived. The Queen, riding in an enormous golden carriage with horsemen in plumed hats, and the horses all decked out in splendour. The crowds erupted into a giant roar.

'The picture's so clear, isn't it? Amazing.'

'Yes. It's just incredible. Just think what they can do with this. You'll never need to leave the house!' said Caroline, then she sighed. 'Oh, doesn't she look beautiful? So . . . regal.'

'How much do you think that's worth then? That hat?' said Mr Fisher, as the shot followed them into the abbey.

'It's a crown. Who knows? Priceless, probably. Or at least a million, I should think.'

It was pomp and ceremony, an almost tribal display, like I had never seen before. Hundreds of officials in grand coats and cloaks, fur-lined and gold-trimmed, carrying objects like 'the orb' up to what they called 'the great altar'. It was like something from a past age, King Arthur or a giant real-life fairy tale. Pages, admirals, earls and then Her Majesty herself, gliding up the nave in a great long cloak.

Carol jumped a little and smudged glue from her scrapbook all over the carpet when the choir suddenly burst loudly into a chant of 'Vivat Regina'.

'That's scary,' she said, looking warily from behind her book. 'What are they doing?'

'It's part of the procedure. It means something. In Latin. I don't know. Long live the Queen, I think.'

Then she sat down and swore to do her queenly duties, like a kind of wedding ceremony to protect all the countries, including at that time Canada, South Africa, Pakistan and Ceylon, as well as Britain itself. Her voice sounded quiet, and when she signed an official document she was a little conspicuous as a woman among men, before she was led away on a great big chair, covered up like a four-poster bed.

'The ensign of kingly justice and the rod of equity and mercy! What's that when it's at home?' asked Mr Fisher.

'Who knows, but it's all part of it, isn't it? To make sure she does her job properly, I suppose.'

And there the Queen sat, looking small and slightly vulnerable in a great big wooden throne, wearing the crown and holding up a giant object that looked like a golden broomstick.

'I'm hungry,' said Lily suddenly. She had seen enough.

'You've been eating all morning!' said her mother.

'Don't worry,' Mrs Fisher told her. 'That's what it's there for. Go and help yourself, love.'

Once the ceremony was complete the atmosphere relaxed, and Lily and Carol began sticking pictures into the scrapbook together, while Bobby went outside to play. Mr Fisher showed Katy the back of the new television set, and Caroline and Mrs Fisher started clearing away the plates. I looked at the clock on the mantlepiece. It was time for me to get on the beat, and back to reality.

That evening, as I walked through Market Place, the town was abuzz with excitement. There were parties in houses, one at the Town Hall, and the remnants of a few street gatherings scattered along the roads. Children walked across town dressed as pirates, cowboys and gypsies, and I even saw one pair of adults dressed up as the walking wounded, all wrapped up in bandages, as a kind of parody of all the people who had been injured in the crush when crowds tried to get a glimpse of the Queen.

'Was it all worth it?' a sign on their bandages asked. I think most of us agreed that it probably was.

Soon after the coronation, another news story hit the headlines again. The trial of John Christie had begun. Just weeks after we had huddled round the television set watching the Queen in all her finery, we were gripped by another national drama. At the station, opinions were running high on what the outcome would be. The case rested largely on the definition of insanity.

Christie himself took the stand and gave a blow-by-blow account of the murders, agitatedly pulling at his ear and rubbing his chin. His defence argued that no sane man could have done what he had done to all those women. The prosecution argued that he was sane, as he knew what he had done was morally wrong, because he himself admitted it was unlikely he would have committed the acts in front of a police officer.

After four days of trial, and the jury deliberating for four hours and twenty minutes, they found him guilty. There was no appeal and he was sentenced to death, hanged at Pentonville prison on 15th July 1953.

After the drama of the trial died down, the public soon moved on from the national hysteria of the past few weeks, and life in the little market town returned to normal. I continued to make my points as dutifully as I had for the past two and a half years. I was sent to the local hotel about a theft; I reported a woman for leaving her car unattended with its engine running; and I served a summons. We had a visit from the Inspector of Constabulary. It was as though nothing much could ever really change in Richmond. Would I be here for ever, I wondered, walking up and down these streets?

One afternoon I bumped into Joe McGregor in town, in a suit. I had never seen him dressed like that before, and when he stopped to say hello, I saw that he had red eyes and a shrunken look.

'Morning, Joe. Everything OK?'

'Not exactly,' he replied, and wiped his nose with his sleeve. 'It's the missus. She passed last week. I held her hand as she went. But she was in a lot of pain, poor lamb. Nothing we could do.'

'I'm so sorry, Joe,' I said, touching his arm gently. But I knew that whatever I said, no words would comfort him. He was alone.

'Funeral's in a couple of hours. I've just some . . . something . . . to do first. Can hardly remember what. Papers to sign and things. I've had a trouble remembering it all.'

'Oh Joe. I had no idea. I'm so sorry. I'd come and pay my respects but I'm on a shift this evening.'

'Don't worry. There'll be a fine crowd. Last night I'm sure I heard her, you know. Talking. Beside me in bed. Just whispering or something. Saying my name. Then when I looked, just an empty space. The pillow. But I could still smell her. Strange.' His voice began to crack a little. 'Anyway, I can manage. You be on your way. You don't need to be troubling yourself with death and all at your age.'

As I watched Joe walk up the road slowly, I thought what a contrast it was since our first meeting all those years back, with Bertie the escaped bullock. Funny how things change.

When I got back to my digs that night, Malcolm was

sitting in the kitchen with Caroline. I had been expecting him this weekend, but he'd come over just to say hello before he caught the bus up the road to stay at the farmhouse. He seemed a little on edge and I wasn't sure why.

'Shall we take a walk? Down the castle?' he suggested.

'It's late but . . . why not? I could use some fresh air. You know old Mrs McGregor passed a few days ago. Poor Joe. I only found out today. I hope he'll be all right in that old house on his own.'

We walked in silence down the road for what seemed like ages, then across Market Place. The sun had set not long ago, and it was just getting properly dark. The air was humid, moths and insects flying about in the streetlights and the last few swifts high in the sky.

We walked along by the river for a while, hand in hand. Out of nowhere a big brown and speckled fish swirled up out of the water and caught a fly on the surface.

'Trout, probably,' said Malcolm.

I watched its shiny back continue to curve across the surface of the water as it made its way along the river, picking off insects.

We sat down on a bench and looked at the castle, the whole of Richmond stretching out in front of us. Suddenly, out of the blue, Malcolm turned to me, reached into his pocket and pulled out a small blue box. My heart fluttered for a moment, as though someone had jump-started it momentarily.

'I've never . . . you know. Not sure how to do this. But will you . . . ?'

He opened the box and there inside was a gold ring with three diamond stones set inside it.

'How did you . . . ?' I breathed in deeply and looked inside the box, unsure what to do.

I thought about Joe and his wife, and the end of their world together, and how the cycle just continues, on and on. One ends, another begins.

'Yes,' I said softly, and he put the ring silently onto my finger. I squeezed it, and then his hand.

That night as I slept, though, it wasn't the ring and Malcolm that swirled about in my mind. It was that brown fish, its shiny back and swirling tail. It was like a sign. Though I had no idea of what.

The next day, at the station, I showed my ring to Doris and she squealed with delight. The lads all patted me on the back and the Sergeant shook my hand. Someone brought in a cake a bit later and we had a bit of a celebration.

But as the noise of congratulations rung around me, I felt like I had gone inside my head for a moment. I was suddenly far away, looking down on my own body from above. I was gripped with a sudden uncertainty that this was the direction I really wanted to go in. Housewife. Wife.

It was as if I was on an uncontrollable roller coaster, and there was no getting off now, no matter what.

For the next few months, though, before the wedding, and all the fuss that goes with that – dresses and cakes, family and friends, deciding where we would live – I remained, for the moment at least, Pamela Rhodes, Miss. Bobby on the beat.

Acknowledgements

Thanks to Jo Wheeler for her help (and a little 'poetic licence'). All place names, other than Richmond and Redcar, have been changed, as well as the names of the characters I've described.

He just wanted a decent book to read ...

Not too much to ask, is it? It was in 1935 when Allen Lane, Managing Director of Bodley Head Publishers, stood on a platform at Exeter railway station looking for something good to read on his journey back to London. His choice was limited to popular magazines and poor-quality paperbacks – the same choice faced every day by the vast majority of readers, few of whom could afford hardbacks. Lane's disappointment and subsequent anger at the range of books generally available led him to found a company – and change the world.

'We believed in the existence in this country of a vast reading public for intelligent books at a low price, and staked everything on it'
Sir Allen Lane, 1902–1970, founder of Penguin Books

The quality paperback had arrived – and not just in bookshops. Lane was adamant that his Penguins should appear in chain stores and tobacconists, and should cost no more than a packet of cigarettes.

Reading habits (and cigarette prices) have changed since 1935, but Penguin still believes in publishing the best books for everybody to enjoy. We still believe that good design costs no more than bad design, and we still believe that quality books published passionately and responsibly make the world a better place.

So wherever you see the little bird – whether it's on a piece of prize-winning literary fiction or a celebrity autobiography, political tour de force or historical masterpiece, a serial-killer thriller, reference book, world classic or a piece of pure escapism – you can bet that it represents the very best that the genre has to offer.

Whatever you like to read – trust Penguin.